Mark Steel has performed as a stand-up comedian since 1983. He co-wrote and performed four series of *The Mark Steel Solution* and has written and performed three series of *The Mark Steel Lecture* for Radio 4. He hosted the Radio 5 sports programme *Extra Time*, wrote the book *It's Not a Runner Bean*, produced a weekly column for the *Guardian* and now does so for the *Independent*. He lives in London.

Also by Mark Steel

It's Not a Runner Bean

Reasons to be Cheerful

From Punk to New Labour through the Eyes of a Dedicated Troublemaker

Mark Steel

Scribner

First published in Great Britain by Scribner, 2001
An imprint of Simon & Schuster UK Ltd
A Viacom Company

3 5 7 9 10 8 6 4 2

Simon & Schuster UK Ltd
Africa House
64–78 Kingsway
London WC2B 6AH

Simon & Schuster Australia
Sydney

A CIP catalogue record for this book is available from the British Library

ISBN 0-7432-0803-X

Typeset in Sabon by SX Composing DTP, Rayleigh, Essex
Printed and bound in Great Britain by
The Bath Press, Bath

Acknowledgements

I would like to thank Mac McKenna and Pat Stack, with whom I spent many joyful hours discussing the various periods I was writing about, though often we'd end up in a stupor from which none of us can remember what was said. Martin Valentine provided a similar service and, crucially, a room in which to write the thing. Jonny Geller was astute enough to tell me what was wrong with my first draft. So however shit you consider this is, if it wasn't for him it would be worse. My partner Bindy deserves many thanks. And my son Elliot deserves boundless praise for not once doing what would have been a classic three-year-old nugget of behaviour, and calmly pressing 'delete' to whisk days of labour into the parallel universe occupied by lost words from computers.

Lastly I must thank Tony Cliff (1917–2000), without whom this book, and so much else, would not have been possible. Including the survival into the twenty-first century of the following joke, which he told so often, as a reminder that all we are up against is what's in our own heads.

An Arab businessman comes to Britain to buy a cooling system for his palace. So he visits a factory where they're made, and the managing director tries to sell him one, but the Arab is distracted because at twelve o'clock the hooter goes. He watches everyone leave and nudges the manager. 'Look, look,' he panics, 'your slaves are all leaving.' 'Don't worry, they'll be back,' says the manager. The Arab is so stunned he can't concentrate, but at one o'clock the hooter goes and, as predicted, everyone comes back. At the end of the day the manager says to the Arab, 'Well, would you like to buy a cooling system?' And the Arab says, 'Sod the cooling system, get me ten of them hooters.'

Introduction

The people I find most infuriating are the perenially miserable: the sort who say 'just my luck' or 'story of my life, that is'. I feel like saying to them, 'Look. If you are a Hutu from Rwanda who accidentally strolls into an armed Tutsi warrior camp, then you are entitled to go "Huh, just my luck. Story of my life." But if you've gone down the shops for a packet of biscuits and they've run out of your favourite sort, shut the fuck up and put up with it.'

For much of the last twenty-five years, some of the most disconsolate people have been found amongst the section of society that wishes the world to be more equal, more, shall we say, socialist. Thatcher, then Blair and their big business chums can appear to have had everything their own way. Worse, in Britain people are often told to 'stop talking about politics, it only causes arguments'. But you can only have that attitude if politics doesn't appear to affect your life. If the house was burning down, and one group was urging everyone to 'run through the flames' while someone else shouted that the only chance was to jump, even my Mum wouldn't say 'Stop talking about fires, it will only cause a row. Now let's have a nice cup of tea and burn to death.'

Away from the sleepiness of Westminster, the period covered in this book has presented many reasons to be cheerful. Because politics is about more than ministers and by-elections, treasury statements and passionless automatons reciting their dry, wizened statements on *Newsnight*. So, although this book is about politics, it isn't about 'politics' or politicians. And although it's a personal account, it isn't about me. Instead, this is a story of the frustrations and exhilaration of the twists and turns, the slow drips and sudden explosions that have affected all of us over those twenty-five years. It's the story of momentous events seen through the eyes of one individual playing a small part in those events.

For nothing ever stays the same. Even since finishing this book there has been revolution in Serbia, and an enthusiastic, largely nose-studded movement has developed around the world to confront bodies such as the World Bank and the International Monetary Fund. Maybe, by the time this is published, Tony Blair and his free market chums will have been swept away, rendering this entire book out-of-date. Wouldn't that be just my luck, the story of my life?

Chapter 1

I'll start with the happy ending; I don't like Tony Blair or New Labour. I've never liked them and I knew all along I didn't like them.

This is the optimistic outcome of the twenty-five years covered in this book. Not that many other people like them, though lots thought they did, because they didn't feel anything better was possible. So polls showed Blair as the most popular Prime Minister of the 20th century. But who do you know who liked him? No one. He was the most unpopular most popular person there had ever been. He reminded me of an irritating idiot at a party, who everyone wishes would leave, but no one dares tell him to because everyone thinks he's everyone else's friend.

Being aware of not liking him is the culmination of a journey which, to begin with, I didn't know I was on. Adopted children sometimes go to great lengths to discover their natural parents, feeling it would explain how they are what they are. But few of us consider the events and trends, booms, crises and political upheavals that swirl around us, whisking us through the markers of our lives.

In fact we are prisoners of our times. We can live by the philosophy that if we show initiative, we'll be rewarded with promotion and wealth, but only because we no longer live in a feudal system in which power is inherited. No peasant in the 12th century believed that if he worked extra hours each day on Lord Hertfordshire's estate, he might end up as his son, and inherit Hemel Hempstead. Someone might be a vegetarian, but had they been around 500 years ago, they would have skinned rabbits joyfully, and if they'd found a tofu-based sausage, grassed up the owner as a witch. And a person may identify themselves as proud to be a Londoner, and a supporter of West Ham. But had they been taken from birth and brought up in the Amazon, they wouldn't have grown up flogging second-hand canoes, and yelling 'You're shit and you know you are,' at a family of baboons.

The first influence on my political direction was to be brought up in Swanley, on the border between outer London and Kent. Most people brought up in small towns complain about the lack of entertainment, and the soporific atmosphere, and many insist that their particular example is worse than any other. But telling someone from Swanley about the tedium of your small town, is like saying to Nelson Mandela, 'I've had hassle from the old bill myself, so I know how you feel mate.'

There was no cinema, no venue for bands, no theatre, and in a town two miles long, about one and a half miles wide and consisting of 25,000 people, there were three pubs and a Chinese take-away. There was a small sports centre, which almost everyone went to, but what difference did this make? When you're a sixteen-year-old boy, if a girl agrees to go out with you, you can't say, 'Great. Let's go weight-training.'

But the lack of facilities was only part of the problem. Swanley was built around domesticity. Its population had quadrupled in ten years, not because it offered work, but because it offered housing, out of the hubbub of London. So its *purpose* was boredom. The stultifying listlessness of the place seeped through the emptiness of the new estates and the deserted main road, which pottered past a fenced-off stagnant pond, Woolworths, and away up to the big city that was Sidcup. Swanley was *never* busy. If you were out after eight o'clock, you'd see only the odd lonesome individual walking their dog, and a feel a camaraderie, the way you might if you met someone up a mountain on Christmas Day.

Boredom is a state of mind, rather than a lack of things to do. So the honourable attempts to combat the lethargy by setting up a pottery class or amateur dramatics group didn't affect the overall atmosphere. There were no collective activities, not even a regular market place. There was no cultural mix, not even a curry house.

When I was fifteen, a group of us would meet in the evenings and play records. Occasionally, for a change, we'd wander the streets. We'd drink a tin of beer between us, pull up someone's flowers, and one night we smashed every pane of glass in some poor sod's greenhouse.

Maybe it's no coincidence that so many revolutionaries come from small towns. Marx was from Triere, Robespierre from Arras, his protégé St Just from Picardy, Lenin from Simbirsk, and Trotsky from the Ukrainian town of Bobrinetz. When Trotsky was 15, I wonder if he spent evenings hanging around a Bobrinetz bus shelter, destroying a peasant's allotment while sipping a third of a tin of Heineken, and thinking, 'There's got to be more to life than this.'

The philosophy of my generation was shaped in part by the notion universally held during our childhood, that as time went on the population would become wealthier. From the war onwards, the economy had been booming, and every year brought a life-changing new gadget; fridge, washing machine, TV, vacuum cleaner or car. Your kids would have an easier life than you, jammy sods, with 'all the opportunities we never had'.

Everyone at that time believed that, within reason, you could choose the job you wanted, and follow it for the rest of your life. 'What are you going to be when you grow up?' adults would ask with annoying regularity. If you didn't know, you'd get a follow-up statement that went, 'Take my advice son, get a trade.' Followed by that wink which that generation did when talking to ten-year-olds. But it's a question you just don't hear any more. It would sound as archaic as 'forsooth sire', or 'two-bob bit'.

The worst that could happen would be to end up in an unskilled job.

'I know where you'll end up,' a chemistry teacher screamed at me when he caught me skipping a lesson, 'You'll end up DRIVING A VAN.' These days they must sit down with the bright kid of the class, and say, 'If you continue with this high standard of work, study hard, get your GCSEs, go to university and come out with a good degree, with a bit of luck you could end up driving a van.'

My parents' generation had been promised security and gradual material improvements. If they worked hard and saved a bit each year they could end up in a nice house, full of china ornaments, that their parents could only have dreamed of. And for many the promise appeared to have been kept.

My dad was the son of a bus driver, spent the war in the navy, and worked in an engineering factory through the fifties, until he became the local insurance man. On an average wage, he bought a garden with a bungalow front and back. He could believe that hi-fi stereos and James Last box sets came to those who grafted. As a result, my dad bought things, like a commemorative plate wrapped in crinkly paper inside a furry box to mark cricketer Colin Cowdrey's hundredth hundred – because 'that'll be worth a few bob one day, son' (wink).

Almost every line of thought from that generation led to money. The response to any career mentioned was either 'good money in that' or 'not much money in that'. If someone bought you anything that looked slightly classy, like a wooden model aeroplane, they would say 'look after that, and one day it could be worth a lot of money'. I wonder if any of us ever took them up on this advice, and at the age of thirty visited Sotheby's, smugly inquiring, 'How much can I expect for this little beauty?', presenting a nine-inch brass tram from the Isle of Man.

My mum worked sometimes, part-time, though it didn't seem to matter much if she didn't. 'I'm going out to get a job,' she said, and walked fifty yards to the electric organ factory, where she was told she could start the next day, in the manner of new characters in *Coronation St* wandering into the Rovers to get taken on by Mike Baldwin. But there was one enormous exception to the notion that material possessions were a reward for graft: *them*.

Sociologists and economists concoct elaborate categories to describe classes in society, but to most of that generation, there was only one class apart from their own; *them*. If my parents had devised these socio-economic groupings, the top category wouldn't have been 'managerial and executive', or 'A and B1' but 'la-di-da types'. Them who didn't appreciate money because they'd always had it. Them who have prawn cocktails and wine so often they've forgotten it's a treat. Them who watch BBC2.

As an engineer my dad must have been a member of the strong post-war unions, which secured rapidly improving pay and conditions. And there lies the contradiction of that generation. They believed their share of the stability, and holidays in the Isle of Wight, bungalows, a health service and vacancies at the organ factory, were what they'd earned as a class. But twenty-five years of that stability meant that it was possible to ignore the wider questions concerning how society works. My parents were never shop stewards or members of the Labour Party. But they were part of the reservoir of people who felt the post-war world would give the working class a better deal than the whooping cough and means tests of *their* parents. So they voted Labour in 1945 and felt part of the order which introduced the welfare state.

By the time I was a teenager the Labour Party was in decline from its peak of one million members. But the enthusiasm of that period left a legacy, which hung in the air breathed by countless children of the seventies. There was us and there was them. We work harder than them but they've got most of the wealth. And that's not fair.

During the general election of February 1974, my mum made a new friend at work and we went out with her family, just before polling day. As her friend left, my mum gave a contented smile and said, 'She's voting for Mr Wilson. She says he's a good family man.' She was so pleased, not just because it would be one more vote for Labour but because it meant she was one of us.

During that election campaign I made a speech supporting Labour to the six people who went to the school debating society. I tried to be a politician, arguing that only Labour could rescue Britain from the economic shambles that Ted Heath etc., etc., but really I was bursting to shout, 'It's not fair! Some people are born rich and stay rich and everyone else is born poor and stays poor and it's not fucking fair.'

The teenager of the early seventies was made aware of the power of the unions. Every Saturday night on BBC1, Mike Yarwood did an impression of Vic Feather, general secretary of the TUC. The machinists in Mike Baldwin's factory had a well-organized union, and the drivers from *On the Buses* ran rings around their inspector, Blakey. The Strawbs had a top-ten hit with 'Part of the Union'. Cartoons in the *Sun* portrayed union members as huge ugly hairy men with 'union power' on their t-shirts. And every night on the news there was talk of a strike or what to do about the problem of strikes in general.

Strikes, everyone agreed, were bad. The question was never whether they should be supported or opposed, but always *how* they should be opposed. If someone on TV had said, 'well, I *support* the strikes', it would have sounded as odd as if there was a discussion about how to deal with a fire, and someone had said 'I support the fire, and hope it spreads to the basement'.

And there were the effects of real strikes: bread shortages, schools shut for the day and power cuts. I didn't care much what happened in the strikes. But they left an indelible impression on everyone of my age: unions mattered.

There was another feature of the times which shaped the psyche of the seventies child: the generation gap. It's often assumed there's always been a generation gap, but there can't have been. In the 1740s, did parents despair at the younger generation, because their kids' Maypole dance was two skips to the right, whereas in their day it had been three to the right and one to the left, making them wonder how they had the cheek to call it music? Again the turning point was the post-war boom. Before that, teenagers got up to mischief, but the same mischief their parents had got up to. And parents of 1990s teenagers may prefer the Jam to the Prodigy, but they don't stand in the doorway with a screwed-up face, muttering, 'Why can't you listen to "Beat Surrender"; something with a tune.' Whereas being a teenager in the 1970s was like being raised by a tribe of wolves.

They didn't understand us, nor we them. As we worshipped Deep Purple on a fiver's worth of plastic mono gear, they had huge wood-panelled stereos with headphones and everything and used it once a month to play Mantovani. 'Turn that racket down. There's no need to have it that loud,' they'd shriek as one across the country, but they were wrong. It can be as quiet as you like if you're playing Henry Mancini lift music, destined to end up as background to 'News from Ceefax'. But there's no point in having Johnny Rotten squeaking 'I am an anti-Christ, I am an anar-chiste' at two and a half decibels.

It wasn't just the music. We had no respect, had it too easy and wouldn't have to do National Service. Monty Python was 'stupid'. And we were never far from a lecture about how lucky we were. They'd been through a war to earn their twenty-five years of boom. Now we were going to get it free.

We could nurture an opposite resentment: was that it? The best that life could offer was a trade, a mortgage and a set of porcelain jugs behind a glass cabinet? 'Michael up the road has got a job in a bank,' my mum told me in a pointed tone. I didn't know why, but I knew things made me angry.

As an angry thirteen-year-old, during one of my first days at the main building of Swanley Comprehensive, the headmaster Dr Henry caught me eating a banana in a corridor. This was an outrageous breach of the school code, he told me, and demanded I saw him in his office, which I did, for over an hour. It may seem a trivial rule to me, he insisted, but if we only kept to the rules we liked, where would that lead?

A breeze of violence blew constantly at the school. It was perfectly normal for someone to sneak up behind you, knee you in the groin so that you'd crumple into a throbbing heap, and shout 'Dead leg my son'. There was one class which played a game called 'Beat Your Head In', in which a group of lads sat in a circle. Then a hard lad turned over a playing card to each player in turn, and when someone got a Jack, everyone shouted 'beat their head in' and beat their head in. Which I always wanted to suggest at family gatherings to alleviate the torture of rummy.

What made me even more angry was the suggestion that these were the best days of our lives, and that even the hardships were serving the purpose of preparing us for later life. Which clearly wasn't true, as it's unusual in an office job for the filing clerk to sneak up behind you, boot you in the jaw, shout 'Kung Fu my son', and for everyone to burst out laughing.

The school did run a scheme called the school council, a sort of union we were told, in which a delegate from each class attended, to raise issues at a monthly meeting with a senior teacher. I stood and got elected and went into the first meeting with a huge list of demands.

'Right,' said Mr Young, who looked like, spoke like and made as much sense as Michael Howard. 'The main item on the agenda is how to fund the house Christmas coach trip,' he went on. I didn't know much about unions but I was sure the Tolpuddle Martyrs hadn't been sent to Australia for discussing the Dorset agricultural labourers' Christmas coach trip. The trip was discussed and Mr Young said the meeting was finished, unless anyone had anything else to say. I put my hand up and complained about the number of broken chairs in the house block. This wasn't a matter for the school council, I was told. So I complained about the school fund, whereby every pupil had been asked to contribute 50 pence towards the school budget. Then about the lack of cricket equipment, the rudeness of the maths teacher, why we had to do woodwork, the filthy toilets, and worked my way through an endless list as the other delegates drifted back to their lunch break.

Once a week these meetings took place, each one following an identical pattern. Mr Young would slowly grind through an opening report about the coach trip as if he was Clement Freud on *Just a Minute*, and I would follow with a string of demands, like a victorious general in a conquered province. Then everyone else would go, 'Phoooo, shut up Steel.'

The school council was a sham, I announced to the class, so we must strike a gesture to expose its fake authority. 3BX had a similar cast of characters to any class in history. There was a genius, who would force the teachers to say, 'Does anyone *apart* from Andrew have the answer?' It had a compulsive liar, who told us he owned a flamethrower, and that his uncle held the world record for eating gherkins. It had a mad kid, a girl who swore at teachers, and a kid who stank. And it had Julie Jensen, who in two and a half years no one had heard say a word out loud. Frail and nervous, she sat in the corner of every lesson, turning bright red even when her name was read out for the register. Julie Jensen, I decided, should take my place on the school council. So I got her agreement, resigned my post, and we held a new election with a recommendation to vote for Jensen, who was elected unanimously.

I can't have been the first person to have thought of a gesture like this. In Libya, China and Stalinist Eastern Europe, where government-run village committees and workers' councils had no influence over anything more pressing than the Christmas coach trip, someone must have done the same. So that somewhere in the Ukraine in 1935 a robust Politburo official will have greeted a new delegate, saw him go bright pink and hide behind a desk, and thought, 'Is someone taking the piss?'

After that, my opposition to the things that made me angry was back to just being angry. Being naively politically angry and teenage angry at the same time makes for a lethal psychological disorder. Not only did I walk home from school in a foul explosive mood but I couldn't be sure whether the cause was the war in Angola or because I fancied Cheryl Jackson and she was going out with that twat from Caxton House. It's a condition which probably now has a scientific definition, like 'confused barbarism/erection syndrome'. *Crossroads* made me angry because people watched it and took it seriously and my mum discussed it on the phone with her friends and couldn't she see it was BOLLOCKS. The Bay City Rollers made me angry. How could these daft girls like a song that went 'we sang shang-a-lang'? Anyone could make words rhyme if they just made them up. Couldn't they see?

Conversely I adored anything which appeared to challenge authority, even the films of Von Daniken, which claimed there was an international conspiracy to hide the truth about spacemen visiting the earth in ancient times. Von Daniken could have looked into the camera, and purred, 'Zis wall painting, in ze ancient Inca temple of Los Margheritta, clearly shows stone-age man loading denim and other synthetics into a fast-spin washing machine'. And I'd have thought, 'Why must governments hide the truth? The bastards.' Pink Floyd sang 'The General is sat / While lines on the map / Move from side to side'. Yeah, that was so true. That *is* what they do, those generals.

Authority, I worked out, was what made me angry. But that was confusing. I was angry with my dad because he was an authority, but angry *about* my dad because he was working longer and longer hours, which was making him ill and depressed. I was on the side of the poor but it was a poor woman who worked in the newsagents and snarled 'clear off' whenever we went into the shop. And the poor kids were the best at playing 'Beat Your Head In'.

Then one day in 1975 I saw in the newsagents a copy of the *Morning Star*. 'The paper of the Communist Party' it said on the top. Wow. Communist wasn't a thing you admitted to, it was a term of abuse. It was like seeing a newspaper with a heading 'The paper of Shitheads'. Ted Heath had blamed the ruin of the country on 'reds under the bed', and every trade unionist on the news denied they were any such thing. With Labour in power it was truer than ever. Strikers and campaigners were accused of being communists and were always outraged at such a slur. And these people *admitted* it on the front page of a newspaper.

I was fascinated, and hovered over it, eventually taking it to the counter while trying to look casual, burning with anxiety as if I was buying my first packet of condoms. I was certain they'd all talk about it after I'd gone. Maybe they'd inform the school, or my parents or the police or a special unit that tracks down people who've bought communist newspapers.

The words inside seemed genuinely shocking, evil, like the rantings of a devil worshipper. The social contract, which the unions had signed with the government, and which everyone hoped would result in industrial peace: they were *against* it. The Shrewsbury builders, who'd been jailed for smashing machinery: they *supported* them. And Russia, they supported Russia.

I skipped school for the afternoon, and sat in the spectators' gallery at the swimming pool, gazing in awe at every paragraph. From a distance I must have looked like a typical teenage boy, drooling over a porn magazine. And that's how it felt. If I'd been with a mate I'd have been grunting, 'Woooor, look at that, greetings to the toolroom workers at British Leyland'.

Here it was, a direction for all that anger. This was anti-authority on a grander scale than I'd ever imagined. From now on I'd be a communist and drool in the shocked expressions of whomever I told. 'So you support Russia,' people would reply, 'where anyone who opposes the government is put in jail.'

'They've got me there,' I'd think. 'Lies of the capitalist press,' I'd answer.

But here was a contradiction in communist Russia's role in shaping ideas at the time. It meant that communism was easily dismissed, as a system that led to dissidents being chucked into a Siberian gulag. But it also meant it had to be admitted there was an alternative to capitalism. In school and in the media, when the possible methods for running the world were being discussed, communism took its place as a serious player. Though I'm not the sure the Siberian labour camps were full of shivering prisoners thinking, 'I may have lost another toe from frostbite, but at least the existence of the Politburo helps to broaden the mind of a stroppy kid in Swanley.'

At the same time I was learning something else about authority; that sometimes you could get away with not doing as you were told, as long as you were prepared to carry on not doing it. If you skipped school you got detention. But what difference did that make, if you didn't go to the detention either? All they could do was give you double detention and treble detention until you owed them thousands of years of detentions. So I stopped going altogether, and the headmaster wrote a letter summoning me to his office, where he told me I was expelled.

Fantastic! The punishment for not coming in was not being allowed to come in. It was like a judge sentencing a bank robber to being paid £50,000. 'I knew you were trouble when you first came here', said Dr Henry the headmaster, as I turned to leave for the last time, 'when you questioned my ruling about where you were permitted to eat your banana.'

But the terrain of post-school life was shifting. The post-war boom was over, and in 1976 the unemployment figure reached one million for the first time in forty years. Then the pound collapsed amidst Chancellor Denis Healey's dramatic appeals to the International Monetary Fund, who demanded enormous cuts in public spending in return.

Most people may not have understood the causes or implications of this crisis, but everyone knew it was a crisis. The security and predictability which had lasted thirty years had been snatched away, and under a Labour government. There was resistance to Healey's measures but it was in contrast to the Heath years when opposition was led by the organized working class and was underpinned by the idea there was an alternative to the Tories, which was Labour.

Now we *had* Labour, so radical opposition was confused, divided and as a result usually defeated. To the angry teenager, the Labour Party had lost any sense of radicalism. Callaghan, Healey, Merlyn Rees and David Owen even *looked* like establishment buffoons. They'd appear on the news, nervously making pronouncements and opening swimming pools, like the secretary of a winning bowls club who's been asked to pose for a local newspaper photo, pompous and slightly surprised to be so important but clearly loving it.

Periodically I pledged to join the Communist Party, but always hit the obstacle of Russia. I was an angry young man in need of an icon and Leonid Brezhnev fell short on several counts. It wasn't just his age, though as he doddered and shuffled along with Jimmy Carter at the arms talks he didn't quite match Marlon Brando in *The Wild One*. He oozed establishment and unjust authority as much as any Western leader. You certainly couldn't imagine *him* getting in trouble for eating a banana.

I wasn't the only one affected by this sense of frustration at leaders of traditional anti-establishment parties appearing to be more establishment than the establishment. Opposition movements became anarchic, especially amongst youth, and raged randomly against any symbol of authority. Which created the perfect conditions for punk.

The Jam said they would vote Tory and few of their followers were bothered. It would have seemed even more bizarre if they'd announced to crowds of frantically spitting youth, maniacally shaking their heads and wearing a nine-inch-diameter badge of the Queen with a safety pin through her nose, that they should give Jim Callaghan one more chance. Punk made directionless anger legitimate. Local bands might perform a song about the evils of the arm trade, followed by an equally vicious one about 'the bastard bus conductor on the 21A'. With lyrics like 'You're a fucking bastard / For kicking me off your fucking bus / Just 'cos I never had no money / What's it got to do with you?' I wish I'd written one called 'I'll Eat My Banana Where I Fucking Well Like'.

Punks, like communists, were evil. So buying the Clash album from a Dartford record shop was like buying that first *Morning Star*. I waited for several minutes by the 'C' section, pretending to be flicking through Johnny Cash and Creedence Clearwater Revival, before I plucked up courage, made my way to the counter and said, 'I'll have that please.'

Back home came a seminal moment, the first few bars of 'Janie Jones' on side one. While the lyrics were indecipherable, the meaning boomed out of the chipboard speakers and echoed around the Swanley walls. It was all right to be angry. You be angry mate. There's a whole generation of us, expected to be grateful, well how about this for gratitude – 'Career opportunities, not one will ever knock / The only job they offer you's to keep you out the dock'. So it wasn't just me.

After a succession of dismal jobs in offices, kitchens and selling watches on building sites, I got a real career opportunity, serving petrol at a garage in Dartford. The hours were seven to six, five days a week, and I took home thirty-three quid. It was owned by a good-looking ex-public schoolboy in his twenties called Tim Brise who, like the Earl of Hertfordshire, had inherited the business from his dad.

He employed three mechanics, whose job was to retune and perfect Brise's rally car, which he raced every weekend. During one of my first days there, my colleague returned from the toilet to see a woman in a fur coat with a poodle, parked on the forecourt. 'How long has she been there?' he screamed. It was Mrs Brise, mother of garage-owning Brise. 'What is the meaning of this delay?' she barked, with a lengthy 'h' at the start of 'what', while I scampered out to her. For protocol stated that Mrs Brise didn't have to ask.

So I checked her oil and her tyres and water and polished her wheels and dashboard. I wiped her windscreen and wing mirrors and headlights, and all the while her poodle yapped and her fur bristled with contempt. And I smiled a false smile as she stood over me and pointed to patches she imagined I'd missed.

Once a day Mr Brise would saunter through and check on progress with the retuning, and I'd watch the mechanics laughing and gesturing with him as they wiped their oily hands, flattered to be considered worthy of minutes of his time.

But the job had a redeeming feature: a carpet company with a fleet of lorries who would fill up with diesel and had an account with the garage. When we filled one of their lorries, we wrote the amount on a sheet of paper, which the driver would sign, which was then sent off for payment at the end of each week. So if the lorry took twelve gallons, we'd write sixteen on the sheet, and take the monetary equivalent of four gallons of diesel from the till, splitting it with the driver. But the scheme went the way of all workplace scams. It was so easy, so why not put ten gallons in, and write it down as twenty. Until one driver said, 'Stick two gallons in mate, and write it down as twenty-five.'

Then another fleet of lorries started doing the same, until I was spending the whole day sharing fivers and tenners with lorry drivers. It got to the point where I'd be paid my wages and think, 'Oh yeah, I'd forgotten all about the wages.' One day a driver came in for petrol in an Anglia estate, so I asked him how much he wanted for his car and bought it off him there and then.

One Friday afternoon Mr Brise called me into his office. 'You don't need to come in on Monday,' he said, as if he was doing me a favour, 'as we've found someone to replace you.' A man in his fifties with an HGV licence had recently been made redundant, and had walked around the garages of Dartford asking for a job. He could do my job for the same wages and drive trucks as well. For most of his adult life that driver had probably never imagined he'd ever have to walk the streets pleading for work. He had nothing against me personally but he'd slung me on the dole. Except he hadn't, it was Brise who'd done that. I couldn't have complained if I'd been sacked for fiddling the carpet company but I wasn't. I was being sacked because the world economy had slumped, the pound had collapsed, the IMF had demanded Denis Healey deflate the economy further, meaning less goods were sold, so less goods were being delivered, so truck drivers were laid off and had to plead for work in petrol garages.

All this raced through my mind as I stood in his office. 'What do I do?' I pondered in rage, and though I didn't know, I knew the worst thing to do was nothing. 'Fuck you,' I screamed, and slung a cup of coffee in his face and a typewriter against the wall. 'That's it,' I said out loud as I got in my Anglia to drive home, 'I'm joining the Communist Party.'

But a new form of politics was spreading; a youthful, vibrant movement loosely connected to music and anti-racism. The punk scene, which had started as an anarchic tantrum, even flirting with fascist insignia in an effort to cause outrage, was developing as an opposition movement. Rock Against Racism organized gigs in every area of the country and 'Power in the Darkness' by the Tom Robinson Band was a rallying cry, not just against authority in general but the specific enemies – big business, racists and bigots. It wasn't just me: there were loads of us.

The amorphous blend of musical rebellion and political activism coalesced in the form of the Anti-Nazi League, which was launched at the height of the punk period, and in particular at the ANL carnivals of 1978. So explosive was the blast of this movement that its fallout permeated into the deserted streets of Swanley. In the punk era even people in Swanley went to see bands, though never in Swanley itself. (There was an attempt to set up a weekly venue in the working men's club at nearby Farningham, but on the opening night the lead singer of the main band was stabbed by the Sidcup 'Soul Patrol', so the idea was abandoned.)

We heard about the ANL carnival at gigs and through the music press, and felt the carnival was part of our world. Two of us went, possibly the highest turnout to a national demonstration there's ever been from Swanley (though to be accurate my mate Jim was from the village of Eynsford). Neither of us had any idea what would happen when we got there. What is a march, we pondered. Do you actually march, in step, with someone yelling at you to get in line?

Instead 100,000 ambled joyfully from Hyde Park to Brockwell Park in Brixton. All the scenes which would become so laboriously familiar, the hordes of leaflets thrust at you from all angles, the flamboyant but awful drumming outfits, the chanter screaming into a megaphone and becoming increasingly, thankfully hoarse, it all seemed so thrilling. And there was Aswad and Tom Robinson and Elvis Costello, and instead of feeling angry I felt jubilant because now I was *doing* something.

And there was the dramatic tension surrounding Jimmy Pursey. Pursey was the lead singer of Sham 69, the rawest of punk bands, who'd picked up a skinhead following, some of which supported the fascists. He'd been asked to appear on stage at the carnival, after which rumours had swirled around the nation's youth as to whether he would or not, the tension building in the way it does before an announcement about a cabinet resignation. Then the matter was cleared up, in a style which should be studied by politicians or football managers, before they appear at press conferences. An announcement was made that there was a special guest. Out came Pursey, and made a speech which went, 'They said I wouldn't be here. They said I hadn't got the bottle. Well I'm FUCKING HERE!' And then he went.

Strolling out of the park towards Herne Hill station, I bought a copy of *Socialist Worker*, and started to read it on the platform. There were the same devilish articles supporting strikes and the overthrow of order. But in tiny print, under the heading 'Where We Stand', was one sentence which caught my attention. 'Russia, China, and Eastern Europe are not socialist, but state capitalist.' Of course. Capitalist, but everything owned by the state. That was it. Everything still run for profit, but instead of companies taking it, the state had it. It seemed so obvious. It was like watching the end of a murder mystery but one that had gone on for three years. It *was* possible to be a socialist and not support Russia. Stalin was the murderer all along.

I filled in the form to join, imagining that this was a simple decision I'd taken that day. But as I wrote my name and address my hand was guided by the smug smirk of Jim Callaghan, the doddering of Brezhnev, by Tim Brise and Mike Yarwood, by Trotsky and Stalin, Joe Strummer and the miners' strikes and Dr Henry.

Now that Russia was cleared up, I could do something, be a proper socialist, play a part in a highly organized movement dedicated to overthrowing the system. I sent off the form and no bastard got back to me for over a month.

Chapter 2

A letter eventually arrived explaining that the nearest branch was in Gravesend. It came on headed notepaper, which seemed disappointingly formal. Maybe I was expecting a tap on the window in the middle of the night and instructions for a secret meeting in Zurich. Someone would be contacting me, the letter said. Oh my God. I re-read the bit in the paper, above the bit about Russia. 'Only the mass action of the workers themselves can destroy the system.' Destroy the system. And they had my phone number.

Part of the attraction had been the sheer devilry of it. Surrounded by the banality of Swanley's timid cul-de-sacs, buying papers from communists and filling in forms in Trotskyist papers was simply naughty. When asked 'Well what would *you* do to liven up the town?', what a lark to avoid the predictable replies of a snooker hall or a cinema and plump for destroying the system. But now they were really going to ring, these revolutionaries.

What if my mum answered? That would be embarrassing for both parties. Can revolutionaries live at home with their parents? Surely no Italian mother ever answered the phone and said, 'It's for you dear, it's the chap from the Red Brigades.' It had all seemed so clear when I filled in the form, but now it seemed dangerous. Then one of them phoned and during our conversation I said the words, 'I'll come along to your meeting this Thursday.' As these words came out, I felt the bolt of half-panic, half-adrenaline that results from knowing you've said it now and there's no going back. It was the sensation I imagine you'd feel if you said 'All right then, I'll do the bungee jump' or 'Chris, I'm going to risk the sixteen grand and try answer "B"'.

What would they be like? Everything I'd read or heard about

revolutionaries told me they were weird, shady fanatics, committed to destruction and evil. I might set off for the meeting and never be seen again, having been kidnapped, forced to change identity and put through a de-capitalism programme in a concrete basement in Karachi.

I'd recently started working as a milkman, with a round in the village of Horton Kirby. Suddenly I felt such a fraud, engaging in jolly banter with the housewives on their semi-detached doorsteps. What would they think if they knew their milkman would soon be spending his evenings trying to destroy the system? The whole village would be in fear that I was planning to poison their yoghurt and ride triumphantly past on the float as they all spluttered to death, cackling, 'This is justice for the historic crimes of the rural petit-bourgeoisie; HA-HA-HA.'

But equally, how could I be a sincere revolutionary – and a milkman? Would Che Guevara have carried the same charisma if there was film of him in a black beret and blue overalls, saying, 'Good morning Mrs Osborne, extra cheese this morning?'

The meeting was in a pub, a dingy lifeless pub. A front perhaps. I sat on my own, watching each person who entered, wondering whether they were one of them. Each new face that came in could have been the one soon to be staring at me to assess my commitment, in the twilight of an upstairs room accessible only through a secret passage.

Then a teacher arrived with what I was to learn was a classic activist stance, arms uneasily around a bundle of papers and leaflets, all slipping from her grasp while she contemplated which ones to save from pouring on to the pub floor. 'You must be Mark,' she said and we went into a freezing function room and put out too many chairs.

Then a permanently stoned hospital porter arrived, and a member of the Gravesend Surrealist Society, who explained how he'd spent the afternoon in the high street giving out blank sheets of paper.

When everyone had arrived there were eight of us. There then followed the process which takes place in any organization when there's a new arrival, whether the aim is to overthrow the prevailing order or stage amateur dramatics to the village. Organization and new person circle each other delicately while, unbeknown to the new person, the familiar exchanges between the group have been suspended as they weigh up their guest. Until one of them, to the embarrassment of their colleagues, says something like, 'Here Terry, I've still got some of that whizz left over from Steve's party.'

The meeting began with a discussion on local activities organized to oppose the National Front. And there was talk of visiting a picket line at Tilbury. Some of them, it turned out, had been at Grunwicks. Most of them had been at the clash between the police and the ANL at Lewisham. All of them had been at events which ended up on the news, provoking my mum to say, 'Ooh isn't it dreadful.'

It was like being a kid meeting a bank robber. I wanted to say, 'Wow, mister, so do you actually throw stones at the police and stuff? Cor, have you ever been arrested?' But I couldn't help worrying what people like old Mrs Scott from over the road would say if she knew I was at a meeting with such troublemakers.

To everyone I knew, people who carried placards and chanted slogans and threw missiles weren't people that you met. They were one of the types that only existed on the news, like drug dealers and people who throw kittens in rivers. It wasn't that their ideas were wrong. When Mrs Scott came over for a coffee and the news was showing pictures of protestors hurling rubble at retreating policemen, she didn't object that this strategy was contravening the rights of free speech. She just said, 'What must their poor parents think?' Explaining the historic role of fascism would be as futile as excusing football violence by saying, 'But the Charlton fans are getting Bolton back for taking their end at the Valley, Mrs Scott.'

The most consistent political message I'd been brought up with was to keep out of trouble. If the news showed a border skirmish in Mexico and we knew someone whose son was in New York, there'd be a short gasp, followed by concern that this might involve Bill and Mary's boy who was out there somewhere. Apart from that, and 'Ooh isn't it dreadful', the only other reactions to news items was a fantastic ability to make them trivial. There might be scenes of Lebanese guerrillas in balaclavas running out of a building to lob grenades and my mother could say, 'Oh look, it's raining there as well.'

It all amounted to the same message. Don't go near people who cause trouble. And here I was, sat with them. Even better, occasionally one of them would say something like, 'The police are right bastards.' This phrase shouldn't have been shocking but these were organized troublemakers, so it was different. It was like the difference between hearing someone up the pub say 'Noel Edmonds should be shot', and hearing the same words spoken by the Godfather. Maybe someone would prise open the floorboards, pull out a shotgun and fire a volley at the next panda car.

Everyone who joins a group which is based on an ideology becomes a mass of contradictions, supporting a new way of thinking but not automatically losing everything from their past. Someone who rejects their violent past to become a pacifist will still have the urge to punch someone from time to time. And when someone becomes a socialist they bring with them remnants of the prejudices and attitudes they've formally rejected. Just as when someone converts to Islam, they must occasionally think, 'Well just a *bit* of bacon can't hurt.'

So the first instinct I had to overcome was that you shouldn't get in trouble. Nominating Julie Jensen and getting expelled was one thing but hanging about with this lot could end up getting me arrested. This fear was jumbled with the liberating realization that other people in the world believed in socialism but didn't like Russia. There may have been only eight of us, but that made our forces eight times stronger than I'd previously reckoned.

Then someone would say something off the end of any scale I was aware of. The Communist Party, someone said, were too right-wing. Aaaagh. If I'd joined the Communist Party, I'd have been the most left-wing person in Swanley. I remembered how shocked I'd been at seeing that first *Morning Star*. But this lot thought the Communist Party were right-wing! I couldn't wait to try this out on the relatives. 'I decided against joining the Communist Party.'

'Well thank goodness for that.'

'You see, they're too right wing.'

I doubt whether any of the other seven had the faintest idea, as we periodically whacked the heater to get it working again, that I was discovering a whole new world as if I'd wandered through the wardrobe door into the land of Narnia. They routinely packed away their leaflets, unaware that I was awestruck at the discovery of seven kindred spirits. I was observing the same dutiful procedures as everyone else but seeing a magic spiralling world of mind-expanding energy, like someone hallucinating on magic mushrooms in a supermarket. Where I was thinking 'Wow, posters', they were probably thinking 'What the bloody hell are we going to do with this lot?'. Where I was thinking 'Now let's talk about Stalin', they were probably thinking 'It's fucking freezing'.

Then I found out that one of them was gay. Fantastic! I knew I supported the right to be gay but I had no idea I'd ever meet one. He asked me where I worked but I just wanted to say, 'Blimey, so you're really actually gay then. You really do go out with other blokes and get on top of each other and everything. Well I don't mind. That's right, I do – not – mind. What do you think about that?'

To grasp the enormity of this moment is to understand that back then there was no Julian Clary or George Michael, or Barrymore or Chris Smith or Ellen or Stephen Fry. Public figures could be like Larry Grayson or John Inman, but on no account could they admit to actually doing that thing with other men. In fact hardly anyone used the word gay. There were poofs, queers and benders. In pub etiquette, to call someone a poof was to crank up the stakes a couple of notches from cunt. In a typical jovial name-calling session in my local pub, all turned sour when one person called the other a poof. Suddenly it all went quiet before the addressee snarled, 'You can call me ANYTHING – but don't call me that.'

In pub culture, a thousand social acts could render you vulnerable to doubts over your non-poof status. Buying flowers, going to the theatre, cooking your own dinner, staying in on a Saturday night, not knowing the difference between a Triumph Herald and Triumph Vitesse, taking two goes to park your car in a tight space and so on. Any man whose appearance could in some way be described as vaguely effeminate would get calls of 'Oy, here he is, don't bend over'. 'Backs against the wall,' we'd say, as if gays are likely to go into a pub and think, 'Ah they're off their guard, I'll fuck the lot of them.'

But it was all in the name of a peculiar form of discrimination, in that we didn't really believe gay people existed. We knew they spoke in squeaky voices, wore lipstick and said 'ooh ducky', but none of us had ever seen one. We were like Ancient Greeks, terrified of monsters that were our own creation.

And I was no better than anyone else. At a New Year's Eve fancy dress party in 1977, I went as a poof. Pink shirt, cravat, handbag, the lot. I must have thought I was terribly amusing with hands on hips, wishing everyone a happy New Year, ducky. But the youth movement which impressed me throughout 1978 was unequivocally opposed to anti-gay prejudice. How could I support this movement; the music, the marches, the badges, but be opposed to one flank of it?

In a sense I arrived at a similar position to some gays when they first come out, at their most outrageous and camp, flaunting their newly discovered sexuality in a reaction against the years in which they've kept it hidden, as if they're making up for lost time. I wore bright pink badges supporting gay rights and said 'There's nothing wrong in being gay' loudly in public places, even if the conversation was about the difference between a Triumph Herald and Triumph Vitesse.

I was greatly enjoying the shock value of the gay issue. And now I'd met one. A real one, who really did fancy other men. And I wasn't shocked. Much. Though I still couldn't believe they really did THAT. Someone arrived and sat next to the gay man. 'That's Peter,' the branch secretary told me, 'He's David's, er, friend'. Why didn't he say boyfriend? He must have considered it because he hesitated. But he must have worried that I'd think, 'Well it started off fine, with them planning an illegal stampede through the streets to confront fascists. Then they talked about overthrowing the state – which was fair enough. But then it turned out one of them was queer! Fuck that for a lark.'

I wallowed in my newly discovered environment, partly as a retreat from the rest of the world. Best of all though, these people *wanted* trouble. In their eyes, people who cut their employees' pay or attacked minorities or ruled Iran *deserved* trouble. And to an eighteen-year-old living and working and drinking amidst the stultifying tedium of a small town, trouble is fun, especially when it's aimed at a bigger enemy than a greenhouse.

*

Just one thing perturbed me. The attractions of socialism were obvious, so why couldn't everybody else see it? Surely everyone could see it was ridiculous to have one and a half million people unemployed, while there were countless valuable tasks which could be carried out. And we'd all be miles better off if everything was determined by human need rather than profits, wouldn't we? Surely the only reason every working-class person in the world wasn't a socialist was because of Russia. Everyone was thinking, 'I would be a socialist but Russia's socialist and I don't like Russia.' But we had an answer. Russia *isn't* socialist: it's shit. Or, if you like, state capitalist. Still capitalist, but everything owned by the state, see. SEE? Obvious. All we have to do is tell everyone and they're bound to see it. How can they not?

Surely if the other seven had really tried they'd have got thousands of others by now, so obvious was the force of our argument. I decided to rectify this. I'd start with the unemployed, who'd be certain to join us in their entirety once we pointed out that the answer to unemployment was socialism but that Russia wasn't socialist, it was shit.

Using another member's duplicator I produced my first leaflet. This involved typing the text on to a stencil, which was then attached around the drum on the machine. You squeezed ink into a hole at one end, turned a handle and as the inky leaflets peeled off you felt like a threat to the state, in a way you don't get from fiddling with your software and nipping down to Prontoprint. The first few would come out covered in splodges of goo, then some would come out properly before half a dozen inexplicably stuck together and the last fifty became increasingly faint as the ink ran out. But so much effort was involved in the production that you ran your fingers over the finished bundle as if you'd crafted the most intricate ceramic vase.

The next morning I went on my own to the dole office. The first claimant approached. 'Are you unemployed?' I asked him. He said that he was. 'Do you want to be unemployed?' I asked. He said that he didn't. 'Well I've got a way of getting you a job,' I told him and gave him a leaflet.

What must they all have thought as I repeated this routine all morning? Some of them probably thought I was about to offer them a spot of mini-cabbing. Some may have thought the leaflet was one of these things that claims you can become a millionaire in a fortnight. Maybe they even got as far as the bit about Russia, still thinking 'I expect they want me to sell insurance'.

My strategy was simple. They'd read the leaflet, thinking the arguments made perfect sense. Then they'd realize that the ideas they'd accepted were socialist ideas. Then they'd be hit by the part that said we didn't support Russia. Finally, on their way out, as they were eagerly absorbing these revelations, I'd confirm that they were coming to the next meeting, which was advertised on the bottom.

About eight said some form of 'yes'. But it wasn't 'yes!', it was 'ay what, er, yeah what' as they shuffled past. So I marked them down as definites. Most of them ignored me, or mumbled a head-down, no-eye-contact 'um oh cahoo dunno mate', the international language of anyone walking past a madman trying to attract their attention. So they were put down as possible.

Then I made my calculations. 'Let's not be overoptimistic,' I thought, 'Let's imagine we only get *half* the possibles.' So there were eight definites, and maybe another ten on top. My thinking continued, 'So if we get eighteen, and next week they all do the same, even if they're not as successful as I've been, and only get, say, ten each, that will mean we'll have one-hundred-and-eighty members. Then if they all go and get ten each . . .'

Over the next few days I'd run through these calculations about once an hour. Sometimes I'd get as far as capturing the entire British state, which I'd estimate at taking between three months and a year, depending on how optimistic I felt. Once, I remember getting this far and thinking, 'Then we could start on France.'

On the night of the following meeting I arrived half an hour early, eager to meet my unemployed disciples. A while later, the other regular members arrived and I told them there was a whole crowd coming down from the dole office. They seemed surprisingly unimpressed. Ten to eight. Any minute the first ones would be here.

One minute past eight. Now it was time for that process whereby the human mind convinces itself that the reason someone hasn't turned up is you gave out dodgy instructions. Arrange to meet someone at the cinema at half past seven, and by ten to eight you'll convince yourself that you said Tuesday instead of Monday and instead of 'cinema' said 'aquarium'. I once arranged to meet someone under the Eiffel Tower at one o'clock. When they weren't there at twenty past one, I found myself thinking, 'Or is there another Eiffel Tower in Paris?'

And it dawned on me, as I sat in the pub, that I hadn't specified morning or evening. I was convinced they'd all come at eight o'clock in the morning. Occasionally I'd hear the squeak of the door opening and bolt round to see someone come in and walk straight to their mates at the bar, obviously a regular. Ten past eight. Everyone had their drink, the heater was on and the same number of chairs were out as usual. The others started moving into the room and I lagged slowly behind, protesting that we ought to wait a while. 'Hmmm,' they said, as if I was six and asking them to wait for my imaginary friend.

The meeting wore on but I could no more pay attention than if a girlfriend had dumped me ten seconds before the agenda was read out. As with any feeling of catatonic gloom, there were odd spasms of naive hope. 'Maybe they're all coming in one van and it's broken down and in a minute they'll all come bursting in,' I'd wonder; the equivalent of 'Maybe she'll change her mind, leave him and come back'.

Once again I was in a different world to everyone else around that table. But now all was darkness. This wasn't just the humiliation of being stood up on a date or of no one coming to your party. This was a searing rasping notice that the project I'd embarked upon wasn't going to be completed by the overwhelming logic of the socialist argument. One year from now we wouldn't be living in a socialist paradise with a little statue of me outside Gravesend dole office.

If ten of those blokes from the dole had turned up, I'd have been disappointed. If one or two had turned up, I'd have been inconsolable. But there were none. In all probability there had never been a single moment when any one of them had considered coming at all. Just as a five-year-old child, in a period of one hour, can go through every emotion from misery to euphoria and back again, my political naivety had taken me from fear to jubilation to manic overoptimism to despair, all in the life of one leaflet.

This was the moment I had to make a decision. Deciding to change the world had been easy but sticking with it was the real challenge. It was like the difference between pledging around closing time to enter a marathon and rethinking the matter half a mile into the first day's training with a choking pain in your ribs.

As defeats in the labour movement go, my experience was not up there with the General Strike or the Spanish Civil War. But there must have been people at the end of those events who had a similar feeling to mine after this meeting: our case is so strong – why can't everyone see it? Nonetheless, there were still eight of us. And they'd had it tougher, as the last one to join before me had joined a group of seven.

I just wish the membership card had had a note on the bottom, 'Socialists can go down as well as up'.

Chapter 3

Being a new member of a political group feels like your first few days at school or in a new job. Everybody else seems so familiar with their surroundings that it doesn't seem possible they were ever new themselves. Then someone says something like 'As long as it doesn't end up like one of Alan's fish' and everyone roars with laughter.

And everyone else knows the rules. 'Can you take some papers?' someone asked me, and I said I wasn't sure how many I could afford. How was I to know that the procedure is to take a bundle, read one, sell one, hand in the money six weeks later and six weeks after that sling out the rest.

Then there's the jargon. 'Can you keep lookout on a flyposting team?' I was asked; the equivalent of asking a 16-year-old office clerk on his first day to nip up to stats and Xerox 10 A4s of a B65. The person who asked me wasn't my boss, he wasn't a teacher, he couldn't sack me or give me detention but I still stared back thinking, 'What do I say, what do I say?' Lookout and flyposting sounded like fun but how could I be sure that if I said yes, he wouldn't say 'Ah splendid' and hand me a rifle?

And comrade? That seemed a bit grandiose. Fair enough if you've been marching through Spain, hurling grenades at Franco's army, but we just met in a pub in Gravesend. And there was a new set of political rules. People talked about sexism. What was that, I wondered. Were sexists people who thought the same about women as racists did about black people? Which meant they wanted all women to be kicked out of the country? Did they say, 'I went down Peckham the other day, there were millions of them, I was the only male face there.' Surely not.

Then it was explained that pin-ups and page-three girls were sexist. Thank God I wasn't a socialist when I was fourteen, I thought.

Almost as tricky to comprehend was the etiquette of the weekly meeting, especially on weeks when there were only four or five of us. We'd all sit around a pub table chatting, then at eight o'clock the same group would stroll into a back room and sit round a table with one person opening the meeting and thanking everyone for coming. Then there'd be a formal meeting with people putting their hands up and waiting to speak, and afterwards we'd all go back to the first table again.

Part of the tradition in the British left was that weekly meetings should finish with a series of meaningless announcements. 'Right,' said the chair with unfounded optimism as they prepared to read them out. Then everyone in the room picked up their beer glass and shuffled outside, while the chair informed everyone about a picket outside a town hall in somewhere like Swindon. As if anyone was likely to hear this through the chatter and think, 'Oh, I'll take a day off work and go to that.' There was usually something about a showing of a film with a discussion afterwards, about a Central American village that's being slowly poisoned by a nearby rubber factory. Then the poor chair waved a piece of paper, telling everyone to raise the motion written on it 'in your union branch or wherever you can'. I was always fascinated by 'wherever you can'. As a result of this request, maybe there was someone who went to their mother and toddlers' coffee morning and tried winning support for Republican prisoners in the H-blocks.

By now the most eager to leave will have got as far as the door. At which point there would be a sharp clap of the hands, the type you make when you catch a cat licking your butter, and an authoritative, 'JUST A MOMENT. These announcements *are* important.' Then everybody stood in silence, rocking backwards and forwards in readiness to set off again, like schoolkids who've just been told, 'The bell is a signal for me. It is NOT a signal for you.'

I wonder if this happens at meetings of other groups. So the Women's Institutes' meetings end: 'If anyone happens to be near Haywards Heath on Thursday morning – JUST A MOMENT. These announcements *are* important – there's a tour of the Juicy-Spread marmalade factory at nine a.m.' But if these matters *were* important, they wouldn't have been left to the announcements, though as a tediously keen new convert, I didn't know the rules. So as the chair half-heartedly waved motions and leaflets about, I was furiously scribbling the details on to a piece of paper, desperately trying to keep up like someone who actually follows the recipes on a cooking programme. One such announcement concerned the Shah of Iran.

Towards the end of 1978 there were demonstrations of a million people through Teheran, the Iranian capital, and an oil workers' strike was threatening the Shah. The dictator responded, chiefly through his secret police force known as SAVAK. Shanty towns suspected of harbouring militants had been bulldozed. And while only 1 per cent of Iranian peasants had any access to medical facilities, 40 per cent of the country's budget went on arms. One of the chief suppliers of those arms was Britain.

There wasn't time for any of this in the announcements though. Instead there was a garbled sentence about a protest outside the Foreign Office on Friday night, something to do with David Owen and the Shah. The announcement probably ended with '. . . if anyone can make it on Friday night'. But I heard it as '. . . if there's enough of us on Friday night we'll force David Owen to resign, after which state power can only be moments away'.

So on Friday night I arrived outside the Foreign Office and mingled with about thirty demonstrators stood around with placards and a bloke shouting into a megaphone. At this point the matter uppermost in my mind was embarrassment. If you arrive at a party on your own, not knowing any of the other guests, at least there's the opportunity to talk to people. But it hardly seemed appropriate, at a protest called against the selling of tanks to a madman who used them to bulldoze villages, to say, 'Excuse me, I'm Mark. Er, did you have to come far?'

And everyone else seemed to know what to do. The megaphone man would shout 'David Owen', then everyone would shout back 'Shah's puppet'. Should I join in? What if there's some hidden rule that I'm not aware of, like you don't shout back after every fifth 'David Owen'. Then I might shout 'Shah's puppet' by myself, while everyone else put their head in their hands, lamenting that now the whole thing was ruined. So I'd call out 'shawel's puppel' quarter-

heartedly and self-consciously, occasionally looking round to check
that no one was watching. Then a policeman wandered slowly and
deliberately over to the megaphone man and said something the
rest of us couldn't hear. 'I've just been told,' said the protestor, 'that
we are no longer allowed to continue our protest against David
Owen arming his gangster friend . . .'

In mid-rant his megaphone was snatched by a team of coppers
who'd encircled him. Then a van pulled up, about a dozen more
police piled out, grabbed the placards and passed them to
colleagues who systematically snapped them all in two. Then five
or six protestors, including the one with the megaphone, were
bundled into the van.

I couldn't believe the casual way this was taken by everyone else.
'Oh my God they've arrested them,' I was squealing. 'Why don't we
go and tell someone, this should be in all the papers. They can't be
allowed to do that and they've got the megaphone and there wasn't
even any warning . . .'

'Yeah, that's what they're like,' said everyone else.

I wasn't used to a world where it was expected that someone
would be arrested. Arrested, as far as I knew, was big news. If my
mother heard that there'd been an arrest of anyone vaguely
connected to her life, she'd announce it in the gravest terms as a
newsflash. 'You know the woman who works in the bakers on
Saturday mornings. Well last week her brother was arrested!' she'd
say, in the voice a newsreader reserves for telling us about a plane
crash. So surely this incident would be a major item on the news. I
was like a four-year-old, uncontrollably excited at spotting a
regular object and screaming 'Look, look, look, an egg cup' at his
unimpressed parents.

What would Mrs Scott over the road say if she knew the police
behaved like this? Your first police violence is like losing your
virginity, or your first curry. No matter how much you thought you
understood the process, nothing prepares you for the actual
experience. I knew in theory that the police force was a corrupt and
violent institution. But I didn't seriously honestly think they'd
arrest people for nothing and break their placards – in *practice*.

All the years of being brought up to believe the police were
friendly souls, was it all a lie? The road traffic lectures at primary

school, PC Plod in *Noddy*, *Dixon of Dock Green*, *Police 5* with Shaw Taylor, films at the big school in which affable coppers warn you never to accept lifts off strangers. Parents, teachers, scout-masters making sure you understand that in the event of anything suspicious, find a policeman. Officer Dibble in *Top Cat*, news items with sergeants assuring us they were doing everything possible to find the culprit. Every image of the police told you they were marvellous. But I'd seen them. Not heard about or read about but seen them, right there, bundling innocent people into a van and snapping their placards.

The next day I scoured the newspapers. Why was there nothing about the unprovoked arrest of five or six people? 'They just bundled in and snatched the megaphone,' I'd gibber at everyone I met for the next two weeks. 'Well there must have been a reason,' I'd be told. 'NOOOO. I'm telling you, I saw it . . .' I'd scream. An even more infuriating response was: 'Well if someone makes an official complaint through the correct channels, I'm sure it will be dealt with.' But none of them could grasp that I'd seen them doing it. I felt like one of these people in science fiction films who sees a spaceship and gets told by everyone to try and forget about it. At work, at home, in the pub, everyone was sure I'd got it wrong. Sometimes I'd get the surreal reply 'Well if you weren't there it wouldn't have happened'. Aaaaaaagh. By this logic you could justify the decapitation of any passing stranger on the grounds that it wouldn't have happened if they'd been in Huddersfield.

There was one other lesson to be drawn from the experience. Those around David Owen, if not David Owen himself, did take notice of protests. Handfuls of demonstrators may not directly alter government policies on arms deals but they do serve as an irritant. If nothing else, it spoils their day to the extent that they ask the police to break the demonstration up, so even a small protest reminds them that opposition does exist. People who regard such protests as pointless should imagine how much happier ministers would be if they never had to face them. When they travel to an armaments factory, or a photo opportunity wearing a silly hat in a bakery, they must think, 'Oh I do hope I don't have a mob of protestors today.' These people are human, and they'd rather be greeted by dignitaries shaking their hands, without a howling posse

of demonstrators waving placards and drowning out the sycophantic speeches with a megaphone.

But also, a protest has an impact on those who agree with the
aims of the protest but who've gone elsewhere on their Friday
night. A snippet in the newspaper, a misreported semi-mention on
London South East, a scrambled report from someone who was
there, gives anyone in opposition the most important assurance of
all, that they're not alone.

There must have been thousands at different meetings around
London who heard about the David Owen protest in an announcement, and subconsciously took a beat of encouragement from the
fact that it was taking place. Even though by that time they were
heading for the bar with not the slightest intention of going. And I
could watch the news from Iran over the next few weeks from a
slightly altered perspective.

Each night the news showed the massive marches, heaving with
a million vibrant demonstrators who could sense they were within
sight of toppling a major dictator as they chanted and thrust their
placards into the air with a confident urgency. Only the most
wretched cynic could fail to be moved by the huge numbers,
beamed into our televisions as they assembled under the
magnificent structure which straddles the main street in Teheran.
And I could view this in the smug knowledge that due to my
naivety concerning the rules of socialist meetings, I had played my
humble part. SAVAK – the Met, bulldozed villages – broken
placards, a million in Teheran – eight in Gravesend, one world –
one struggle.

Chapter 4

Becoming an active socialist in the late seventies was like arriving at the end of a brilliant party. I was arriving at the time others were leaving and garbling that I should have been there earlier. 'You mean you weren't here for the miners' strikes and dockers' strike and bringing down the Tory government,' old hands would say with sympathy. There was still the odd shriek of jollity, enough to confirm that if I'd got there earlier I'd have witnessed some cracking revelry. But mostly it amounted to the odd council workers' strike, the equivalent of the last sausage rolls and bottle of Liebfraumilch, while everyone else got into their cabs and went home.

There were still many people who considered themselves active socialists. The Labour left, embittered at the surrender of their government to the bankers, was growing. The Communist Party retained the support of thousands of trade unionists and the anti-racist movement alongside the punk scene could mobilize thousands more. But as unemployment grew and the certainties of the post-war years faded under a Labour government, the centre ground in society was moving rightwards.

This combination made for a polarized society. A large minority actively supported strikes and campaigns but the majority were hostile to them. The Silver Jubilee was celebrated by countless street parties but loudly despised by anyone with the Clash album. One trend which sprang from this political friction was the rise of the badge.

Campaigners took delight in climbing aboard trains, packed with commuters oozing with respectability, sporting a bright bold badge saying 'Abortion Rights NOW!' or 'Ireland – Britain's Vietnam'. It became possible to locate certain badges at 60 yards through crowded shopping centres. 'That woman carrying a rubber plant's wearing an anti-nuclear power badge.' Then, as long as you were wearing a badge or two yourself, you'd give each other a friendly nod as you passed, in the way that owners of Morris Minors beep each other on country lanes. There were badges saying 'Defend Our Unions', 'Disband the SPG', 'Fight for the Right to Work' and 'Help the Police – Beat Yourself Up', which at the time seemed sharply satirical. The badge culture was an example of how people can be proud of standing up for a cause, whereas no one is proud of being 'realistic'. Who would wear a badge saying 'Support the Right to Work Without Jeopardising the Target Inflation Rate'?

And in the fallout from punk almost every council estate had a band and every band had a badge. So it was possible to collect enough badges to cover a jacket or shirt and wander around as a mass of slogans and adverts for obscure punk bands. Amongst my badges was one for 'Kent County Cricket Club'. People must have wondered whether that was a band or a cryptic anti-nuclear message, never imagining it was the badge for Kent County Cricket Club.

Occasionally I have a flashback to the badge age and see someone sixty yards away in a shopping centre wearing a bright yellow badge. Sensing a kindred spirit, I prepare for the mutual nod and notice it says 'Judo For All', or 'HMV Record Store'. I got half-way through the nod once before realizing the badge said McDonald's and felt annoyed all day that this wanker was probably thinking 'Ah, someone else who appreciates a Thick Shake'.

In the winter of 1978/79, however, one organization swept the board with all badge awards: the Anti-Nazi League. In that period there were probably more people wearing the little yellow badge with the arrow than wore mini-skirts in 1968 or platform shoes in 1973. Fascist candidates had won council seats in Blackburn, 44,000 votes in Leicester and 119,000 votes in the GLC election in London, which was 5.7 per cent of the total. Almost every town had a branch of the National Front and one of their leaders, Martin Webster, became a national celebrity.

Living standards were falling for the first time since the thirties. The polarization of society was creating an air of violence, as crime grew, strikes became bitter and punks snarled through suburban high streets. A number of books appeared predicting social breakdown, including one which claimed the combined forces of left-wing groups, Rastafarians and the IRA were plotting to take over the country. Which, if successful, would have made for brilliant arguments in the cabinet. 'When you light that spliff, can you make sure it doesn't go near the semtex.'

As inflation roared, while demonstrations and urban youth remained visible, a corner of society felt under siege. Certain shop-keepers, small businessmen, aspiring salesmen who drank in saloon bars on Sundays in thick pullovers, all sought the economic stability of a few years ago and the respectability of an imaginary erstwhile golden age, a world without punks, long-haired students – and blacks.

From this circle came the backbone of the National Front. The NF candidate in Gravesend was a greengrocer. In Sevenoaks it was Michael Easter, who owned a chemist shop. In most areas the leading figures were disgruntled small businessmen or farmers. They had to recruit frightened pensioners and disillusioned unemployed youths, but without their small business heart their movement would have withered and died.

A widespread explanation for why this movement eventually declined is that extremism is not 'the British way'. Does this mean fascist groups in Britain can achieve 5.7 per cent of the vote but never 5.8 per cent because that's not British? Does it mean that marching and waving flags could never catch on here, as it would interfere with afternoon tea? And that if British fascists didn't like a book, instead of standing in a circle and throwing it on a bonfire, they'd *sit* in a circle and criticize the grammar? Fascism wasn't the German way either until 1933. It wasn't the Italian way until 1922. Just as until 1867 parliamentary democracy wasn't the British way.

My first sighting of fascists in action was when a punk band called the Lurkers played at Thames Polytechnic in Woolwich. There was nothing especially political about the event, until around 50 fascists took their shirts off, revealing t-shirts displaying the British Movement logo. 'Sieg Heil' they all chanted and set about attacking everybody else in the room. The band itself was attacked and dozens of people were pummelled, left to lie in a corner screaming for help. Stunts like this were common and a lesson in the tactics of fascism. One argument was that the way to defeat these people was by making their arguments look stupid. But it was doubtful whether it would have made much impact, as a sixteen-stone skinhead rammed his fist into your eyeball, to point out that he may well be descended from a Roman.

It was to provide a genuine opposition to these characters that the Anti-Nazi League had been formed, in the aftermath of the battle at Lewisham. The ANL had three aims. The first was to expose the National Front and similar groups as fascists. The second was to create a culture in which fascism wouldn't be tolerated. Musicians, actors and sportsmen were encouraged to make anti-Nazi statements. Anti-Nazi groups were set up in workplaces, schools, and football clubs. Over 100,000 people went to each of the ANL carnivals in London. And countless people wore that little yellow badge.

Thousands became adept in the art of removing NF stickers. After a while, you could reach out and yank one off a post box without even breaking your stride. But what a bastard if one was well stuck down. How many people at that time were late for work because their route had taken them past a particularly stubborn sticker? Because once you'd started, to leave it even half intact was an admission of defeat. So you'd stand for five minutes, scratching alternately with a key and a two-pence piece. Eventually you could resume your journey, having reduced this sticker to four torn white corners and no middle. 'That,' you would say to yourself, 'is a Nazi-free post box.'

The third aim of the ANL was to physically stop the NF from carrying out their activities. John Tyndall, leader of the NF, had said, 'Our great marches, with drums and flags and banners, have a hypnotic effect in solidifying the allegiance of our followers so that their enthusiasm can be sustained.' But marches are nowhere near as hypnotic and solidifying if everyone taking part has to run behind a bus shelter, using the drums to protect themselves from a shower of rubble.

In Dartford, which had a large Asian population, there was an NF group, of which the most prominent members were Irene and Thomas Nobbs, who never went anywhere without their Great Dane. Every Saturday they gave out leaflets in the shopping centre, extolling the virtues of repatriation, while their hound sniffed and harumphed, unaware of its proximity to people of such destiny.

So just before Christmas 1978, a local branch of the ANL was formed, comprising two SWP members, a nurse from the women's group, a Communist Party member, two from the Labour Party, my mate who'd gone to the carnival and a vicar. And every Saturday we'd stand by the shopping centre handing out leaflets opposing theirs. Sometimes they'd spit at us and sometimes we'd snatch their leaflets and chuck them in a puddle.

Once, two enormous skinheads walked past wearing badges saying 'Pogo on a Communist'. 'We'll get you later,' they chuckled and nearly did, hurling their massive frames between bewildered shoppers in pursuit of us, in an American TV-cop style chase, until a friendly car screeched alongside and we jumped in, sped off and thanked our anti-fascist stranger. For tens of thousands of people, incidents like this amounted to just another Saturday morning in 1979.

Mrs Nobbs always seemed more enthusiastic than Mr Nobbs. She'd whisk out her leaflets with great authority, emitting a curt 'Here you are' like a Victorian headmistress. While Mr Nobbs, unshaven and somewhat overweight for an exhibit of the master race, held the dog lead and garbled obscenities at any shoppers who took exception to his presence.

One day, via the local paper, Mrs Nobbs dared me to call her a Nazi to her face. This was the stuff small towns are made of. 'Mrs Nobbs,' I said the following Saturday morning, a contingent of about fifteen standing on either side, like extras from *High Noon* awaiting the showdown, 'You're a Nazi.' She took no notice at all and gave out another leaflet. I was so disappointed. Had she no sense of drama?

The day she really let rip was when she was talking amiably to a bystander, who also had a large dog. 'Don't listen to her,' I scowled, 'She's a Nazi.'

'I beg your pardon,' said Mrs Nobbs in a shocked shriek, that you might expect if you said 'cocksucker' to the vicar's wife. 'I am *trying* to talk to my friend about dogs,' she said. And for a moment I actually felt sorry. The legacy of being a teenager, enduring the constant feeling that you're disrupting important adult life, made me feel momentarily guilty for bothering her while she was just talking to her friend about dogs.

In the spring of 1979 came Dartford carnival in the park, with dog-handling displays, pony rides, homemade cakes, an RAC recruitment stall and a spinning wheel stall. We knew in advance there would be a spinning wheel stall, because a security guard from the park had seen the application forms and tipped us off that it would be run by Mr and Mrs Nobbs and their friends, to raise funds for the NF. But to prevent anyone knowing, the council had allowed them to apply under the name of the Dartford Angling Society.

For certain local dignitaries, the annual carnival provides their raison d'être. They can stroll amongst their citizens, posing for photos as they hand over a cheque to the hospice appeal and present a trophy to the winning tug of war team. So it must have flashed through their minds that the whole year was in danger of ruin when they heard that a group of protestors with leaflets, placards and megaphone had surrounded the stall promoted by the Angling Society.

Our informer was inaccurate in one detail, in that the NF stall turned out to be a lucky numbers game. So before the protest could begin, we had to perform the classic task of amateur agitators, crossing out a mistake on 500 leaflets and correcting it in biro. I bet that as the French revolution was starting, someone was adding the letter 'l' to hundreds of leaflets, muttering '*I* didn't know there were two "l"s in Bastille'.

But most importantly, there they were, the same people who spent Saturday mornings handing out leaflets promising repatriation of immigrants, barking 'Roll up, roll up, pick your lucky numbers, three goes a pound'. Had there been a debate? I wondered. Was there a moment when a dozen Nazis were divided into two animated factions, one screaming 'We'll make more money with lucky numbers' while the other yelled back 'But I spent all last night making the bloody spinning wheel'.

The NF were astonished at our arrival, especially Mr Nobbs who cried out 'Oh for God's sake, leave us alone'. But you can't blame them for being astonished, as this must have been one of the only protests in history to have taken place about a lucky numbers stall.

We implored the public not to have a go at picking any lucky numbers, as this was a fascist lucky numbers stall, and prevented them from getting any custom at all. Though the general reaction was not outrage at the fascists but utter bewilderment. There must have been people who went home that day believing we were a group hostile to the concept of lucky numbers stalls in general, perhaps connected to mention of them somewhere in the Bible.

But the dignitaries were as embarrassed as the NF were outraged. 'Surely there's some way of coming to a compromise,' they insisted, visibly sweating that this could end up as an item on Radio Kent. We probably hadn't helped our standing with the council by stating on our leaflet that, 'Dartford council, by allowing the fascists to be here today, are openly supporting all the National Front stand for.' Everything: from increased subsidies for British farmers, to the deportation of blacks and secret celebrations of Hitler's birthday, Dartford council, according to us had proved they openly supported the lot.

After two hours came a problem we hadn't considered. People started to leave. Someone had to pick up their kids, someone had promised to do some shopping, and our numbers were dwindling. So we struck a deal with council officials, whereby we promised to leave the carnival alone as long as a large sign was erected pointing out that this was a Nazi National Front stall and that people were advised not to contribute to it. The council agreed and we left. Though I'm sure some people would argue that by abandoning our posts we were openly supporting all the National Front stood for.

The exuberant chaos of local activities was magnified many times over by the unrelenting mania of the national demonstrations. Counter-marches are unique, in that no one's sure where they're going, as it depends on the last-minute rearrangements of the fascists and the police. So every single person amongst the thousands who attend, as they arrive asks the nearest person 'what's happening?'

But no one ever knew the answer. Eventually, a group of fifty or more would walk in the same direction and everyone followed. They might have all been going for a burger, but as everyone joined them it would go around that the fascists were definitely this way. So even if they *were* going for a burger they would now believe that the fascists are this way anyway and abandon the burger. Then a group of six people would run across a car park, screaming 'They're over here. This way. For Christ's sake you fucking idiots, they're over here.'

But did they really expect that, as a result of their yelling, a thousand people would change direction and follow a route which went over a wooden fence and through Woolworths? Although, if instead of six people screaming it had been someone muttering at the back that the fascists were apparently that way, within seconds word would have spread and there'd have been a stampede through the pic 'n' mix.

Yet some people would have the ability to shout 'over there' and find that as a result everybody ran over there. It must be a magical gift to have one of those voices, as their shout would come after twenty or more other shouts of 'over there', all of which had slid away like sand through fingers. It's surprising how a phrase containing three syllables can start strong, gradually peter out and end up as barely a whistle, but that's what happens to most people when they shout 'over there' to a crowd of strangers. But some people are blessed. They must be the same people who can start a chant at a football match and find that everybody joins in.

So we'd all run over there, although they were never there. But amidst the exasperated groans of demonstrators catching their breath, gazing in all directions like the Sweeney when they've lost a criminal, was I the only one thinking 'Thank fuck we can't find them'?

After a period of inactivity, someone would decide that one of the onlookers from a pub was a Nazi, because his hair was shorter than anyone else's. 'Nazi, Nazi' a contingent would shout. The onlookers would watch in fascination, until the one with short hair gradually realized the venom was aimed at him. Then he'd make a face that said 'What? Me?' As you would, if you were having a quiet lunchtime drink and then thousands of demonstrators converged on the area for the sole purpose of spitting at you, specifically *you*, from the middle of the road.

At the end of one of these days everyone would drift on to trains and coaches, with no one sure whether we'd won or lost. Days like these make you realize how misleading are the maps punctuated by arrows and dotted lines, which clinically describe the movements in major battles. Even when there are no guns, smoke or cannon, but a few thousand people with round yellow placards, chaos reigns. I bet the Battle of Hastings ended with hundreds of soldiers wandering in a daze, saying 'I think Harold's won'. At one point a rumour probably swept through the ranks that the enemy was just over this hill, and some will have seen a crowd, charged forward and then realized they were lunging into an equally bamboozled posse from their own side. And at the end, whole platoons probably waited by a designated spot, moaning that this was where the horses were supposed to be half an hour ago to take them home. And that they were bloody starving, but because of the battle all the local inns were boarded up and had notices saying 'No Normans or Saxons welcome'.

Often I'd wonder whether my presence had achieved anything at all. Months later I'd meet people who had been on the same counter-demonstration as me and they'd swap stories. Everyone had a tale; of stumbling across wayward groups of fascists and chasing them through a boating lake. Or of nicking a road digger and parking it on the route of the NF's march before legging it over a breaker's yard. 'Huh-huh,' I'd titter, in that way you laugh when you ought to be impressed but aren't sure you believe a word of what someone's told you.

Though really I was just dreading them saying, 'And what about you Mark? What's your favourite story of things that happened to you, you personally, that day?' For I would either have to lie, or say, 'Well it was incredible, right, because I got there, and then we went over one way, and around a bit and back, and then I bought a pasty and went home.'

Back on the coaches, a few would scream in macho angst that if everyone else wasn't such a coward we could have been far more destructive. But even if we'd forced the entire NF membership to flee the country on a rowing boat, these people would have shouted that the whole day had been a disaster, and if only we hadn't been so weedy we could have smashed their oars as well.

All this was to miss the point of the ANL. The exuberant

schoolkids who distributed the badges, the tenants who formed groups to wash off the graffiti and the security guard who risked his job by tipping off the local group about the lucky numbers stall were the real army that defeated fascism in 1979. It should be *celebrated* that most people who attended the counter-demonstrations weren't hardened brawlers and were probably secretly frightened. For it proves that thugs can be beaten by ideas.

And the marches themselves, even at their worst, forced the fascists to shuffle along their route protected by thousands of police, their flags hidden and their vitriol drowned by the ebullience of the demonstrators. More commonly their march would be re-routed by the police, usually into a park or industrial estate, eventually stuttering out altogether as it became impossible for the police to guarantee their safety. In Gravesend, the police announced to the 300 people who were stood in the road that the NF march had been abandoned altogether.

It was this momentum which led 7,000 people, on a Monday night just before the general election, to the Asian area of Southall. Three years earlier Gurdip Singh Chaggar had been murdered there by an NF-inspired gang. Now the NF had organized a rally in the town hall, to be addressed by Martin Webster, and most workplaces in the area had responded by going on strike.

By now the routine was becoming familiar. Just as baffling, but familiar. I arrived at the station and followed everyone else, then came across a crowd in the road. 'What's happening,' I asked, and nobody knew. Everyone tried to peer over the mass of people to see what was happening. Every time you asked what was happening, you felt you were being a nuisance for wanting to know, as if you'd arrived late at the cinema and kept asking who was that bloke with Al Pacino.

Occasionally a section of the crowd would shout, so everyone else would shout and the adrenaline would rush because something might happen. But today did seem different; the hanging around was less confused and more purposeful; hundreds were sat in the road. There had been a series of arrests throughout the day as demonstrators were gathering. In the following weeks came dozens of substantiated reports that the police had been taunting Asians all afternoon. The 5,000 police were moving with a rigidity and purpose I'd never witnessed and they were flaunting the presence of the notorious Special Patrol Group, with riot shields and truncheons.

In these situations the police are like a pub brawler. The only thing I ever learned about fighting was how to tell when a bruiser was showing off and when he was really shaping up for a bundle. You can apply the same lessons to the police. They stiffen, they focus their eyes, they breathe more heavily or something, I'm not sure what. But whatever it is, they give off a sense that crackles like a darkening thunderous afternoon in summer, swirling litter through the streets and spitting its first drizzle before a ferocious storm.

Now the rumours weren't of where the fascists were but of arrests; and in the middle of the main road, where the front row of demonstrators sat gazing up at the front row of the police, scuffles were breaking out like the border clashes that lead to all-out wars. Then at various points, to the left, to the right, the eerie multi-clippety-clop of a team of riot cops trotting in line and stopping at a pre-determined spot. But most people are bemused; it looks almost funny. The upbringing runs so deep you just can't imagine they would attack a road full of people, even when you've seen them snatch a megaphone and snap placards.

The police must study horror films, for they seem aware that nothing is more terrifying than silence. They know the impact of their presence would be ruined if they started beckoning, and shouting 'All right then you slag, do you want some?' So they wait, not moving, not responding, like those Raptus dinosaurs in *Jurassic Park*.

In the distance is the tension of another arrest. A placard is launched at the policemen making the arrest. More arrests, more placards and occasionally the heavy tapping of another movement of police. Everyone stands still, from motivation, fascination, excitement and disbelief that the police will really launch an all-out attack. At certain times, one second can be the complete opposite of the one which follows. And when that second came, it was the armoured lines of police running furiously into the crowd as everyone screamed and ran in all directions. Individuals were selected, apparently at random, and groups of six surrounded them before they disappeared under a flurry of waving batons.

The tactic is called crowd dispersal but the most unlikely reaction is that everyone will disperse. Anger exploded in all directions and missiles launched through shop windows, setting off alarms. Vans hurtled into the main road from side-streets and the back doors flew open to reveal a team of police diving out like bank robbers in an old English comedy. Someone, probably for reasons that the police themselves didn't know, would be selected, pursued and if caught, battered.

And so it went on. Manic aimless fleeing, interspersed with periods of calm as the police regrouped, while battered demonstrators stood in the middle of the road and yelled. Then a van would screech beside you and you all ran again, some shrieking, some swerving to avoid a swinging baton, but all collectively knowing when to stop.

Yet somehow none of this seemed as terrifying as it should have done, probably because I couldn't quite believe it was happening. No matter how many people who hadn't done anything I saw getting battered, I still felt that they wouldn't wallop me because, well, I hadn't done anything.

In the chaos I found two friends from Dartford and two Asian men who took us to an Indian café they claimed to own but evidently didn't. They seemed to feel exhilarated by the episode, so now I didn't know what to think. I couldn't deny it had been exciting, compared to an evening in Swanley. But on the train home I had no guide as to its outcome apart from the rush of my own adrenaline.

The next morning I eagerly turned on the radio news. What would they be saying about the thing that I'd been at? They were bound to be discussing it with avowed reverence and I'd been there. Whatever else they said, I heard four words – 'Death of a teacher'. As we were fleeing backwards and forwards, one of the teams from one of the vans had looked around, pointed at Blair Peach, pursued him and killed him. One teacher who, it emerged, was afraid of events like this and had twice been attacked by NF members, who on one occasion severed a tendon in one of his hands.

I was veering between numbness, shock and guilt at having come away with a sense of excitement. But there wasn't time for either, for already the torrents of predictable bile were flying. Every paper, news bulletin, politician, police officer and respectable member of society was yelping at how this demonstrating mob must be stopped. A man had been killed, so we must have immediate and decisive action . . . against those who'd been attacked! It was as if these people were all suffering from some collective psychological illness, whereby they got people who'd been battered and killed mixed up with the people who'd battered and killed them. Maybe, when these people watched thrillers, they spent the whole film thinking 'I hope they catch the evil bastard who was killed at the beginning'.

From the way it was reported, there must have been people who thought, 'What on earth made those violent Anti-Nazi people want to kill that poor teacher?' I'd hear protestations from workmates and co-drinkers who'd repeat the line of the press and I wondered whether it was all an elaborate international wind-up designed to drive me mad. 'Look,' I'd repeat, 'Dozens of demonstrators, but no police, were hospitalized. 340 were arrested. A musician had to have a testicle removed. An immigrant advice centre was demolished. And Blair Peach is dead. So which side was the most violent? Eh?'

Listening to fruitcake views – that the firemen's strike was organized by the Kremlin or that social security gives every Pakistani a new car – always feels like a two-pronged assault. There's the depressing experience of hearing someone talk such rubbish. But just as exasperating is that the argument is so blatantly illogical, causing the same frustration as if someone insists it's Tuesday on a Thursday.

Most galling of all is when someone insists that they know better than you what happened, not even acknowledging that you were there and they were at home. But of course the majority of people just accepted the official version, with which they were being bombarded from every angle. They'd been through the same experiences as I had, hearing every day that the police were there to protect them. Trying to convince them that the police had run riot and murdered someone was like saying, 'You know those burglaries that have been going on round here. The person doing them is your mum.'

The people who accepted the truth were the people who'd

experienced the police at first hand, such as the trade unionists and
Indian Workers Associations who campaigned against the cover-
up, and the 15,000 who went to Blair Peach's funeral.

In the following weeks, the pathologist who'd conducted the post-
mortem on Blair Peach concluded that the weapon which killed
him was a 'hosepipe filled with lead shot, or some like weapon'. An
inquiry discovered that SPG officers' lockers contained dozens of
weapons like this. It also confirmed which SPG unit, consisting of
six officers, the murderer came from. Whichever one he was, he
never received as much as a £10 fine.

Southall left an indelible mark on all who were present. Rather
than discouraging the participants, events like these solidify the
determination of everyone who attends. They serve the purpose of
an initiation ceremony in a cult group; anyone there would always
be, at least partly, defined by the fact that they were. Southall was
the most explosive and, because of the murder, the best
remembered of the counter-demonstrations. It was also the last of
the major confrontations, as the spring of 1979 marked a turning
point in NF fortunes.

For the reason why, you have to see these events through fascist
eyes. You may have been a cynical teenager, thrust into a world in
which the full employment, rising living standards and guaranteed
housing enjoyed by your parents were being snatched away. But
there were blacks with jobs and blacks with houses. If only we
hadn't given everything to the blacks, you'd think. So you were
drawn to the force that dared say this publicly. But every time you
put up one of their stickers, it was torn down. Every poster and NF
graffiti was removed. Some of your idols made statements condemning the party you were attracted to. You were abused when
you gave out leaflets and every time you went into a public place at
least one person was wearing a badge aimed directly at you.

You were invited to rallies designed, in Hitler's words, to 'make
the worm feel like a dragon'. But you'd wake up in the morning and
grimace at the prospect that, at best, you'd shuffle fifty yards
around a car park behind 2,000 policemen, protected from 10,000
demonstrators. Then, you were even surrounded when you tried to
raise money with a stall offering lucky numbers. With such

methods the ANL succeeded in splitting the weekend racist from the dedicated fascist.

The protests, counter-marches, leafletting and picketing of stalls in parks were all individually chaotic. But the whole picture showed that a growing confident fascist movement was strangled at a crucial stage. In the May 1979 election, the NF stood 280 candidates, whose average vote was 841, just over half their average in 1974. Irene Nobbs lost her deposit. The National Front never recovered and by the time of the next election they'd dissolved into a spiral of internal feuding.

One explanation for their decline was that Margaret Thatcher stole their support, with her speech about people being swamped by an alien culture. But why were fascists capable of launching violent attacks in 1978 but not five years later? Were the British Movement supporters who attacked the Lurkers gig thinking, 'I would have kicked that bloke's head in but now that Mrs Thatcher has promised to introduce tough legislation I'll let him go and grow my hair.' In France, the National Front of Jean-Marie Le Pen *increased* its support every time conservative politicians made racist speeches in an attempt to attract his supporters.

The argument that Thatcher ruined the NF is classically British, in that it imagines no political action has an impact outside of parliament. Are they saying the millions of leaflets, badges, stickers and placards, the gigs, the carnivals and demonstrations had no effect at all? That disillusioned people considering a vote for someone appearing to offer something new weren't influenced by the constant reminders that these people were brutal, violent and fascist? But one speech from Margaret Thatcher and they all changed their mind? What a depressing thought then, if fascist parties return. Because the only way to stop them will be to persuade the leader of the Conservative Party to make a racist speech. Maybe he should chuck a brick through a curry house window. Then the fascists wouldn't stand a chance.

No one can say how strong the fascists would have become if the ANL had never existed, although Martin Webster and John Tyndall both wrote that its effect was crucial. But more than any statistics or quotes could reveal, the decline of their dream was etched on to the face of Mr Nobbs as I bumped into him in a

Dartford pub, about a year after the election.

'I can't understand you,' he said. 'Why did you have to do that to us? After all, I'm a socialist, just a National socialist, that's all.' He fumbled in the pockets of his shiny and slightly too short trousers, rummaged through the change he found and gave a little relieved grunt once he'd amassed enough to buy himself one more drink. 'Our people have got nothing,' he said, and repeated the word 'nothing'. But he said it in the way an old man might say 'I gave her everything' about the wife that left him twenty years ago. It wasn't a vision for the future but a yearning for why this future would never be.

'It was the wife who went on about it more than me,' he said. 'To tell you the truth, I'm much happier walking the dog.'

Chapter 5

The dead were left unburied. It's a fact. As incontestable as Nelson's one eye or Edison inventing the lightbulb. It's as if the full title of the year 1979 is '1979 – when the dead were left unburied'. It became known as the Winter of Discontent and from then on no discussion of trade unions was complete without warnings of returns to the days when the dead were left unburied.

Take the *Mail on Sunday*'s report on the 1998 strike of electricians at the Jubilee Line Extension. 'It's the Winter of Discontent all over again,' it began, before describing strikers as 'industrial gangsters', 'wreckers dressed in donkey jackets and carrying placards', 'infiltrated by militant troublemakers' and 'surrounded by burly pickets'. (How do you infiltrate electricians? Do you hire a box of fuses and wander round muttering 'tut-tut, someone's made a right mess of this'?)

It should have continued: 'And in a dark reminder of the gloomy days of 1979, the electricians even refused to bury the dead! "But it's not our job, we're electricians," snarled unshaven pickets, when we handed them a shovel and corpse and told them to start digging.'

Teenagers reading about the winter of '79 must imagine that was all trade unions did. They collected dead bodies, dragged them into the manager's office and said, 'Give us a rise or we're nailing these to your desk.' There must be people who think that in 1979 corpses were randomly scattered across roads, so that from a distance they looked like the first speed bumps. And that bemused housewives would ring the council, asking if there was any news as to when someone could take Uncle Alf away, as they were having a new settee delivered and there wouldn't be space.

The strikes of that winter were in response to four years of government pay limits. Between 1975 and 1978, prices had risen by 50 per cent but wages by only 30 per cent, making this the first time since the war in which living standards had fallen. Throughout that period there was a barrage of propaganda informing us that wage rises caused inflation and therefore made us worse off. Every politician, every newspaper and *Nationwide*, the early evening news programme on BBC1, regularly said so.

A graph would appear showing how high inflation would be if wages rose by 5 per cent. Then they'd say that if wages rose by 10 per cent, inflation would be *this* high, and another graph would come out with a line spiralling off the edge, like the line to tell you how much has been raised for the *Blue Peter* annual appeal.

For four years the propaganda had worked. But in the fifth year, workers at Ford, oil tanker drivers, lorry drivers and bakers struck to break the government's pay limit. Then followed one-day strikes by hospital workers, journalists, civil servants and council workers, including, in some areas, gravediggers.

As the winter progressed, the press frenzy escalated. Honest men were prevented from working by burly pickets and one day a journalist from the *Daily Mail* contacted the senior clerk in a Liverpool morgue. After several assurances that there were ample places for the dead to be stored, he conceded that, in the event of the most freakish circumstances, it was conceivable there may be a problem. 'Now the dead are left unburied' screeched the next morning's paper. Newspapers became like those church bulletins in which every article leads to the same point. Except that, instead of a piece about the FA Cup Final somehow arriving at Jesus, it would end up as yet more proof that the unions were running the country.

The *Daily Mail* had a cartoon strip called 'Focus on Fact', which usually told you things like who invented the post box or how cheese is made. Suddenly one week its subject was 'The Unions'. In the first strip, over a notice saying 'school closed until further notice', came the facts: 'Unions now have legal freedom to close factories, hospitals and schools, deprive workers of jobs, hurt the sick and the weak, to increase their slices of a shrinking national cake.' The solution they proposed was to elect the woman whose whole career was dedicated to opening factories, hospitals and schools, to creating jobs and protecting the sick and the weak.

You almost expected to see crossword clues like 'Coming together before Jack to leave the dead unburied perhaps (5)'. Or for the weatherman to say 'luckily there will be some strong wind this evening, which should waft away the smell of those unburied corpses'. The subtext to every tirade about the dead being left unburied was that the mountains of stiffs piling up in local parks and libraries were caused by the Labour government and would all be sorted out by Thatcher. In other words, it was the result of Labour being soft on the unions. Which lacked a certain logic, as the strikes were only taking place because Labour was confronting the unions.

But while the media claims were painfully exaggerated, the winter was dominated by strikes. There *was* an enormous pile of rubbish in Leicester Square, courtesy of striking dustmen, which for a while became a national monument. People would ask whether you'd seen it, in the same way they might ask if you'd seen *The Texas Chainsaw Massacre*. Which should have provided an exhilarating boost to the career of a budding troublemaker. Instead there was a dour sense of gloom descending on the labour movement which the strikes couldn't hide. It was difficult to play a part, because none of the strikes reached beyond their own corners. Those involved made few attempts to link them together, a mistake that wasn't made by Margaret Thatcher or her press. There were none of the support groups that became a feature of strikes in the eighties. So it felt like being a football fan whose role was reduced to watching and hoping.

This was especially frustrating as the media regularly announced that it *was* the extremists who were causing the strikes. The president of the Food Manufacturers' Federation declared about the lorry drivers' strike 'the whole thing was planned six months in advance. Who by? The SWP – I have no doubt'.

Throughout Britain then, the nation's lorry drivers were taking their orders from groups of eight people who met once a week in freezing pub function rooms. After all, lorry drivers are renowned for being particularly weedy and easy to push around. How did we organize it? Maybe drivers would hear a code like 'the pussycat is ready' on their radio, then think 'that's the signal from that stoned hospital porter in Gravesend' and screech immediately to a halt.

And what a fascinating detail, that it was planned 'six months in advance'. Which gives the impression of an underground bunker full of Trotskyists marching in orange boiler suits purposefully around a giant map of Britain, with lights depicting every city and every motorway. While the grand leader, wearing an eyepatch, sits on a raised platform banging his fist on a table and screaming 'Not a single biscuit is to enter Southampton'. And opposite him a digital clock displays the number of seconds left until the strike begins.

However absurd, this statement and similar ones filtered into everyday conversations. In the pub my own mates would make comments like 'I've got to hand it to you, you've organized this to perfection. They've even run out of sugar at International Stores'. Others would ask me for advice on matters such as when we could expect the next delivery of pork to the Swanley area; or whether the strike would still be on in three weeks' time, as that's when their dad's building firm would need a new supply of cement.

I'd find it hard to admit, let alone explain, that, far from being the Godfather of the lorry-driving fraternity, I longed to be on first-name terms with a single lorry driver. So this was a tremendous boost to the ego. I couldn't get anyone from the dole office to a meeting but apparently with a snap of the fingers I could be responsible for a total absence of margarine in Exeter.

The 'outside agitators' theme, I came to realize, is a stock response to every strike or campaign which gathers a momentum. Partly, the company spokesmen, the ministers and journalists who adopt this line are creating propaganda. They're aiming to scare supporters of the campaign into thinking they're being manipulated by sinister figures with ulterior motives. The campaign to keep the swimming pool open is merely being used by these outsiders as a cloak for their real purpose of world domination.

But when the president of the Food Manufacturers' Federation made that statement, he almost certainly believed it. It's as if those at the top of society are incapable of believing that working-class people are intelligent enough to get cross without being told to. But if one group of outsiders turns up with a leaflet, they start thinking: 'It turns out I'm oppressed and miserable, and the only cure is to stand outside the plant linking arms, and looking burly. Off we go then.'

During this flurry of theories on outside agitators, I saw an episode of *Blue Peter* which for some reason included an item about the French Revolution. After telling us what a well-dressed and charming woman Marie-Antoinette was, the narrator told us that 'agitators from outside the area' rode through Paris on horseback spreading lies about the queen and encouraging revolt. This was accompanied with a shadowy drawing of men in cloaks tossing leaflets into the streets. I'm not suggesting a conspiracy here, along the lines of MI5 having an undercover spy in the scriptwriting department of *Blue Peter*, but the narrative had a distinctive early 1979 touch about it. Though if it *had* been drafted by the secret service it would have ended up 'but after they beheaded the King, even *they* took the trouble to bury him'.

Just as absurd, for anyone who's attended a few demonstrations, is when the press reports that there was an 'organized' force from outside the area. Organized! How little they know. If only the true outside force, the police, had the same level of organization as most demonstrators. Then the inspector would arrive half-an-hour late at the assembly point and splutter, 'Oh no, the sergeant's locked the truncheons in the boot of the panda.'

But in any case, why shouldn't a nurse actively support striking lorry drivers, or a lorry driver support striking nurses, even the stoned ones? For one thing, to do so is simply to display the human caring response that most of us are brought up to aspire to. If someone crossed the road to defend an old man being set about by thieves, they'd be very surprised to find a journalist behind them, haranguing them for interfering in a dispute that was nothing to do with him.

As the Winter of Discontent progressed, a new buzz-phrase was discovered: secondary picketing. It was always said in the tone with which people describe a new low; a practice carried out by fiends already as awful as we thought possible, but who have found a way of being even worse. Secondary picketing was simply a new name for the practice of picketing a workplace that wasn't your own, in order to ask the workforce to support the strike. But for most people, to admit during the winter of '79 that your son was a secondary picket would attract more shame than anything. 'Well there's one consolation,' your neighbours would say if a box of heroin was discovered under your floorboards, 'at least he's not a secondary picket.'

To anyone who believes the *Daily Mail* version, the reality of picket lines is an enormous disappointment. There are usually three or four people walking on the spot and rubbing their hands to keep warm, having being stood near a gate for several hours, and if it weren't for one of them wearing an armband, you'd worry that they'd been misled into thinking they were at a bus stop. The myth of outside agitators visiting picket lines to stir up trouble is even further from reality.

Most picket lines in the late seventies were outside obscure plants at the far end of remote industrial estates, next to a stretch of warehouses. The nearest object that would burn was probably twenty-minutes' drive away. The pathological troublemaker would have to arrive at the picket line with an armful of air rifles and try to persuade the strikers to shoot pigeons, on the grounds that it was the only thing possible to do that was naughty. Usually there were a couple of policemen stood a few yards from the pickets, occasionally coming across to ask 'How long are you lads thinking of staying here?', as they were desperate to get back in the warm themselves. In these circumstances it's doubtful whether the outside agitator's best approach is to shout 'I'll show you how to win this strike' and kick one of the coppers in the crotch.

This became clear to me on my first ever picket line at Littlebrook Power Station in Dartford. I wandered nervously along a muddy track and there they were. Now I realized the outside agitator's real dilemma: once you get there, what do you say? Which led to the same process as if I was walking up to a woman at a disco. I'd had plenty of time to work out my first line – 'Hello, I'm from the SWP and I'm here to support your strike.' Then one of them said 'oh, right' and looked quizzical, while the rest of them carried on talking about horseracing; the equivalent of the woman's friends pulling faces behind her. I half expected one of the other pickets to whisper 'uuugh, he's got no chance' and for the others to start giggling.

So I stood there, and stood there, and went through a variety of possibilities for a follow-up line. What must they have thought? They might have assumed I was a manager's son, sent down to elicit some inside information. It's more likely they were just perplexed as to why a long-haired teenager covered in badges for obscure punk bands would drive to this remote piece of wasteland by the Thames to quietly watch a group of workers in a dispute about overtime payments standing in a frozen huddle.

It must have seemed as strange as if you were mowing the lawn and looked round to see someone saying 'hello mate, I'm here to urge you on'. Eventually I selected my next line: 'So how's it going then?' He came back with a deluge of trade union jargon, words like 'differentials', phrases like 'convenor for the combine' and abbreviations for every regional divisional sub-committee throughout the NEC of the GMWU.

'Oh good,' I said, and wished this was a disco so I could quietly retreat to my mates. I stood there a while longer, rubbed my hands in the cold while desperately thinking of something else to say, until I came up with 'I don't suppose you fancy joining the local branch of the SWP then'. Which was the equivalent of standing silently by the woman, who's clearly taking no interest, then as the record stops saying, 'You wouldn't fancy a bunk-up, would you?'

There was a whole world of trade unionism out there and you couldn't go barging into it without having some idea how it worked. You might as well turn up at a hospital and announce that you've come to help carry out some heart surgery as you've heard that they're understaffed.

I was becoming more and more confused. I was an official enemy of the state, so what did I have to do to get into the middle of a series of strikes creating mass outrage? Shouldn't I be speaking at mass meetings of gravediggers? Instead, the main way the Winter of Discontent impinged on my daily life was to make me undergo an identical conversation several times a day on my milk-round.

About forty of the villagers bought their Sunblest medium-sliced bread from me each day. As the bakers' strike began, I was allocated only a few loaves of (scab) bread, which I kept for the old and infirm on the round. On day one of the strike, the occupants of the first house in the village marched up their gravel path and shouted over the sunflowers that instead of the usual loaf today they'd like seven. 'Seven?' I said. 'Seven,' they confirmed, 'because of the bakers' strike.'

'But I haven't got seven for the whole village.'

'Why not?'

'Because the bakers are on strike.'

'But you're not a baker, you're a milkman.'

At this point it was handy that I was confused about the role I was supposed to be playing in events, as this restrained me from following my instincts. Which was to shout, 'Does that mean you reckon I bake my own fucking bread? Maybe I milk my own cows as well, you brainless rural twat.'

Instead I explained that although I was a milkman, the dairy ordered its bread from a bakery – where bakers work. 'Well how many loaves have you got?' they asked.

'Six,' I said.

'Right, I'll have them.'

'They're for the old people.'

'Well I want them.'

'But they're for the old people.'

'Can't you give them to me?'

'No.'

'Well how many can I have?'

'None.'

'None? But I want them. Why can't I have them?'

'Because they're for the old people.'

'Well it's a bloody nuisance, this bloody strike. That's what's wrong with this country, too many people who are just downright selfish.'

And several times a day I endured a variant of this with villagers, their *Daily Mail*s flapping behind them on the doorstep. But what confused me further was that despite wanting to scream at these people I couldn't dislike them. They were so removed from the tensions of life up the road in Swanley that they could hardly be expected to empathize with a baker or lorry driver furious about his productivity deal. I imagined that if a striking lorry driver did turn up on their doorstep, they'd offer him some homemade marmalade and fudge, as long as he hadn't been secondary picketing anywhere that was muddy as they'd just got a new cover for the sofa.

But then came a piece of luck that would give me the trade union experience I needed. One morning, while reversing my milk float out of a driveway, I backed it straight through a BMW that belonged to the wife of Dave Charnley, ex-light-heavyweight boxing champion of Europe. In a chilling rerun of Teddy Kennedy's incident at Chappaquiddick, I panicked and sped off, as much as you can in a milk float, hoping no one had seen me. But they had. This time when I was sacked, it wasn't quite so easy to blame the economic crisis of capitalism.

But what a coup to then get a job in the telephone department of the Post Office at Elephant and Castle. And, during the training week, a one-day strike was called! I was going to be on strike! In truth the union agreed not to call out anyone who was on a training course but I didn't have to take any notice of that. 'Will the strike affect us?' someone asked at the course. 'Listen,' said the instructor, a robust and forceful woman (you could almost call her burly), 'if any of those pickets try to give you any trouble, you come straight to me and I'll give them a piece of my mind they won't forget.' It was a speech that summed up the atmosphere. The consensus was that picketing was an epidemic and this intimidation required a handful of heroes prepared to stand up it, backed only by the meagre forces of the management of industry, the press, the government, the opposition and the police.

To most people working there the strike seemed remote, called by distant union officials who had little more regard for the workforce than the management had.

I spent the strike day on the picket line, but as there were several different unions represented in the building I couldn't work out whom we were supposed to be stopping from going in. Better to try and stop too many than not enough, I considered, and approached the first person walking past. 'Excuse me, this is an official picket line and I would like to ask you to support the strike for a decent wage,' I said, pleased with the correct blend of politeness and assertion. 'I'm the fucking cleaner,' he said, having listened patiently to the end, adding, 'I've only nipped out for a packet of fags.'

Relating to workmates as a socialist is a precarious business at the best of times. You need to be respected as articulate, accepted socially and acknowledged as capable of doing the job. Then you need to be stroppy enough to be admired as resilient, but not so belligerent that you're a liability; thoughtful enough to suggest ways of advancing causes that you can get people to agree with, but willing to stand stoically alone on more difficult issues. Even then, at certain times, you can find yourself doing very little advancing causes and a lot of standing stoically alone.

'Isn't it disgraceful,' the woman who sat behind me at the Post Office would say, almost every morning, 'that these people have worked so hard and have to pay so much tax?' referring to *Daily Mail* articles about the trials of the wealthy. I would counter with all my statistics at the ready, while she insisted that if I were rich, *I'd* want to keep all my money. 'But that's not the point,' I'd say, getting agitated, 'The rich don't defend people on strike, going "well if you were a gravedigger, *you'd* go on strike for more money".'

The trough of my depression took place when a memo came round from the managers, advising staff we were no longer permitted to bring bags of chips in for dinner, as the smell 'encouraged others to disrupt their work and go out for a bag themselves'. And one woman said 'well you can see their point of view'. I wanted to shake her. And slap her and throw water in her face and say, 'Look into my eyes. No you can't see their point of view. It's stupid.'

Nor did anyone ever seem to back me up in my other main forum of debate: the pub. 'Let's have a look at your paper, mate,' someone said one night, having spotted my *Socialist Worker*. I handed it over hopefully and he ripped it up and threw it on the fire. The laughter that ensued was borne not of hatred but derision, which was more humiliating though probably not as painful.

Around this time, the government finally collapsed and had to call a general election. The outcome is well known and undeniable. The reasons for this outcome are assumed to be equally well known and undeniable; ridiculously high rates of tax and the dead were left unburied. Which led to an unstoppable tide of support for the Thatcher revolution. But does this make sense?

Thatcher's Tories won 43 per cent of the vote out of a turnout of 75 per cent. Also, the measures she became associated with were not the same as those on which she won the election. Forty-three per cent voted for what she said she'd do, but they wouldn't necessarily have voted for her if she'd campaigned on a platform of what she would *actually* do. Then her famous poster wouldn't have shown a line of unemployed, with the slogan 'Labour isn't working', but a line of people clocking on in a steelworks or pithead and the slogan 'We'll have this lot on the dole for a start'.

Nor was it true that the election was fought between Thatcher's free-market individualism on the one hand and Labour's utopian egalitarianism on the other. The previous five years had been the first time since the war that the gap between rich and poor had grown. Labour had also cut public spending by £12 billion. Chancellor Denis Healey boasted that the government was 'the first in many years which has given monetary policy the importance it deserves'. And a columnist in the *Financial Times* wrote, 'I cannot for the life of me think of any reason why anyone should consider voting Conservative at the next election. In terms of what Mrs Thatcher's Tories have to offer, we are already served by about as good a Conservative government as we are likely to get.'

Labour's problem was that they were not only conservative, they were failed conservatives. There was a crisis, which everyone could feel. We were in a changing world, in which we could no longer be certain that hospitals would improve, or that school-leavers would get jobs, or that if you had a job you wouldn't be superseded by a lorry driver prepared to tour the petrol garages of Dartford.

There was a gloomy foreboding about the start of 1979. Punk, rising crime, fascism, violent demonstrations, and the new aura of uncertainty fuelled a sense of impending turmoil unknown during the post-war era of stability. Visions of the future became increasingly pessimistic, creating the popular theory that the world would be frozen in an imminent ice age. Tom Robinson predicted, in his song written in 1978, the news in winter 1979: 'All the gay geezers were put inside / the coloured kids were getting crucified / a few fought back and a few folk died / in the winter of '79'.

Whatever political view you were advancing, the point you were compelled to start from was that something had gone badly wrong. Labour, having presided over this descent, had nothing to offer to put it right. Nobody saw the Labour government as a brave but failed body. Instead they looked beleaguered and desperate, having abandoned their programme in order to satisfy the IMF and then done deals with, in turn, the Liberals, the Scottish nationalists and the Ulster Unionists in a scramble to cling to office. Then Jim Callaghan announced he'd be proud to cross a picket line, which accepted that unions were the problem.

They could have challenged the assumption that unions were 'running the country' and suggested that millionaire press barons like Rupert Murdoch did not have the common person's interest in mind when they used their newspapers as forums for union-bashing.

They could have retorted that there were other unelected bodies with more clout than the unions. It was the IMF who imposed the cuts in spending and coerced the government into 'giving monetary policy the importance it deserved'. The secret service had run a farcical campaign to undermine Labour. But instead, by trying to appear tough on the unions, Labour entered a game that only the Tories could win. Thatcher simply had to huff that 'we've tried your way, and it doesn't work'. Labour's promises to bring down unemployment or 'cure industry of confrontation' looked like those of an adulterous husband pleading to his wife 'oh go on, give me one more chance'.

Tories, on the other hand, could appear dynamic and vibrant, armed with a new solution, a determined war against the unions, and instead of a reluctant conservatism, an unashamed worship of the right to be rich. That woman in my office, who insisted that I'd have done the same if I were rich, had probably been a Tory for years. But now she felt a sense of destiny, confident that few people would oppose her thought for the day each morning, even if they didn't agree. And so it was in every workplace and every pub, where the Tory could be the cocky one, knowing that those in favour of Labour would be floundering.

Every crusade needs a slogan to summarize the decay of the order it aims to overthrow. And as the sense of portentous unease crackled as far as the cul-de-sacs and three pubs of Swanley, the followers of Thatcher stumbled across a theme which tapped the anxiety in the atmosphere: the dead were left unburied.

Slogans don't have to be true to be successful but they do have to connect with the truth. The image of a backlog of corpses being stacked up outside cemetery walls struck a chord not just because of hostility to unions but because it seemed to encapsulate how unstable life, and now even death, had become. The result was not that masses of working-class people switched their support to Thatcher. But it did make it impossible to be enthusiastic for Labour. The only coherent argument as to why anyone should vote Labour was that the Tories would be even worse. Millions still voted Labour, out of class-based loyalty and because, however weak it sounded, the argument was right – the Tories *would* be worse. But in such an atmosphere, the middle ground that determines election results was destined to tip the Tory way.

Nonetheless, it was the first time I'd voted and I felt so important. More than my first fag, first beer or first day at work, that stroll into the polling booth made me feel so adult. I almost expected an official to stop me half-way through and say, 'Oi, piss off and come back when you're older.'

The night itself is now regarded by many as a moment when darkness descended upon us, like the start of an 18-year-eclipse and yet the general mood amongst people who despised Thatcher was despondent but calm. The next morning, as she waved and smiled and made her hideous speech about bringing hope, I drowned her out with a deafening blast of 'Babylon's Burning' by the Ruts, and looked forward to her demise.

I set up an SWP branch in Dartford, assuming that everyone vaguely on the left in the area would immediately join. I must have imagined that they all thought, 'I agree with socialism and agree that Russia is state capitalist, but the nearest branch is in Gravesend and I'm not going all the way down there. I'll make do with the Labour Party as it meets on Watling St.'

I got the addresses of everyone in the local Communist Party and went round to visit them. 'Yes?' asked a bemused Stalinist in cycling shorts at the first address when I knocked at his door. 'I've come round to tell you that there's now a local branch of the Socialist Workers Party,' I told him, with the garbled enthusiasm of a radio advert for a carpet warehouse. 'Look,' he said, and pointed to the pile of *Morning Stars* next to me in his porch. 'Yes,' I said, 'but now there's a local branch of the SWP, so I was wondering whether you might join it.' His expression was similar to the one he'd have if I'd said, 'I've just moved into the area so I was wondering if you could let me have your wife. Yes I know you're her husband but I've moved in up the road now, you see.'

I was nineteen, brimming with unjustified confidence, and determined to win over any and every audience. I explained to my mum how workers' militia would operate, to which she said 'well as long as it doesn't get you in any trouble'. I argued with everyone at work that Northern Ireland Catholics were historically justified in supporting the IRA. 'Well I don't know about that dear,' said the tea lady. When I saw Bob Dunn, the newly elected local Conservative MP, I told him how a socialist society would distribute food throughout Dartford. And I was genuinely trying to win him over. I was the same when I spoke at a local meeting addressed by the head of the Kent Police. If I'd met the Pope, I'd have tried to recruit him to Marxism, and afterwards have been convinced that I'd have succeeded if I'd only had another half-an-hour.

Six months after my arrival on the socialist scene, we had Thatcher. So it's just as well I didn't think things through more thoroughly. Or it might have occurred to me that far from my presence heralding an era of international class struggle, I was a bloody jinx.

Chapter 6

It's hard enough being a nineteen-year-old boy as it is, spun through a whirlwind of love, lust and emotional confusion, without the added anxiety of being a novice Trotskyist under a newly elected Margaret Thatcher.

Like most boys of that age, I was constantly torn as to where to direct my passions. I was in love with Anna Ford, Debbie Harry, Chris Evert, Poly Styrene from X-Ray Spex, Lieutenant Uhura, Anthea Redfern, Suzy in *Coronation Street*, Astrid Proll, convicted terrorist from the Baader-Meinhof gang, the woman who worked part-time in the newsagents, someone who accidentally gave me a snog on New Year's Eve, a woman who was pressed against me from St Mary's Cray to Catford on the train one morning, and Stephanie. Especially Stephanie. She worked opposite me all day, just two desk-widths away and was torturously gorgeous. But she'd voted Tory. Didn't I have enough anguish to deal with, without that cauldron of emotion poured on to it?

She was three years older than me and had just married a dashing Greek, so my chances of cementing my affections were not good. But by voting for Thatcher, she'd even put herself out of reach in my dreams. I would have to imagine not just that she abandoned her Mediterranean groom for the scruffy badge-covered clerk who lived with his mum, but that she also abandoned her approach of 'I don't really know why I voted Tory, I just did' in favour of a Trotskyist perspective.

Then, to add to the trauma of getting to grips with sex, I had the dilemma of getting to grips with sexism. This was the toughest challenge of all to the ideas I'd been brought up with. I could imagine sitting in my dad's working men's club, arguing around the red Formica tables, across the frothy-headed light and bitters, that industry should be in the control of the workers. Or that Russia was state capitalist. But I couldn't picture myself presenting a case for why they shouldn't gawk at girlie calendars.

If ever my dad saw a model posing in a paper, or Pan's People, or a girlie calendar, he would make that deep 'pwwwww' sound, like the growling of an angry cat. Then my mum would sort of tell him off, exclaiming 'I don't know', as if he'd been caught taking an extra biscuit. He took great pride in showing everyone his screwdriver that had a picture of a woman on the side, whose clothes disappeared when you tipped it upside-down. Gawking seemed to me a natural response of the human body. Hearing that socialist men shouldn't leer at women was like being told that socialists shouldn't sneeze.

At school I'd upheld my dad's proud tradition, gawking at the inevitable magazines as they circulated the classroom. At that time, if any TV programme dared show a topless woman, every boy who'd seen it would spend the next day exclaiming excitedly that you 'saw a bit of tit'. At sixteen, working in an office, I would join my male colleagues in a pub in Smithfield to watch the strippers on a Friday.

If it was sexist to gawk at women, was it sexist to find women attractive at all? Was 'chatting someone up' allowed? How did socialist couples ever meet in the first place? Surely, I thought, it's hard enough as it is, that experience of sitting on a settee at one in the morning, occasionally catching each other's eye, the last dregs of coffee growing undrinkably tepid as you contemplate when to make your move. Now on top of that I had to worry that if I leaned over and asked her to bed I might be dividing the working class.

Nonetheless, the next time someone in the office showed me a picture of a page-three girl in the *Sun*, asking 'Wouldn't you like to get your hands on that?', I said I thought women were more than just objects to gawk at. To which the reply was a blank confounded gaze, followed by 'Are you a poof then?'

Apart from the difficulties of arguing the non-sexist cause, I was baffled as to what constituted an acceptable personal code of behaviour. I became even more confused after a meeting in London, when I went to a pub with one of the organizers of the Right to Work Campaign, his Australian girlfriend, another woman and a steelworker. It was agreed that we'd get a couple of beers and stop at the organizer's flat, which we went to in the Australian's car. I'd bought some books at the meeting but she suggested I left them on the car seat as she could give me a lift to the station in the morning.

So I went upstairs, had a beer or two and crashed out on the sofa. Until I was woken up by the sofa being gently, and then less gently but rhythmically, nudged by four increasingly frenetic legs. The settee was still a few inches from the back wall but eventually the force of the thrashing limbs pushed it tight into the side of the room, so that now it was being rattled and thumped with nowhere to go. As the nudging became more ferocious and the accompanying squealing more animated and less harmonic, I lay frozen and still, wondering what on earth was the correct thing to do. Far more annoying than being woken up was the conundrum of who this was down here, with their limbs flailing beneath me. Surely not the steelworker. At his age you don't have sex up against a settee, hoping the bloke on it doesn't wake up.

But the Right to Work man and his girlfriend had gone to bed, which only left this other woman. This was worse than playing Cluedo. It almost occurred to me to say as politely as I could, 'Ahem. Look, I don't mind but could you please just tell me which ones you are.' But then the door burst open. 'You fucking bastard,' screamed this unmistakable Australian voice and the settee shuddered to an abrupt halt. It was just as well I had to unravel this mystery, as I might have been tempted to yell 'thank fuck for that, I was beginning to have trouble holding on'. Clearly the Right to Work man was two-timing his girlfriend in the next room and making no attempt to keep quiet. A whole new gamut of riddles ran through my mind, as I lay on a now still settee.

Had he got out of bed, saying that he was getting a glass of water, then on the way to the kitchen managed to get off with this woman in the sitting room? Did he assume that this transgression would not be found out? How was he planning to explain the grunting and settee clumping? Did he imagine his girlfriend was lying in bed, thinking 'there's a lot of noise, there must be some all-night bailiffs repossessing the furniture'. Or that she'd assume a pig she'd never noticed was roaming through the living room.

'Oh come on,' he pleaded, but he was going to have to be inventive to get out of this. And in the ensuing three-cornered eruption, I had to lie utterly still, playing dead, like they tell you to if a tiger takes an interest in you. Until, predictably, the Australian screeched 'fuck you' and stomped out of the house. 'Shit,' I suddenly thought, 'what about my books?' And for a few seconds I pondered the option of calmly climbing off the settee and saying, 'Before you go, I don't suppose I could grab my bag from your car could I?'

It took me a while to appreciate that left-wing people had ferocious arguments – about anything, let alone shagging within earshot of their girlfriend. I was still so delighted there were other people who agreed with me on the major issues, I witnessed arguments between socialists with the bewilderment that overcomes kids when they see their parents arguing. I'd enquire to a long-standing member, 'Why are they shouting? Doesn't Alan agree with the theory of state capitalism any more? Can't you make them stop?' And when I discovered what they were arguing about, I'd understand it even less. It would turn out to be about some bollocks like whether socialist women should wear mini-skirts or whether anti-racists could be skinheads. I'd just think, 'I'd be ecstatic if I could get anyone at work past "Are you a poof then?"'

Nonetheless I felt a thrilling sense of discovery, of a purpose to history, a thirst for education, a new and exciting, if sometimes baffling, set of social rules. Then I had my first public success, at a mass meeting in Swanley following an announcement by Asda superstores that they were planning a branch in the middle of town. To make way, several streets would be demolished, along with a section of the park and the library. I got to speak, and finished with a shriek that the reason the board's assurances sounded so phoney was because they were only interested in one thing, 'their stinking, lousy profits'. And everyone cheered. It felt like the first time you have a semi-conversation in a foreign language. Blimey, if you do it right, they actually understand you!

There was a common witticism that the Socialist Workers Party had no workers and wasn't much of a party. But a major part of my re-education took place in the vibrant lefty leisure scene with its continuous supply of gigs and parties. And proper 1979 lefty parties, with someone asleep on the floor while everyone danced around them to 'Night Boat to Cairo', a group in the garden chanting 'The workers united will never be defeated', an empty pot of chilli by a kitchenful of unwanted rice, an enormous argument on the stairs about an issue such as whether anyone would take speed in a socialist society and a bang on the door from a vanload of police.

At the annual Socialist Worker weekend in Skegness, parties echoed through the night around the damp depleted huts that passed for accommodation. I had a party in my room but at one o'clock received a visit from a leading SWP member, the magnificent Duncan Hallas, who'd been sent to tell us to stop. At four o'clock he was the last one there and I had to ask him to leave as I was falling asleep. If someone had thought of it, they could have claimed that Trotskyism was the new rock 'n' roll.

And far from there being 'no workers', there were loads of them. There was Billy Williams the electrician, who got thousands of votes standing against Frank Chapple for leader of the union. And Val Dunn, gloriously Northern, mumsy but hard-as-nails steward in the bakers' union. And Jimmy Fitzpatrick, admirable Scottish firefighter who'd emerged as a charismatic steward in the firefighters' strike. How much I admired these people, who knew how to be stroppy and organize a union, and knew which were the scabs and which were the cleaners.

I wonder whether anyone has ever felt as joyous in Skegness as I did that weekend. A whole holiday camp full of people who had supported the lorry drivers and didn't call black people 'coons'! And loved getting pissed! And there were all these talks, about Zimbabwe and the Tory union laws and China and Malcolm X. Even the dullest driest stuttering speaker had me spellbound. In the bar, if I overheard a comment like 'Mao's revolution was based on the peasantry', I would marvel at how anyone could be so knowledgeable.

Paul Foot's lecture on Louise Michelle, a leader of the Communards in the Paris Commune, left me breathless, the way you feel after seeing *Casablanca* or the Jam. And I caught my first sighting of Tony Cliff, originator of the theory that Russia was state capitalist, and as such a founder of the organization to which

I belonged. His demeanour exuded everything I wanted a revolutionary leader to be. He was short, bald and splendidly Jewish with a tuft of white mad-professorish hair leaping unkempt from either side of his head. Arms flew in every direction as he enthused about the Spanish Civil War in a croaky Palestinian accent, each syllable distinct, so that the word 'every' would be three syllables rather than the English two, and each 'r' pronounced with a slight cat's purr. 'What rrru-bbish!' he'd proclaim, with an operatic roar and gesticulating like a rabbi, referring to a quote he'd read out from someone like Shirley Williams. And yet the whole performance was delivered in an effortlessly endearing style, packed with gags and tangential anecdotes with the aplomb of the finest rural storyteller.

Arriving back at the office, I must have seemed like a child excitedly returning from his first visit to the circus. My workmates, especially Stephanie, probably weren't as moved in the conversation about our respective weekends when I cackled at high speed about 'a talk on Rosa Luxemburg, and a party and this brilliant Jewish bloke right, and this bloke I met from Barnsley . . .'

'Have you heard of Louise Michelle?' I asked, preparing to re-enact as much of the talk as I could remember.

The social life of the left reflected our political activities. The anti-Thatcher movement contained differing ideas on how to oppose her but everyone agreed we had to *do* things. The Dartford women's group campaigned with us against Tory MP John Corrie's bill to restrict abortion rights. There were regular large demonstrations, against troops in Ireland, the Tories' first anti-immigration act and unemployment. Every inner city area had its alternative venues and left-wing bookshop, plastered with anti-Thatcher posters, especially the one with Maggie lifting a purse from an old woman's handbag.

We got into the *Dartford and Swanley Chronicle* on nine successive weeks, for stunts like a picket of the Tory Party jumble sale and crawling under a fence into the park at two in the morning to spray-paint the war memorial with anti-military slogans.

Through this activity, most of it barking mad, the issue of sexism began to come into focus. Clearly, if you spent all day alongside women seeking support for the abortion rights protest, it would seem a little unsavoury to announce that, as you were in need of a little relaxation, you were going to the White Swan, which promised 'the tastiest strippers in South London'.

As people unite, their self-esteem and respect for each other grows. And if you respect someone, you wouldn't really want them bending over while sliding off their g-string to 'I Need Love' by Donna Summer in front of a horde of filing clerks going 'wo wo wo'. Clearly there was a difference between genuine sexual attraction and making a grunting 'woooor' noise at a topless woman on a calendar. Anyway, that was how I rationalised it, as it meant if I was ever in with a chance with Debbie Harry, I could follow it up without transgressing the laws of socialist etiquette. As well as making more sense, this formulation seemed considerably more optimistic than the other explanation I was hearing for the meaning of sexism, which was that all men are just pigs.

My dad, for example, had never rejected the liberal approach to women's role in society, he'd just never even considered it. When I was eleven, my mum had to go into hospital for two days, so she prepared a series of meals ready to cook. Even then she had to slowly run through the instructions regarding toasting bread and turning the cooker on and off with care and precision, as if she was addressing the SAS on a mission into Central America.

'You're going to have to help me out here son,' he said, hesitantly entering the kitchen as if he was stepping out of a lunar module on to the moon. His task, with my help, was to turn on the gas ring to boil the ready-peeled and salted potatoes and then dish them up. Which may as well have been a challenge on *The Generation Game*, as boiling water flung itself out of the pan and potatoes were hurled across the floor in the ensuing chaos. I find it hard not to imagine Bruce Forsyth stood there, screaming, 'What are you doing? Turn the flame down, no DOWN for goodness sake!'

Years later he was astonished when I cooked a meal, as if I'd done something genetically impossible like breastfed a baby. But in the post-war working-class world, he'd been brought up with exactly those values and could no more be blamed for adopting them than 14th-century peasants can be blamed for thinking the earth was flat. Even he had the capacity to change and yet the view of some feminists would be that he was the oppressor, equivalent to a slaveholder or medieval baron. The concept of him representing those who benefit from society's divisions therefore seemed somewhat ironic when he had a breakdown and had to spend the rest of his life in a mental home.

Even the richest can have breakdowns but they wouldn't end up enjoying the hospitality of an institution like Stonehouse Hospital. As you climbed the stairs to my dad's ward, you were greeted by the welcoming aroma of overcooked cabbage, followed by the first of many requests for 'a fag mate, or a bit of baccy, ay, or a fag, I say have you got a fag, or a bit of baccy'. And then along the threadbare carpet, the stringy underneath bits exposed except at the edges, past an imaginative array of things that were broken. Chairs, chessboards, windows and a quarter-size snooker table with ripped felt, a length of one cushion missing, over half the balls missing and no string in the pockets. While in one corner a radio, perhaps on a station especially designed for such an environment, seemed to constantly play songs like 'Happy Talk'. And in the background, from the other end of the ward, a television blared out the early days of afternoon programming so loudly that it buzzed with distortion.

Everyone wore slippers, most of the patients were in their dressing gowns, everyone shuffled and no one walked, which probably accounted for the state of the carpet. In one corner a Polish man held bitter animated conversations with himself. There was a meal a day, a tea-trolley twice a day and medication several times a day. But Dad, who would know when I was visiting, would be waiting in the one armchair which wasn't surrounded by its own foam stuffing. He'd be in his fraying jacket, old red tie and shoes. 'Hello son,' he'd say, with a grin, welcoming me with an offer of a cup of tea and asking if there was anything at all I wanted, as if he was showing me into his stately home.

'It's good to see he's still alert,' I'd tell myself to think, knowing that in this place it was best to be as gaga as possible. Then I'd sneak him out of the building to the nearest pub, where we'd have more honest conversations than we ever had when he was at home.

Then the time would come to take him back, where he'd insist that if I wanted a cup of tea, he only had to say the word and it could be arranged, such was his influence. This wasn't a lunatic asylum, he insisted, it was a men's home. There *was* a Stonehouse mental institution, which he'd heard people talk about, but that must be further down the road somewhere. This was just a men's home.

As I left, we'd shake hands with that mutually firm grip that goes on for a second or so beyond the normal handshake, that negates the need for either party to say anything else before parting. Descending the stairs, I'd look back just once and he'd always be watching. Then I'd stroll to the bus stop, brimming with a cocktail of sadness, guilt and anger, though always in differing and unpredictable ratios.

His condition seemed to place him in the worst of all worlds. He could engage with people, understand a joke and maintain his dignity, but his memory was erratic and his reasoning unorthodox, to the extent that he needed continuous supervision. After two years of him being at home, attending the institution on certain days, it became an intolerable burden on my mum, so he had to go there fulltime.

How little it would have taken to alleviate the worst of this situation. How much would it have cost, compared to the billions Thatcher was unleashing in tax cuts, to create Health Service posts which could have enabled him to come home regularly under supervision. Or to place the most coherent patients in a separate building, away from the most tragic cases like the gibbering Polish man. Or to organize the occasional day trip. Or at least to mend the fucking snooker table.

More striking still was the upside-down logic of a society that depends on obedience. Dad was clearly not contented with his quality of life. Which to anyone sane was the only sane attitude to possess. Yet every spark of discontent he displayed was viewed as further evidence of advancing insanity. One day, he slipped out to the bus stop and despite having no money persuaded the bus driver to take him to Dartford. From there he pulled the same trick with another bus driver to get to Swanley and walked home, popping into the newsagents on the way to convince the owner to let him have a packet of fags on tick.

Surely any right-minded society would view such behaviour as a display of outstanding initiative, possibly rewarding them with a senior rank in the armed forces, especially as he did the whole journey with his jumper on inside-out, back-to-front and under his shirt. But not according to the 'banana in the corridor' philosophy of order. So the hospital authorities viewed the matter as 'very serious indeed' and upped his dose of medication.

Early on in his stay there, he was obliged to take part in 'occupational therapy', the basket-weaving I'd imagined was only folklore. Dad tried it for a short while, then stomped off refusing to take any further part, earning his first 'tut tuts' and black marks. This occupational therapy, it seemed to me, was perfectly valid except for the final touch. When someone refused to take part, they should have said, 'Congratulations, you've passed. Here are the keys to some accommodation, this is the warden who'll be looking after you and here's fifty quid for a crate of beer. These other poor sods will have to stay here. They're obviously completely nutty, spending all day weaving poxy baskets just because we tell them to.'

My dad's predicament seemed to sum up the twisted logic of the Thatcherite order I was eager to confront. But the dominant view from the forces opposed to Thatcher was to wait until the next election, when hopefully we could bring back the failures who had preceded her. My dad, I like to think, was more sensible and got on a bus. He didn't succeed. But at least he tried.

Chapter 7

The second day of January 1980 was the first day of the national steelworkers' strike. For Margaret Thatcher and myself, it was called with perfect timing. Occupying Thatcher's mind was her war aim – the Ridley Plan. Designed by her friend Nicholas Ridley, the strategy was to take on unions one at a time, 'starting with a weak union, with little history of strikes' and ending with the jewel of the miners.

The weak union turned out to be the Iron and Steel Trades Confederation (ISTC), which was told that over one third of the industry was to close, with the loss of 52,000 jobs. For those that remained, that year's wage increase would be 2 per cent, at a time when inflation was 20 per cent.

Which meant it was time for graphs again. 'The British steelworker produces this much steel an hour,' the TV expert would say, pointing to a bar chart. Then came the amounts for the German and Japanese steelworker, with mighty blocks towering over the puny British matchbox-shaped oblong. The obvious explanation was that foreign steel companies enjoyed greater investment, and greater subsidies. The French, for example, sub-sidized each ton of steel by double the amount of the British. But the one given was that the foreign steelworker was just faster. German steelworks must have been like an episode of *It's a Knockout*, teams in heatproof suits and visors racing along beams, dragging giant ladles full of molten metal, tipping them in a vat and rushing back to get more, as Stuart Hall cackled that Frankfurt have nearly filled theirs up.

Thatcher was after her first scalp and she had every reason to be confident. One of the strongest unions in the country, at British Leyland, had been taken apart by the chairman when he'd sacked the Communist Party convenor Derek Robinson, and unions were being attacked everywhere. It was a mood reflected around my office. There had been a mass meeting in the canteen, called by the union to end the pitiful campaign to improve pay, at which I gave out a leaflet I'd written. The union official opened his speech by ripping up my leaflet on the stage.

During my own speech, one of my leaflets came drifting towards me in the form of an aeroplane, having been built with the minimum of effort and thrown very lamely. I could have tolerated an orchestrated chorus of 'kill the commie'. But where's the glory in causing nonchalant mild irritation? If the Confederates had really wanted to destroy Abraham Lincoln's career at its beginning, they wouldn't have barracked him during his speeches. They'd have gazed around the room, their feet draped over the chair, while one of them half-threw a badly made paper dart and muttered 'all right mate, don't keep on'.

The union official won the vote by 450 to 70. Shortly after that, the managers set about making my life as difficult as possible, demanding explanations for every spelling mistake I made. I arrived at that point where you lay in bed every morning gazing wistfully at the clock, thinking 'one more minute and then I'll get up'. Then counting down the last seconds of the minute, ending in a sequence of 'three – two – one – hnnn phooo – one more minute and then I'll get up'. Regularly I encountered that psychological trick that your mind and body collaborate on, whereby you feel a twinge of a sore throat and convince yourself that you're seriously ill. At the time you ring in sick, you're ill. You even mean it when you do the 'I'm really sorry about this, let's hope I'm better by tomorrow' call, in that pathetic, rasping, weary voice. Everyone who has ever rung in sick has put on that wasting adenoidal tone, even if the ailment was a broken toe.

So the thrill of a steel strike was overwhelming and from my desk at the Post Office I rang the strike centre in Scunthorpe. There was a slight bolt of adrenaline as the phone was answered in a throaty Yorkshire voice and I was talking to a real striking steelworker. I asked him if he could send some pickets. I had no idea what I thought they should picket but was certain we'd find somewhere.

'Hang on,' said the steelworker and there was some background muttering. Then, 'We've got about thirty lads who are keen to get on the picket lines, so that sounds grand. Now, if you can arrange to put them up and name a place where we can meet you, we should be there by about eight.'

'That's marvellous,' I told him, suggesting a pub in which to meet, and put the phone down. It was a left-wing version of the behaviour of these Nick Leeson types when they stick five million quid of their firm's money on the stock market. I was thinking 'yeah, just go for it', while it would never occur to whoever was at the other end of the phone that I didn't have a clue what I was doing. I feigned a headache, went home and rang round everyone I knew to arrange their lodgings. Then I got a phone call from the strike centre, in which an ISTC official said they were coming to Kent to picket the private steelworks in Sheerness, which hadn't joined the strike. But then my mum heard me arranging places for pickets to stay and went berserk.

'I've seen them on the television, they're troublemakers, that's what they are, God knows what the neighbours would think if they knew you were running the steel strike from my house, well don't expect me to visit you in prison . . .'

How are you supposed to organize a national strike with that going on? What if the union official from the strike centre heard this? They probably imagined I was in a huge hall, the walls plastered with pin-covered maps, occasionally waving a baton and despatching an eager devotee to check out the situation in Maidstone. So how could I explain it if he heard 'and don't go swanning off to meet those pickets without tidying your room'. My mum only calmed down after countless assurances that no steelworkers would be stopping under her roof.

The pub was a cauldron of anticipation. The strike was dominating the news and we were about to play a part in this historic moment. A bus pulled up and a crowd of steelworkers poured in. Everyone who'd come to greet them was sent home with a steelworker more than the number they'd said they could take, until there were two left. Just two steelworkers and me, and a barman wiping tables and unplugging the Space Invaders machine. 'You'd better come with me,' I said.

In optimistic mode I convinced myself there would be no

problem. My mum was sure to be in bed when we got home and a van was coming at six o' clock to take us to Sheerness. As long as we didn't wake her when we got home, there was no reason why she should ever know that her house had been an unlikely refuge for striking steelworkers.

I explained the situation to the pickets and, as we arrived home, turned the key with the silent precision of a safebreaker. I found some blankets, tip-toed into the living room and they followed me in, all of us grimacing at the slightest semi-creak of a floorboard. Gingerly I pressed the light switch, determined to avoid the faintest click. And as the light came on, there was my mum, glowering in the armchair, glancing at the pickets with a sneer as if they were giggling women in orange lipstick and torn stockings, swilling from a bottle of vodka and wearing a sandwich board that said 'we'll do ANYTHING for a fiver'.

'I KNEW you'd bring them home,' she raged. Then, turning to them, 'You're trying to ruin the country, it was on the news.' But her distaste wasn't that they were ruining the country. It was that they got in trouble. To her, it must have seemed the most unlikely experience, that people on the news would end up in her living room. As peculiar as going into the kitchen because you've heard a noise, and finding David Bellamy frying an egg.

The greatest distress however was the question of the neighbours. What would they say? Would they denounce us to the Home Office? It would certainly be the last we'd see of Mrs Speller's homemade damson jam. The van was coming at six o' clock, we all assured her, and would be long gone before anyone in the street was awake. No one would ever know, as they sighed 'isn't it terrible?' at that evening's news, that the figures they were tut-tutting, huddled around a lighted brazier, had slept thirty yards away under Mrs Steel's spare eiderdown. With this knowledge she reluctantly calmed down and went to bed.

There was a popular poster at the time, depicting Margaret Thatcher with axes for arms and a huge caption 'Stop the mad axewoman'. At six o'clock the following morning, a white van screeched to a halt by the front garden, covered from bonnet to back door in these things. 'Waaaah waa waa wa-wa waaaah' went the horn, the driver thumping his hooter as if he was a drummer in a heavy metal band. Then as we emerged from the door, the windows were all wound down and a dozen striking steelworkers launched into a tour-de-force rendition of 'Maggie Maggie Maggie – out out out' in glorious Scunthorpe accents.

One by one, the curtains of the road twitched and flickered as neighbours investigated the noise and wondered why the words 'Stop the mad axewoman' were beaming at them a dozen times over through the Swanley twilight.

The only people more surprised that such a scene could be taking place were the steelworkers themselves. A few weeks earlier, none of the characters being bounced along the floor of the van as it rattled its way to the Kent coast would have believed they would play any part in such an episode. Over the previous years, as they drank, fished, played snooker, or longed for the hooter that signalled the end of their shift, none of them can have imagined that a world slump and a scheme plotted by Margaret Thatcher and Nicholas Ridley would combine to change their lives forever.

The most obvious aspect of their attitude on the picket line was their commitment. As each lorry approached the gate, two pickets, accompanied by the police, were permitted to stand in the January drizzle and ask the driver to turn away. Like a young boy watching his father drive the car, I wanted to ask 'Can I have a go please?'

In contrast to the image portrayed, their mood was polite and pleading. 'This is an official ISTC picket line, and as fellow trade unionists, we're asking you not to enter this plant,' they'd begin, with that hint of desperate tremor in the voice that pokes through when you're trying to stay calm with an overzealous traffic warden or rail ticket inspector. 'We're fighting for our livelihoods here mate. I mean, if Thatcher gets away with doing this to us, she'll do it to you.' Even as you heard this, faintly, from across the road, you could tell the pickets were controlling themselves from snapping and blurting out, 'Look, I've got a wife and baby and live in shitty Scunthorpe, and all there is is a dirty steelworks and fuck-all else and if we lose this strike we're all fucked so turn your poxy lorry round and fuck off.'

But it would have taken a brave driver to turn round. Their union had issued no instructions on respecting the strike and a single driver refusing to cross would be worried about losing their own job. Their torn sympathies were apparent from the small numbers who would hurtle past without stopping. Most of them stopped, leaned out of the window and listened sympathetically, before turning the key to create the depressing sound of a lorry juddering into action and continuing past a disconsolate crowd of pickets, hands buried in pockets like grumpy six-year-old boys, drizzle running off their bobble hats.

The same scenario repeated itself, every fifteen minutes or so, every day, for nine weeks.

Of all the charges made against strikers in a situation like this, none is more peculiar than to call them selfish. To seek a redundancy package could be described as selfish, or to get out quickly and take one of the few non-steel related jobs in the area before the deluge. Or even to come out on strike and treat it as an unpaid holiday. But no balance sheet drawn up by the selfish would lead them to spend their days in the downmarket part of the Isle of Sheppey and their nights depending upon the eiderdowns of strangers.

The more active a striker was, the more likely it would be that he saw the strike not as a fight for his own livelihood but as a struggle to defend communities and jobs for the future. Which may be why one of the most consistent workforces, sending out hundreds of pickets, collectors and speakers was the Shotton plant, which had already been closed before the strike began, leaving them nothing personally to gain from it at all.

One morning at the picket line, we heard a rumble from around the corner. Into sight came about a dozen women, but it was difficult to make out their purpose through a plethora of boom stands, cameras, lighting equipment and an entourage running awkwardly alongside them, clasping clipboards and calling out instructions like 'we're going to have to go wider on the approach shot'.

Then they all returned to their starting position a few yards away and repeated the process. The third time, they got to their marker and the women burst from the middle as if they were about to launch into 'Oklahoma'. 'Leave our men alone' they shouted for a few seconds, which was also the slogan on their placards.

That night, BBC and ITV news each began with a five-minute

report documenting how the wives of working steelworkers in Sheerness had begun a protest against the pickets, which their cameras had just happened to be there to record. After this, there was no problem in arguing that the media was biased.

The educational process of a strike can be complex. Only in dreadful plays performed by middle-class theatre companies does a strike lead automatically to racists suddenly becoming best mates with a houseful of Rastafarians. But the turmoil of a strike makes its participants open to new ideas, as long as someone is there to provide them. The pickets in the van weren't feminists. 'Ay darling, come over here so I can squeeze yer spots,' one of them would howl out of the window to women as we drove past. On the face of it then, the strike hadn't changed him. But supposing someone in the van had said 'Oy. Why should any woman support this strike, when that's the contempt you have for them'? There would, I think, have been an argument between him and his colleagues. Whereas before the strike, a similar outburst would have met with 'Are you a poof then?' The trouble was, I never found out, as I didn't have the guts or wherewithal to try it.

A strike centre was set up in Chatham, from where pickets would be arranged, hardship funds distributed and collections organized. And this place *did* have pin-covered maps across the walls. Local ports were picketed successfully and for the first time in their lives, they felt as if their opinions and decisions mattered. There was delirium when Arthur Scargill led a huge delegation to a mass picket of a private plant in Sheffield called Hadfields and shut the place down. That day anything seemed possible. For a moment it wasn't just a theory. If there was enough of us, we *could* make them do as we say.

For socialists, instead of being thought of as odd, we were *respected* and odd. Two ISTC officials rang to ask if I could take them out fundraising for a day. I led them around a tour of Dartford, strutting into factories and paper mills, brushing through the bendy Perspex doors that led to the workshops, asking the nearest worker where the union rep was and requesting, usually successfully, that they set up a collection.

As the strike progressed, something else became evident that I'd previously known only in theory. Union leaders are desperate to end confrontation at all costs. ISTC leader Bill Sirs made a speech in Wales in which he burst into tears, saying, 'I am prepared to go to jail for the working class.' But experience tells you a union leader is never more untrustworthy than when he's blubbering that he's prepared to go to prison.

To start with, what does it mean? There was never any talk of sending him to prison. He might as well have spluttered, 'I'd shave my head completely bald for you lot if I had to. I would. 'Cos I fucking love you, you're my best mates.'

People who go to prison on a point of principle don't go around publicly announcing that they would do it if the circumstances arose. The union leaders refused to call out all the private steel-works. They made it clear they would settle for a promise of an inquiry. They cancelled a miners' strike in Wales, originally called in support of the steelworkers. They refused to involve women and families in the dispute. And the day after Sirs' speech about going to jail, he announced that the union would comply with a ruling by Lord Denning that no secondary picketing, solidarity strikes or blacking of steel would take place.

Industry could cope with the minor inconvenience of late deliveries and bide their time. At Sheerness, as every passing lorry took its toll on the pickets, their numbers dwindled, an increasing posse could be found in the pub and the openness to new ideas was replaced by a confirmation of disillusionment and despair. Thatcher had expected a walkover. Instead she had to fight a three-month battle. But eventually a settlement was agreed which raised the pay but left management a free hand to close down the 52,000 jobs.

It's fashionable to comment that although Thatcher swung the pendulum too far, 'something' had to be done about the unions. Well this was her first something. As a result communities were torn apart, countless families were ruined and Thatcher passed on to the next round of the Ridley Plan. She was like a Premier League football team that struggles in the third round of the FA Cup against a team from the third division but gets there after a replay.

'Shit,' I thought as the strike began to wane, 'I suppose I'd better go back in to work. I wonder if they'll believe that headache went on for two months.'

Chapter 8

After the steel strike came the year of the giro. Unemployment roared to two million, chased towards three million, and Norman Tebbitt famously said the unemployed should get on their bikes and look for work. Unemployment was the result of the unemployed not trying hard enough. In which case what a peculiar economic century we had.

The population must have gone through a period of laziness at the end of the 19th century, then felt a sudden spurt of energy and got jobs. Until the 1930s, when they got lazy again. Then they perked up around 1938, which was handy as it was just in time for the war. This was fine until 1980, when everyone changed their mind and decided to stay in bed all day, which makes sense as this coincides with the invention of the duvet.

Keith Joseph said the unemployed should get jobs by asking employers if they could work for lower wages than those already being paid. Jim Prior announced that they should offer to work for nothing. But even if they had, those finding work would have done so at the expense of whoever would have got the job if they hadn't applied, so the number out of work would have stayed the same. The only difference would have been that British industry was staffed by cyclists and people capable of living off wild berries.

The unemployment figures weren't affected in the slightest when someone found work at the Post Office, replacing me when I was sacked. I had been asked to visit the manager, who told me to leave the premises immediately. No one seemed at all bothered, though I think I remember Stephanie saying 'see ya then' but that might be my memory playing tricks.

I'd done everything wrong. Given that the times were against me, I should have selected carefully the issues to complain about, attracting a handful of people, instead of mouthing off on everything. And I certainly shouldn't have taken days off to go to Sheerness. Then I may have kept the job and attracted a handful of people prepared to organize a stronger union. But what sort of boring bastard wants to do that when they're 19? Dennis Potter said, shortly before he died, that we should be able to look back on our youth with 'tender contempt'. Exactly. And because I alienated the entire workforce of Erlang House Post Office against me, I'm able to do just that.

Looking through the papers that I was presented with on my dismissal, three things give me particular pride. One is that on my sick record it stated the reason I gave for not coming in one day (when I'd been at Sheerness) was that I was suffering from vertigo. Presumably I must have put on that croaky voice and spluttered that I couldn't come in this morning as I was scared of heights. And that hopefully by tomorrow it will have cleared up and I'll be able to go to the sixth floor again without screaming.

Another reason given for my sacking was that I held a collection around the office for the steel strike, to which several people had contributed.

Best of all was that between the official warnings and bureaucratic documents lay a copy of the note I'd sent to the manager when he'd demanded an explanation for other days I'd taken off. It ended, 'If management consider I have that little pride that I can continue to make an effort towards my work in an atmosphere that has come about due to management's victimization of myself, I suggest they abandon their dogmatic self-righteousness and remember that their employees are people and not just robots to be pushed and shoved in whatever direction they choose.'

And would you believe it? Even that didn't persuade them to keep me on.

I'd been unemployed before but 1980 unemployed was different. It seemed that everyone was unemployed. Every event had two prices, one normal and one for unemployed. Yosser Hughes became the cult figure of the times with his catchphrase 'Gissa job'. And in what must have been some sort of attempt to align with the oppressed, UB40 called themselves UB40.

Across the nation grouplets of doleys slotted into the daily ritual of sitting around each other's houses with a pot of tea and homegrown grass. If one of you had to go somewhere, such as a breaker's yard, you would all go together. Then you'd meander back with an aimless soporific ambling that comes from not having any reason to get where you're going, slinging insults at each other to pass the time.

Within a few weeks of signing on, I lost contact with mornings altogether. Which made signing on a major achievement, as you weren't allowed to do it in the afternoon. The dread of signing-on day would loom three days in advance, as if it was the day I had to get up at five to do a shift in the sewers. Lethargy bred lethargy, until I'd feel a warm glow of creative satisfaction if I accomplished a task like posting a letter.

Then I left home and moved into a Crystal Palace squat, in a road of squats in which nobody worked at all. When I had to get a key cut, which involved a walk of half a mile to the shop and back, it took me three days. I lay in a sleeping bag in a room with a bare lightbulb and a window covered in plywood, and tried to get up but couldn't. In that transcendental state time goes by incredibly quickly. You gaze idly at a corner of the room, vaguely aware of the pips on a distant radio informing you it's one o'clock, then contemplate matters like the shortest route to Tooting on foot and how to make a meal out of a tin of plum tomatoes and an orange. Then off go the pips again and an hour has passed.

On the day I had to get the key cut, there was no point in rushing – until suddenly it was four o'clock and there was a panic. So I got up, but someone had made a pot of tea, and I remember thinking, 'Well there's no point in scampering about and making myself ill when I can wait until tomorrow.' The next day I went through exactly the same process, until at twenty past five on day three, I puffed into the locksmiths just in time, having taken longer than if I'd come from Montreal.

Then there was the problem of money. On the dole you literally run out of money. I had frustrating conversations about this, in which someone would shrug their shoulders and agree it was a nuisance when you had no money. 'But I don't mean "not much money", or "no money until I get to the bank",' I'd grimace, 'I mean NO MONEY.' One of the most frustrating pieces of advice in that situation was information about shops that sell cheap shoes or a kitchenware sale. Because if you've got NO MONEY it makes no difference whether something costs ten quid or twenty quid. You either nick it or go without. You might as well tell someone that Swan Hunters are offering a half-price battleship for only eighty million quid.

One problem this created was getting around. On the underground I perfected the technique of nonchalantly walking past the ticket collector, with scraps of paper in each hand, so that it looked as if I was searching for my ticket. Usually I'd be twenty yards past, before the collector yelled 'Oy, you haven't got a ticket', at which point I'd run off. Sometimes I'd observe the half-hearted attempts of others trying this trick, who perhaps lacked the incentive of NO MONEY. They would get twenty yards past the collector, at which point he'd shout after them – and they'd *go back*. I would watch this with horror, thinking, 'No, you idiot. You've done the hard bit, now just run. He's not going to chase after you and let the whole of London march past with no ticket. And besides, he's about seventy.' It was like watching someone escape from Colditz, getting into Switzerland, hearing a shout to come back and saying, 'Well I'd better go and see what the Kommandant wants or I might get in trouble.'

On days with NO MONEY, buses with conductors were a blessing. They were also the nearest I'll get to the drama of Russian Roulette. Every time the bus departed from a stop, this was one stage nearer to my destination. But at some point, while gazing out of the window trying to appear as dreamy as possible, there would come the awful realization that the bus was chugging up and down on the spot, while a conductor stood by my side with his hand out. At which point I would go through the charade of feeling in every pocket and saying, 'Oh I am a fool, I've left my money at home.' Then came the humiliating walk of the condemned, up the middle of the bus, feeling as if every other passenger was shaking their heads and muttering 'tut tut'. Then as a final blow to the self-esteem, I'd watch a bus disappear into the distance and think 'it's all right for you rich bastards' about the passengers on a 159.

From the perspective of the dole, *everyone*'s a rich bastard.

During a flurry of activity in the summer, I took to bunking the train to Canterbury or Folkestone, heading to the cricket ground and finding a way of slipping in for nothing. I'd gaze enviously at other spectators and the casual way they did things like stroll up to the refreshments stall and buy a pie. And find it hard not to hold them in the same contempt as if they were oil sheikhs, surrounded by their harems and a personal jet at the back of the Leslie Ames stand.

Even free activities have little appeal when you've got no money. You can enjoy a walk across Regent's Park with a tenner in your pocket, because you've taken a decision to go there. But when you've got no money, you're aware you're doing it because it's all you can afford to do. It's like the difference between going on a camping holiday and having to live in a tent.

In one sense being unemployed is the hardest job of all, in that it's relentless. It wouldn't be so bad if the hours were the same as other jobs, so you spent the day in a numb trance or walking to Camberwell to get cheap onions, but at five o'clock reverted to a normal human being with forty quid in the bank and a reason to wash. What a joy it would be to wake up on a Friday thinking 'one more day and then a whole weekend of having enough money for a pint before being back in this sleeping bag'. And at least you'd feel you mattered if a supervisor came round once an hour yelling at you to get back to sleep.

Instead, unemployment impregnates you with an infectious sense of worthlessness that spreads through your whole body to leave a numb vacant slouch, because you can spend all day in a sleeping bag and no one's going to complain, or even notice.

There was a sense of foreboding as the year went on, about how far this mass unemployment would be allowed to go. Especially as Thatcher and her friends were reaching their zenith of unashamed class hatred. It was reported that at a private lunch held in her honour, a top industrialist made a speech which ended, 'Screw them Maggie, screw them till they bleed. We wish you were with us forever.'

Thatcher was adamant there would be no U-turn; the lady, remember, was not for turning. So every day redundancies were announced on the news, over a map of Britain with dots to mark that day's unlucky towns. There were regular reports of middle-aged men, their upbringing and education having geared their whole lives towards a single purpose of 'providing for their family', reacting to redundancy by committing suicide. With fifty or sixty people going for every job, would I ever work again?

A few years earlier most people would have refused to believe there could ever be three million unemployed in Britain. We'd learned at school about the time that 3 million were unemployed but that was history. It was no more likely to take place again than an invasion of the Vikings or the Bronze Age. Most people believed no government could get away with it, which was to forget that anyone can get away with anything unless someone stops them.

And those best placed to do that, the leaders of Labour and the unions, seemed paralysed. Instead of confronting Thatcher they begged for talks with her, but she was in no mood to comply. And anyway, what would they have said? 'Excuse me, but we were wondering if you could possibly only screw us till we bruise?' Local councils adopted the practice of displaying the number unemployed in their borough in huge figures dangling from the town hall.

A popular Steve Bell cartoon of the time depicted a tennis match, with Thatcher, Howe and Joseph on one side of the net armed with cannon, tanks and rocket launchers. On the other side the union leaders held tennis rackets with no strings and the engineers' leader Terry Duffy was buried, just the top of his head and ears poking above the ground, as he pleaded 'Is this low enough for you ma'am?'

The sense of hopelessness was exacerbated in the squats, where it took me a while to puzzle out what anybody did at all. Some of them called themselves artists, which impressed me until I knocked on the door of a painter called Brillo. He invited me in and told me that he hadn't been out of the house for three weeks because 'I've been doing some paintings'.

'Oh brilliant,' I said, 'Can I have a look?'

'Ah, well I haven't actually started yet,' he said.

'I haven't actually started yet' was the motto to which the whole area aspired. Someone should have found out how to write it in

Latin, then inscribed it on a plaque and hung it over the entrance to the road.

For months I would be puzzled by the tribe of bikers who would stand in a circle, covered in oil, continuously assembling roll-up fags and garbling about valves and torque wrench settings. Occasionally someone would utter a key phrase, like 'Norton 850 Commando', and everyone would nod their head, smile out of one side of their face and say 'nice'. Eventually I worked out what was especially odd about them – none of them had bikes.

One was called Oily, one was Ape, one was Greasy, and there would sometimes be a surge of excitement in the road as one of them banged on every door to announce they'd got a new bike. So we'd all go round and everyone would stand in awe muttering about a nice set of pistons, and I would wonder whether I was the only one surprised that the bike had turned out to be a pile of bits in a box.

Over the next few months, the machine would go through stages of assembly in their kitchen, then there'd be another bang on the door and an announcement that it had been sold and replaced by a *new* new bike, which we had to go and see. It was my misfortune to share my squat with one of the few residents who owned a fully operational bike. So one unemployed afternoon, I heard an enormous crunch and looked down to see that an axe had been swung through the banisters of the stairs, while my squatmate beamed, 'Now I can park my Ducati in the hall.'

Not that the place blossomed with breathtaking interior design to start with. Two rooms had no floor. And the toilet had been put diagonally in an outside room that was so tiny the door wouldn't shut no matter how acrobatically you arranged your knees. If a peasant from the 14th century had travelled through time and landed in this place, they'd have yelled, 'For Christ's sake letteth me go home.' Though it's a pity that *Changing Rooms* wasn't on at the time. I'd have loved to have seen Carol Smillie's face as we said, 'There you are, do something with that.'

The most dangerous aspect of the area was that the bizarre became normal. It didn't seem odd when someone knocked on your door at three in the morning pleading they were desperate for some peanut butter. One night eight strangers followed me indoors and

started rolling joints in the living room. They explained that this
was the address they'd been given for a party, so I told them they
were in the wrong house. Then they all did that druggy elongated
gutteral 'wooooooooooow right' noise, followed by a chuckled
'ahugh' as they stared into the middle distance, then carried on as
before while I went to bed and left them there. In a pitiful attempt
to bring a dash of aesthetics to the household, I bought a pot plant,
a coleus that sat on the mantelpiece barely visible through junk and
Ducati engine parts. One night I got in from the pub and it was
gone. 'Oh like yeah we smoked it,' said the hippy who'd just moved
in.

No one thought it especially odd when the mechanic who lived
at no. 9 announced that he'd made a discovery – that he could stop
the telephone from ringing by placing a saucepan over his head. Or
when a party one night was brought to an abrupt halt when a
Satanist went berserk with an axe and severed the main power
cable, producing a shower of sparks before plunging the place into
darkness.

For a while it was exhilarating, the antithesis to the stultifying
predictability of Swanleydom, where if the telephone rang after
twenty to nine, everyone would freeze, then someone would snap,
'Who's that ringing at *this* time of night?' In the squats, no one was
racist, no one liked Thatcher, no one liked the police and everyone
smoked dope. But eventually it felt uneasy, being the straightest
person in the clan. If your philosophy is to abstract yourself from
the real world, the next step is contempt for the real world. Not just
those who rule it but those who inhabit it.

I would rummage through skips for furniture and started to feel
superior to the deluded fools who'd thrown out a perfectly usable
rickety chair and then paid for a new one. The area cultivated a
distrust of outsiders, until it felt some of us considered that by
virtue of his uniform the milkman was an arm of the state.

The standard response to my requests for support for the Right
to Work Campaign was 'I want the right *not* to work'. Then the
chuckled 'ahugh' and middle-distance stare. There was little
interest in trade unions and still less in the values of socialism,
because 'they're just more institutions telling us what to do'. It
occurred to me that the aspirations of the armchair anarchists

amounted to a belief that everyone should get on with their own thing, or to put it another way, alternative Thatcherism. Look after number one but pass the joint.

Then, as the summer of unemployment blazed by, a carnival of hope erupted in the distance. In Poland, protests over food shortages led to a strike in the Lenin shipyard in Gdansk. From there a general strike spread across the city and then the country, creating the movement 'Solidarity', which quickly became known by its Polish name of Solidarnosc.

Every television picture or newspaper photo suggested what Polish and Western rulers denied – that the people chanting and marching, screaming into megaphones, packing into mass meetings and confronting their government were no different to the people of London or Glasgow or Swanley.

Poland was sure to have its sexist steelworkers, its stoned hospital porters, its naive activists, bursting and blooming and exploding with theories and leaflets, with speeches, predictions and plans for action. Suddenly twelve million people had written a note to their boss that they weren't robots to be pushed and shoved in whatever direction they chose.

It was one of the lesser consequences of their magnificent movement, and hardly reported in the media at all, but Solidarnosc got me back in the habit of getting up in the mornings. I pledged my own little bit and signed up for the Port Talbot to Brighton Right to Work march.

A walk of that length should start with fireworks, a band, a tearful crowd waving farewell to their loved ones and two booming blasts of a ship's funnel. Instead there were 200 of us in the pouring rain, in a car park outside the Port Talbot leisure centre, while the organizer, John Deason, stood under an umbrella, and said, 'Right, well off we go.'

It made me realize the most extraordinary journeys must have begun in the same mundane way. Jack Kerouac probably left home to the sound of his neighbour calling, 'Ta-ra then. Hope the weather stays nice.' And then wandered to the end of the street to wait for a bus.

Then we walked through the town centre, clad in orange jackets like the ones worn by railway engineers, shouting 'Maggie Maggie Maggie – out out out', a little concerned that this chant could become tedious by the time we approached Slough.

We slept each night in Labour Clubs or town halls where there was a sympathetic council. Fifty Labour MPs backed the march, as did 500 trade union branches. But putting all that in perspective was the reception as we passed through the villages of the Rhondda. Outside every terraced house, villagers cheered and waved us through the winding hilly roads, appearing at first glance like the people you see in Pathé newsreels greeting the Queen. Except the cheering wasn't passive but proud and forceful. And they weren't so much waving as punching through the air with a 'go on' you might shout at a horse you'd backed. Each one had a message as we passed their house, like 'Give it to Maggie when you get there'.

That night, at a miners' hall in Blaenllechau, Paul Foot spoke on the subject of the socialist answer to unemployment and 200 miners crammed into the place. Two hundred! Fuck Gravesend dole office, I should have given those leaflets out in Blaenllechau. The questions they were keenest to ask were those I'd spent several years wrestling with – how would this socialism work, would we all have to be the same, what went wrong in Russia, as they sought an explanation for the condition of their own lives. And all in that formal Welsh politeness. Brother, sister, sir, with respect, the gentleman, and definitely no swearing.

The next day, as we were leaving the village, the police tried to arrest the organizers. We crowded around those they were trying to arrest and the police backed off, with a disgruntled 'yes, well just watch yourself next time'. I was beginning to think we were invincible.

Within days a tribal loyalty emerged, throughout the purple-mohicanned Glaswegians, the cloth-capped couple called Dennis and Edna, the American student, blind Larry and his guide-dog Seeker, and the rest of the 200 diverse characters, similar to that which must develop in military units.

Few military units however would include Gladys. She was seventy-two and had wandered to the leisure centre in the rain to see us off. From there she was persuaded to leave her shopping in the van and march the first mile with us. But she carried on to the lunch break, then to the first lodgings, and slept in a spare sleeping bag in Bridgend Labour Club. 'I'll stay for a second day,' she announced to a huge cheer the following morning. But she stayed for the whole three weeks. By then she'd been interviewed by the *Daily Mirror*, ITN and every regional news programme along the way. By the time we got to Bristol, she was speaking on public platforms. One night, in front of 2,000 people, she finished with, 'One of my neighbours is a po-lice-man. Well I tell you, after the way I've seen them behave to us marchers, I'm never letting him in the house again.'

For the first week, most of the twenty-five miles a day involved the surreal task of tramping across deserted hills, the banner flapping frantically at the front, while we sang to ourselves and to disinterested Welsh sheep. No one had proper walking boots or sweatshirts or rainproof coats, and certainly not wax trousers tucked into thick brown socks. No one did warm-up exercises or was aware that multi-glucose energy bars or hi-protein power drinks existed. It troubled no one that after an eight-hour hike the only washing facility available was a sink in the toilet. Or that you set off for Oxford in the same unwashed shirt that you'd set off in for Swindon the day before.

As blisters mounted, I became accustomed to walking on those bits of my feet that weren't blighted, until the unaffected area shrank to a three-inch strip under each foot, which didn't even have the decency to be in similar areas, so at least my hobble could be symmetrical.

Across the Severn Bridge into Bristol we marched, and then to the Wiltshire town of Chippenham, at one point through the genteel pedestrian village of Wooton Bassett. Some of them probably moved there to get out of the rat-race of Chippenham. And here were 200 unemployed marchers, bellowing what we were going to do with Maggie Thatcher ear-ly in the morning as they moved past the delicatessen and displays of local fudge.

Through rural Berkshire we played a game with the police convoy accompanying us, of speeding up into a semi-trot which they couldn't keep up with. 'Slow down or I'll arrest you,' one of them puffed. Now we were convinced we were impregnable, becoming like a maverick regiment in an army. Another month like this and we could end up like Kurtz in *Heart of Darkness*, going missing and setting up our own colony in Wooton Bassett.

Then we passed Windsor. An advance party was sent to the outskirts of the castle, with walkie-talkies donated by a *World in Action* team who were filming us. The police suspected a stunt and sent busloads of officers to protect it, but it was all a decoy. Unnoticed, the main body of the march had slid down a back road and invaded Eton College.

The judges and spies of the future sped from the courtyard into the sanctuary of the building like iron filings being sucked towards a magnet. Iron bolts were drawn across the vast wooden door with dramatic clumps and the schoolboys and tutors retreated upstairs, to gaze out on the mob they'd been brought up to fear. 'What does one want? The right to gainful employment,' we yelled, feeling like the Viet Cong surrounding the American Embassy in Saigon. It was a perfect protest. Everyone there, on both sides of the wooden door, will always remember as a result that however much you're brought up to rule, you won't necessarily have things your own way. And the event was carried off with perfect discipline. Except that one lad with a purple mohican threw a chair through a window.

As we approached Brighton, it felt as if we were coming to the end of a great thriller, an exhilarating odyssey almost complete but with the big shootout to come. We were also aware, as one is at the climax of an adventure, that although we would meet again, always remembering the camaraderie, loyalty and warmth of the friendships that had developed, it would never be quite the same.

In Brighton, as in Port Talbot, it rained. Except it really rained. Seven thousand demonstrators joined the march to surround the Tory conference and, unbeknown to the rest of us, one demonstrator had secretly obtained credentials and harangued Thatcher from the conference floor, for which he was knocked unconscious by security guards. Outside, the police charged and soaking placards flew back at them through the rain. The spray crashed on to the front from the sea, arrests, snatched megaphones, one last 'Maggie Maggie Maggie – out out out', a TGWU brass band defied climate and mayhem to keep blowing, and we were the main item in the next day's news. One of the main speakers at the final rally was Gladys and I think her shopping was still in the van.

As we left Brighton to go our separate ways, we all felt a magnified version of the conflicting emotions that circulate on the last day of a great holiday. The warm satisfaction of having experienced an episode you'll always cherish, but trepidation about rehabilitation into the routine of normal life. That unsettling feeling that tomorrow you'll be back in the real world and all this will seem like a distant dream. Tomorrow I won't be able to sing the Maggie Thatcher bonfire song in the high street and the police won't be wary of me. No one will cheer me as I arrive, nor demand that I shouldn't be allowed there in the first place. I won't have to hurriedly wash in a basin before the bacon butties run out. Tomorrow I can stay in my sleeping bag all day and no one will mind – or notice.

Chapter 9

It was a resounding moment of joy: to get a job in an administrative office in a London Transport engineering depot. But what a mental trial. The other six people in my department were in their fifties, which would have been fine except they were in their *fifties*, and there was no point of contact whatsoever.

Every day would start with that little office joke, when whoever comes in four minutes late says 'morning' and everyone replies 'afternoon'. Then they would discuss every particle of their previous evening. 'Dorothy made a lovely gravy last night, not too thick, because I don't like it too thick, but with a little bit of chopped onion. I've never tried it like that before – with the onion actually in the gravy. I said "this is lovely, this is, we should try it like this for Sunday lunch" . . .'

Then they would discuss the previous night's telly. Until someone would complain that they quite fancied that film, but saw it didn't finish until twenty to eleven and it's ridiculous putting a film on that goes on to that sort of time. And I'd be quietly filing, recalling that around that time I was dragging a wardrobe out of a skip with a biker who kept screaming like a wolf because he was out of his box on magic mushrooms.

Every single day the boss of the section would take his coffee cup across to the sink, joking as he did so, 'I'm just going over to wash my thing – ha ha ha.' And every day I wished I had the nerve to say 'And I'm just going over to wash *my* thing', then take my knob out and run it under the tap.

There wasn't a single aspect of my life outside that office that I felt I could mention without fearing they would faint or call the emergency services. What would they think if they knew I lived in a squat? I remembered the period in the mid-seventies, when a national paranoia about squatters developed following a rash of news stories. There was an explosion of urban myths, along the lines of 'There was a family in Dartford, they went to the seaside, and when they came back their house was full of hippies playing guitars. So they went to the council who told them there was nothing they could do about it and now they live in a caravan'.

It became fashionable to speak of squatters as if they were ants. 'It doesn't matter what you do, they'll find a way in,' people would say. And it wouldn't have seemed abnormal if they'd continued, 'You can put powder down but they walk straight over it. They'll find a hole in the skirting or something.'

If I'd told them how I lived in a legal squat, in a house which would otherwise have been demolished, it may have undermined any prejudices they had. But now I had the opposite problem to before, I was terrified of doing anything that might jeopardize my job. So I lived a double life, almost like a bigamist. I couldn't tell them where or how I lived. And when they asked if I'd seen *Dallas*, I didn't feel comfortable about saying that I hadn't, on account of being at a district meeting to discuss the strikes in Poland.

So I made occasional small talk, which might have been bearable if I'd had any work to do. But I didn't. Each day a small pile of forms came in, and I had to copy the information on to another set of forms and return them to the office who'd sent them in the first place. The purpose of this was never explained. Nor was it explained what I was meant to do after I'd finished each day's pile, which took less than an hour. So I'd invent games, positioning two paper clips on my desk as a goal and rolling a round pencil sharpener in an arc through the middle. After a month, if this game had been a surprise inclusion in the Olympics, I'd have been bound for gold.

I was so bored I memorized the entire map of the London Underground, eventually drawing the whole thing from memory. At times it would occur to me that I hadn't looked at the clock for a while and I would prepare myself for a check. 'Oh please God,' I would think, 'please let it be later than half past twelve. Oh if it's half past twelve I couldn't bear it. I couldn't stand thirty minutes until lunch. I'll die of boredom, I know I will, and I bet I survive until two minutes to one and *then* die of boredom. Oh please please

let it be ten to one, please oh please oh please.' But with no
landmarks in the day to chart the passage of time, guessing the time
was like judging distance across a desert. So I'd look at the clock
and find it was twenty-five past nine.

I'd cleaned the windows and polished the desk and filed things
and picked up every rogue paper clip and put it back in a box and
was desperate for something to do. Which must have made me the
only Marxist in history to demand that their manager increases
their level of exploitation. Then Jim, a retired Irish railway engineer
with one eye, took over the job of delivering the post. I noticed he
wore a union badge, so I jumped up to awkwardly say 'hello' as he
was leaving, the way you might contrive to greet someone you
fancied. And we talked about Thatcher and Ireland and James
Connolly, and he'd say 'Ah the Tories, they're terrible terrible
people so they are' in that jovial Irish way that makes them sound
cheerful and avuncular even when they're explaining that they hate
someone's guts. Every day when he came in, I'd stop the nothing I
was doing and dive across to the wooden boxes that housed the
post and talk to Jim about H-blocks and Solidarnosc and unions
and why the Royal Wedding was bollocks.

He found it hard to talk about any of these subjects, or anything
else, without ending his sentence with a throaty laugh that sounded
like Father Christmas with a Dublin accent. He even laughed when
he told me how he'd lost his eye in an industrial accident but was
awarded a pittance as compensation, though London Transport
were kind enough to transfer him to the post. Until one day, when
he showed me his invitation to see the board, to collect a clock for
long service. 'I've not even replied. Fockin' bastards,' he said. And
didn't laugh.

During our conversations the other clerks from that side of the
office would join in, debate, laugh and ask questions. Then I'd be
asked to return to the desk where time stood still, gazing across at
the warm jolly people on the other side of the office, like someone
peering over the Berlin wall in a Cold War propaganda film.

Every Monday morning, when I was formally asked what I'd
done at the weekend, I would answer 'nothing much', whatever the
truth. But on the Monday morning of 13 April 1981, 'nothing
much' was such a lie that I was barely able to mouth the words.

*

Much of my social and agitational life was spent in Brixton, which in some company was a shock in itself. When I visited the old pubs of Swanley, the words 'I was down in Brixton', would be enough to elicit one of those long sucking noises, the sort a car mechanic makes before telling you that you need a new gearbox. 'That's dodgy, isn't it?' they would say, despite living in a town that invented the parlour game 'Beat Your Head In'. And it wasn't just Swanley, the reputation seemed universal. I wondered if you could go to the front of the Iran–Iraq war, say you were from Brixton, and find soldiers going, 'Phooooo, that's dodgy isn't it?'

The basis for this nonsense was racism; Brixton = full of blacks = danger. The real Brixton was not 'black' but multicultural, with a large Irish contingent, a Portuguese community, one-fifth Afro-Caribbean and a white majority. And the centre was always youthful, energetic, welcoming, loud and wonderfully mad. Reggae boomed from Desmond's Hip City, a record shop in the market, outside which a Rasta affectionately known as 'Twirler' span round and round all day on the spot, somehow never getting dizzy or throwing up. On hot days, black families would stand outside their houses, a contagious habit that spread to white households, creating the ambience of a spontaneous carnival. And every marginal left-wing paper in the world was on sale at the tube. On one occasion there were twenty-three varieties, a heartening if ironic example of free-market consumer choice.

But two things *had* soured the atmosphere. In January of that year, a fire at a party about four miles away in Deptford had killed thirteen black teenagers. Many people were suspicious that this was the result of a racist attack. Then the police launched Operation Swamp '81. This was an extension of the 'Sus' law, an adaptation of a 19th-century vagrancy act, which allowed the police to stop, search and detain anyone they regarded as 'suspicious'. In four days they stopped 1,000 people in Brixton, almost all black, and arrested 150. On the Saturday of Swamp '81, the swamped area fizzed with tension. Every twenty yards stood a group of police and in every side road were police vans. At each end of the high street were those long green police vehicles that look like rural buses from the 1950s. Never had a normal shopping area been so covered by defenders of order and never had it felt so dangerous.

Later that day a black lad called Michael Bailey who'd been stabbed in a fight was detained by police as his friends called for an ambulance. The police put him in their car and refused to release him, but his friends dragged him out and got him into a cab, which was sent to the hospital. The police tried to stop the cab and a crowd gathered to throw stones at them.

Unaware of this, I had arranged to meet a friend in the Old Queen's Head on the road to Stockwell, on the edge of the centre of Brixton. By the time I arrived at the pub, the roads were littered with broken glass and police cars were squealing aimlessly down the South Lambeth Road and back again. Clouds of smoke drifted from all directions, like tributary rivers converging on a smoke lake in the middle. I walked to the high street, where a marquee which had been erected in front of the police station, with a massive sign saying 'HELP FIGHT CRIME', was melting and collapsing into a smouldering heap. Almost every shop had lost its windows, filling the air with an array of alarms that together sounded almost harmonic. The railway bridge was on fire, Burtons was on fire, the area in front of the cinema was on fire and up the road a racist pub was on fire.

The mood amidst this mayhem was an opposite atmosphere to that of the morning. Now there were no police and an assortment of buildings on fire, and yet it seemed safe. After all, no one was likely to swipe your wallet when twenty yards away was a jewellers with no windows. The crowds were black and white, looters were handing out goods to strangers, selective locations such as the Law Centre and the hippie cinema the Ritzy were left untouched. All the sneering, the sarcasm, the petty smirks, fingers jabbed on chests, cars uprooted in a supposed search for drugs, were rebounding on the police who were as astonished as a wife-beater whose wife finally leaves him.

Explosions appear as sudden, but only if you've not been watching the careful drip-drip of wrath that seethes and festers and spits in impotent frustration, until the crowd is so near to breaking point that one stone can spark a riot. When liberals condemn such action on the grounds that it 'solves nothing', they forget that the unemployed youth of inner cities didn't launch their petrol bombs that summer as a means of solving anything. They just saw the chance to have one night when they could get even, which would stay with them no matter what followed.

What followed for me was that I wandered back to the pub in case my friend was waiting there. Amongst the scattered debris lay a pair of shoes, looted, discarded and looking sadly rejected. I didn't want the shoes. I couldn't have sold the shoes. If I'd taken them home as a souvenir, within a week I'd have dwelled on how much kudos could be gleaned from the things and slung them in a skip. But for some reason, some force, a God of stupidity urged me to bend down and pick them up. There must have been something compelling about the idea of holding them, as if they would provide proof I was really there.

As a result, moments later I was stood amidst the maelstrom of the major disturbance on the British streets since the 1930s, explaining to two policemen as the smoke glittered through the flashing blue lights that I hadn't stolen the shoes, I'd just found them and innocently picked them up. I might as well have said they were the result of a wish I'd been granted by a passing genie. I was arrested, and the events of the next few hours I recorded in a notebook the next morning. If I hadn't, I'm certain I would now be wondering whether time had distorted my memory.

First came the uncertainty, handcuffed and taken to Brixton police station, and left amidst a sea of police as they tore in and out of the yard, sweating and angry. In the semi-distance was a conversation that may or may not have been about me, leaving me straining to catch what I could, like a kid listening to their parents from the top of the stairs.

'Black bastards,' said a copper as he smashed a truncheon into the face of a lad stood about ten yards from me. A line of black youth descended the stairs at the back of the station, each of them with their face covered in blood. I resigned myself to a hiding, comforted that in this state at least they wouldn't bother being sarcastic.

Eventually I was thrown into another van, with the accompanying words 'sorry about the colour sarge'. There were five detainees, handcuffed to each other with a policeman between each convict, making a circle. The last lad in the van was made to kneel on the floor. 'You're stupid, what are you?' asked the copper. 'I'm stupid,' he replied, terrified, but determined not to look weak. 'You're stupid and what?'

'I don't know.'

'Crack' went the truncheon on to the side of his face.

'I don't know,' he whimpered and there was a harder 'crack'.

'You're stupid and black. You're a black bastard. What are you?'

'I'm a black bastard.'

'Can't you get that dog to string up a few niggers,' said an officer to the dog-handler, which says so much about their frame of mind. Because, apart from being appalling, this is meaningless. Dogs can't string people up, even police dogs. But such was the eruption of race hate that stuff like this burst from their minds in a frenzied avalanche of unthinking abuse.

We were taken to Lambeth police station, where all around were young men, almost all black, with different levels of injury. I was made to stand facing a wall, and at intervals of what seemed about a minute, someone would say something like 'what's he doing here? He's white'. One of them, leaning into my face so that his nose touched my cheek said, 'You white shit, whose side are you on?'

'Kiss the wall,' an officer demanded of the next convict along. At the opposite end of the room to me was a door, from which every few minutes a figure would emerge with blood across his face. Which left those of us stood by the wall feeling like children in a dentist's waiting room, watching and wondering exactly how painful it would be when our turn came. And then I was slung in a cell and left to reflect.

The police, it could be argued, had a right to be annoyed after spending the night retreating from showers of petrol bombs. But that doesn't explain the racism. These attitudes weren't the reactions of a shocked body of innocent men, but of a group that had already defined the battle lines of their environment.

I'm certain not every policeman supported the actions and language of their most enthusiastic colleagues. There must have been some who were disgusted, or at least unsure of the merits of this behaviour. But they were in no position to speak out. The atmosphere was driven by the hardliners.

The cell door opened and another white lad was thrown in. He lived on Railton Road, in the middle of Brixton, and told me how a line of police had refused to let him pass to get to his own home. Irritated, he'd pleaded, and as a result was sat next to me in a cell. He paced around the room, occasionally sitting and immediately getting up again, opining with bewilderment about the unfairness of his arrest. 'What was I supposed to do? Why wouldn't they believe me? I've never been in trouble before. One of them pushed me! They wouldn't even listen to my dad. And he's a vicar!'

I burst out laughing at the vicar revelation and he joined in and calmed down. Over the next hour I had the conversation I'd had so often before. The police, I suggested, were an institution committed to preserving the status quo. If they treated all sections of society equally, wouldn't they set up Swamp '81A and stop 1,000 stockbrokers on suspicion of city fraud? Never before had I enjoyed such a captive audience. As the night wore on, we agreed that we were enjoying ourselves. It's so rare you get a chance to enjoy a lengthy uninterrupted dialogue with a complete stranger like that.

Suddenly there was the echoey scratching and clanging of a cell door opening and we were summonsed to separate rooms for interviews. I was told I could make a confession statement or 'be back in the cell until Monday'. I could have demanded to see a lawyer or refused to co-operate, but none of this occurred to me as it would now. The reason may be that back in 1981 the police seemed all powerful, at least in their own domain. Juries automatically believed the word of an officer over a civilian, especially if they were young or tatty or black.

As I signed the statement, they stood eagerly over me as if they were salesmen and I was signing an agreement to buy their timeshare holiday cottage. 'There you are Mark,' they said with cornershop intimacy, as they handed back my belongings in that plastic pouch. And the bonhomie made me wish I'd opted for the kicking.

I was released, relieved and slightly guilty about remaining unharmed, into the balmy Waterloo night, where my cellmate and his dad the vicar had waited for me, to drive me home.

Within days, 'defend the community' meetings sprang up, each packed with hundreds of people. But instead of emphasising the similarities between black and white youth, they emphasised the differences. At the largest of these meetings, a row broke out about which bit of Brixton had been the most heroic.

The first contribution was 'You Frontline brothers weren't worth shit'. Followed by a Frontline brother rolling up his trouser leg and urging everyone to look at his scars. I got to speak and was met with windswept silence, as everyone appeared to spend my whole speech puzzling out what I was doing there. It was as if I was at the wrong meeting and had said 'I'd like to welcome everyone to this year's AGM of the Guildford Rambling Society'. There was one other speaker after me, then someone put on a record at a deafening volume, and minders shoved everyone out of their chairs and bundled the place empty in under a minute.

Another of the meetings was dominated by a black businessman, who spoke at length on the need for the black community to use black businesses only, in particular to place their money with the Bank of Ghana. I enquired whether the board of the Bank of Ghana had been especially active during the riot, reasonably confident that one of their major shareholders wasn't going to trump me by rolling up a trouser leg to show us his scars.

I had one other unavoidable meeting to attend; with a judge to decide my sentence for the Great Shoe Robbery. 'There were many policemen present on the night of your arrest, were there not?' the prosecution counsel asked me. I agreed that there were. 'Then if you weren't stealing the shoes, why didn't you ask a nearby officer if he could track down the owner?'

What a marvellous image. Running across the rubble-littered street, frantically waving at a Panda car as it hurtles cop-show style across a backdrop of crackling flaming clothes shops. Then greeting the emerging officer with, 'Excuse me, only I've just found these shoes and I'm concerned that the owner may be missing them. I mean, you shouldn't wander through this broken glass in bare feet.'

Nor would the prosecution have it that I'd set off for Brixton unaware that the riot was taking place. 'But it was one of the most reported events for years,' he said, 'everybody knew about it.' I decided, just, that the best tactic was not to follow my instincts and say, 'But even major events tend not to be reported *before* they happen. You might as well ask why JFK went to Dallas when everyone knows that he ended up getting shot, you cloth-eared brainless overpaid legal fuckwit.' But I might as well have done, because the jury believed the word of the police. I wonder, if the trial could be rerun today, if the legacy of high-profile miscarriages of justice would lead to a more sympathetic jury, and I would get my 100 quid back.

It probably didn't help that by the time it came to court, riots had spread to almost every major inner-city area in the country.

On the Monday after the Brixton riot, the office procedure ran a little behind, due to an extended session of 'isn't it terrible about those riots'. But eventually they got round to asking if I'd done anything interesting over the weekend. 'Nothing much,' I answered, croakily, after a long pause.

But as I sat in that office, I looked at them and wondered: 'Do you never, not ever, when you're copying out the 100th form of the day, when you think it's ten to five but it's only half past three, consider grabbing that filing cabinet, setting fire to the thing, and lobbing it straight through the nearest window?' I bet you do.

Chapter 10

In the summer of '81, Britain seemed to be two entirely different countries, slapped on top of each other, like two films being shown on the same screen at the same time. In one was the dole, Alexei Sayle, the Beat singing 'Stand Down Margaret' and the Damned playing at the Lyceum on my twenty-first birthday. In the other Charles married Di.

There were vast demonstrations against Thatcher in London, Liverpool and Glasgow, and enormous un-royal events on wedding day. But it was as if we were the same crowd each time, like one of those social groups in which every now and then one of you has a party, but it's always the same people in a different house.

The protest movement wasn't reaching beyond its own ranks of around 150,000 people and it was dawning on those of us that despised her that she was getting away with it. But in no issue was the failure to overturn her more gruelling than in the matter of the north of Ireland. All that most people knew about Ireland was that it was nearly as bad as Brixton.

Then there was the official scrambling for words of condemnation after every bomb. The news would tell us that 'Willie Whitelaw said it was "despicable", while Denis Healey said it was an "outrage".' And I wondered whether the politicians conferred before announcing which word they'd selected. Maybe there were arguments – 'You can't have "hideous" again, you had that last time. You've got "shocking and disgraceful" this time. If we don't stick to the rota, the whole thing falls apart.' If not, how could they be sure there wouldn't be the embarrassment of two people picking the same word? Imagine the news telling us 'Keith Joseph said the bomb proved the IRA were "loathsome". And David Owen, well he said they were, well, er, "loathsome" as well.' Also, wouldn't there have been arguments after the politicians' statements? Geoffrey Howe saying, 'Roy Hattersley has called the latest IRA bomb "monstrous". He is quite wrong. This one was more, sort of, grotesque.'

Anyone in the media who half-groped towards analysing the root causes of the bombs, rather than mournfully shaking their head, crisply pronouncing hideous/monstrous/grotesque, and declaring that the IRA would 'never, ever succeed', was met with howls of protest. It was as if these words were passwords and unless you used one of them in your opening remark, you couldn't log on to the rest of the discussion.

Then, it seemed that any time you were on the verge of per-suading someone through months of patient reasoning that the IRA weren't just sadistic psychopaths, they'd blow up somewhere like an old people's home or a sanctuary for sick and especially furry rabbits.

So you couldn't blame the majority of the population for not being sympathetic. If I did get to a discussion on the roots of the problem, the most likely argument I'd counter would be that it was all down to religion. Which also stood up to very little scrutiny. When loyalist gangs hurled stones into Catholic areas, they clearly weren't thinking 'transubstantiation my arse'.

Occasionally there would be mention on the news of the 'dirty protest' in the H-block jail, in which IRA prisoners lived in a blanket, refused to shave and smeared their excrement on the wall. This was clearly not a strategy destined to win over the floating voter. If you were starting from the point of modern politicians, desperate to emphasise points that would reassure the commuters of Middle England, you probably wouldn't jump up at an electioneering strategy meeting, and shout, 'I've got it – we photo the candidates pasting shit up a wall.'

So Ireland was tough. But it wasn't surprising. I'd never considered what the cause of the conflict might be myself, until becoming an active socialist. Even then, anything which hinted of justification of the IRA was going one stage too far. All the other stuff, about the police and the Communist Party being right wing and not gawking at girlie calendars, I could take that. But this was being outlandish for its own sake.

Until I read *War and an Irish Town* by Eamonn McCann and
saw how the first Prime Minister of Northern Ireland had declared
a 'Protestant land for a Protestant people'. How the Catholics were
effectively denied the vote. How the B Special police had been
formed from Protestant gangs. How the Special Powers Act was
considered draconian even by President Vorster of South Africa.
How the army interned hundreds of Catholics, breaking down
doors and dragging men away in front of screaming kids, with no
formal arrest and no trial.

I felt as if I'd been moaning at someone for being miserable and
grumpy, and suddenly discovered they were suffering from a
terrible disease. I read more books, which brought more shocks.
There'd been the Black and Tans, the famine, the siege of
Drogheda, the Statute of Kilkenny and an expedition by Henry II
in 1169 to supplant the wayward Dermot Macmurrogh. Blimey.
And right on our doorstep. It was like discovering your partner's
been having an affair with a neighbour for years. Though even then
you'd have to be very unlucky to ask how long it had been going
on, and get the reply 'since 1169'.

Like most people, I hadn't even heard of the loyalist groups, the
UDA, UFF and UVF. I just assumed that all the shooting was done
by the IRA. So little was ever said about these organizations that it
must have been common for people to hear that the UDA had shot
someone and automatically think 'IRA bastards, they've done it
again'.

Now I was in the opposite quagmire, knowing more than I could
cope with. I'd reel off how the army had imposed curfews and
torture and no-jury courts, and the reply would come back 'but
they had to go in there and do that because of the IRA'.

'But the IRA didn't exist in 1969 when the army went in.'

'Of course they did.'

'No they didn't. The Provisional IRA weren't formed until 1972.'

'Don't be stupid mate, the IRA have been going for years,
everyone knows that.'

'But they'd collapsed and didn't really exist in 1969.'

'You don't know what you're talking about mate.'

By which time you might as well be arguing about who won the
FA Cup in 1959.

Out of fascination I travelled to Belfast, and was struck by the way the books I'd read were proved to be accurate. The boarded-up shops, disused factories, hobbling old men and dishevelled housing portraying a rolling poverty, the legacy of British neglect in the Catholic areas. Then I'd see the next mural, and the giant red hand and shining white horse would tell me that for the last ten minutes I'd been in the heart of a Protestant area.

This was no South Africa, with the Protestant minority employing Catholic house servants. Their privilege was to be able to point to the clanking of Shorts engineering, and say 'I can do shifts in there for fifty years, but the Fenians can't'.

I strolled into a pub in the heart of the Protestant area on the Shankill Road and became acquainted with a group of lads by playing them at pool. Johnny was nineteen, with the wispy moustache a nineteen-year-old can be proud of, and loved having someone new to talk to. This was just like Swanley. You went up the pub because as a teenager living with your parents, you had to go out to enjoy the luxury of being bored.

After a few pints and games of pool, Johnny asked if I fancied getting some carry-outs and going back to his house with his mates. Using the wonderful taxi system, in which a dozen strangers piled into black cabs, laying across each other like escaping prisoners under a box in a laundry van, we went to his parents' house in Rathcoole. As I stepped into his living room, opening a tin of lager, I couldn't help noticing an enormous framed square of cloth, embroidered with the words 'Ulster Freedom Fighters – we will never surrender'.

'That was given to my da,' he told me proudly, 'when he was away in jail.'

Rathcoole appears to have been plonked on the outskirts of North Belfast with a slightly irritated 'where shall we sling this?' attitude. Until the authorities puffed 'oh, here will do' the way you would with a broken radio when you're tidying the house in a hurry. And as we sat on Johnny's father's decaying settee, in the grey concrete dwelling indistinguishable from the thousands that surrounded it, he told me how he fought Catholics, admired the people who'd shot Catholics and was proud of the tradition of keeping Catholics in as low a place as they could be kicked to.

As he related his hobby and heroes, he gave a mischievous smirk, as if he was a little urchin telling you how he'd been scrumping apples or playing 'knock down Ginger'. Yet there was nothing in his tone which led me to believe he hated Catholics. He never mentioned any specific Catholics, nor anything any of them had ever done to cause him grief. He would kick them and throw stones at them and one day maybe shoot them, but he didn't hate them. No more than a bored teenager who fires his air-rifle at blackbirds does so out of a hatred of blackbirds. What he really hated was being an insignificant teenager, whose only realistic ambition was to be an insignificant adult, with his own grey dwelling on another part of the estate. But as long as he could look with pride upon that framed embroidered square of cloth, he could at least be satisfied he was helping to keep someone lower than him.

I slept on that settee that night, under the beaming framed cloth, wrapped in a blanket. The next day I thanked him for breakfast, made my excuses and left.

Wandering around Belfast, it's impossible not to be impressed with the ingenuity and artistry of the murals, on both sides. I'm sure soppy community workers from London have strolled through East Belfast, seen the beautifully crafted image of King William on his horse, and thought 'I wonder if I could get these creative youngsters to paint a racial harmony mural for the youth centre'.

On the Catholic side, almost every picture addressed one issue – the blanket prisoners in the H-blocks. From murals, leaflets and posters, blurred images of gaunt frail men, cross-legged, huddled in a blanket and clearly shivering, would stare at you with startled eyes through a mat of unkempt facial hair. On the face of it they were crazy, but why were so many men, and in Armagh prison women, crazy in this identical fashion? Every account of the backgrounds of the blanket men and women suggested they were sane rational people. And that if they'd been brought up in Swanley and gone to work for the Post Office, they wouldn't have felt the urge to turn up in a blanket, or wait till no one was looking and put shit all over the filing cabinet.

Until 1976, prisoners who'd been convicted of terrorist offences were awarded political status in the jails. Then this status was removed and they were forced to wear prison uniforms and participate in prison work. They refused, were denied access to the toilet and were left with the choice of floor or wall.

Their demand was for political status to be reinstated for Republican prisoners and to no longer be classified as common criminals. The question became more pertinent towards the end of 1980, when seven of the prisoners raised the stakes by going on hunger strike. This ended with a confused settlement and in March 1981 another hunger strike began, the first prisoner to refuse food being Bobby Sands.

Sands spent most of his childhood in one area – the Rathcoole Estate. The UDA staged a march past his house. He was regularly pursued by loyalist gangs, who on one occasion caught and stabbed him. Demonstrators would stand outside the door chanting 'Taigs out', and eventually when a dustbin came through the window, they moved, no doubt bringing joy to Johnny's da. He was a teenager through the B Special rampages, the curfews, internment and Bloody Sunday. So he joined the IRA. He was convicted of possessing a gun, which on the loyalist side carried an average sentence of five months, but he got fourteen years.

When people asked how the IRA could do such terrible things, I would compare his life to mine. I'd been so angry when the garage owner sacked me. But no one had driven my family from their home. I'd been so outraged when the police broke up the Foreign Office picket. But we didn't see anyone get their door kicked in and dragged at gunpoint into a van. I joined the group which seemed from my perspective best suited to changing the world. And so did he. When I was stupid, I got a one hundred pound fine for stealing shoes. He got fourteen years. While there, he learned Gaelic and memorized novels, and gave lessons in both to other prisoners by shouting through the prison doors. The worst physical pain I'd suffered for my ideas was blisters from Bristol to Chippenham. Bobby Sands was preparing to die on hunger strike.

The IRA did some lousy rotten stuff, but he wasn't a common criminal.

No other campaign is like that around a hunger strike, as matters are a little more urgent than normal. If you were on hunger strike, you wouldn't want to be told, 'Chris is having trouble finding a venue for the benefit, so we might have to put it back a month.' You can't nip into the cell and say, 'The posters have gone missing, so is there a chance you could have a boiled egg or something, so we've got an extra couple of days to get more printed?'

To add to the desperation, in Britain there was virtually no support for them, with one opinion poll stating the numbers in agreement with their demands at 2 per cent. Which left campaigners feeling as if they were watching someone lie on the floor in a pool of blood, while no one else could see them. I organized a Hunger Strike support group among a few of the more lucid squatters, and we stuck up posters and held the odd meeting. There were pickets and stalls in high streets, but instead of the same 100,000 being on every one, it was the same five. But then the MP for Fermanagh and South Tyrone died. And in the by-election, Bobby Sands stood as the 'Anti H-Block/Armagh, political prisoner' candidate.

Imagine what the image consultants of New Labour would think about the chances of a candidate like Sands. Advising him how to give himself a chance, where would they begin? 'If you're going to stick with the blanket, at least get one designed by Armani.'

Every rule of winning a modern election was not just flouted but turned comically upside-down. And on 10 April 1981 it was announced that Bobby Sands had won the election with 30,492 votes and was duly elected as MP.

'Ha ha haaaaaa,' said Jim as he came in with the post, and this day chuckled not after each sentence but each word. And all around people were astonished or aghast, or like me and Jim delirious, but it was a turning point, because from now on you had to take notice. 'They have no status, they are not accepted by anyone,' Lord Carrington, the Foreign Secretary, had said a few days before. Ha ha haaaaaa, well how about 30,492? Does that count as anyone?

What a weird situation it must have been; lying there, cold, sick, insults pouring in from the prison staff, preparing for blindness, agony and death, but newly elected as MP for Fermanagh and South Tyrone. This is a post that all good respectable people aspire to. You could imagine someone who knew Sands as a boy, but had left the country and not kept track of events, having the most peculiar conversation as they were told the news.

'Whatever happened to that little Bobby Sands boy?'

'Haven't you heard? He's an MP.'

'Oh, he's done well for himself. With a start in life like he had, it was more likely he'd end up in some sort of trouble.'

I only wished that the campaign had had more fun with his new status. They should have insisted that Sands was allowed to hold weekly surgeries for his constituents. And then arranged for queues of local residents to stand outside the prison, demanding to be allowed to see their MP about the broken lamppost by the bus stop. The traditional method for Republican prisoners to smuggle out messages was via notes written on cigarette papers and kept up their backsides until visiting time. So Sands should have issued a statement that if any of his constituents was getting hassled by officials from the council, the offending bureaucrat would be getting a letter from their MP.

Thatcher was humiliated by the election, temporarily. Governments around the world appealed to her, as did the Catholic Church. The French government even suggested they wouldn't send anyone to the royal wedding. But it wasn't appeals we needed, it was pressure. Without it, campaigners were left with the slogan that summed up 1981; 'Why won't she listen?'

So on 5 May Bobby Sands died. The state of New Jersey sent a message of 'honour to his courage'. The town of Le Mans announced they were naming a street after him. The Iranian government named the street that the British Consulate was in after him. Five thousand students marched through Milan burning the Union Jack. Barricades were built in Belfast and Derry and the streets were set alight. I went to my office at London Transport and filled the details from one form on to another.

I was devastated, but most crushing of all was to have no outlet for that pent-up assortment of emotions. Imagine telling them at work that I was upset because Bobby Sands had died. They wouldn't have taken issue with me on grounds of supporting terrorists, they'd have just stared in disbelief, as if I'd told them I was unable to work properly because I was too upset about Ernest Bishop being shot in *Coronation Street*. 'Well, that hunger fella died in the end,' said Connie, in an attempt to fill one of the ninety-minute silences that hung over the section. So I turned around, and as calmly as I could, explained about his upbringing in Rathcoole and the civil rights marches and the gunning down of fourteen people who were marching against internment, and she said 'well it just goes to show there are two sides to everything'.

Around once a fortnight, another prisoner joined the hunger strike, so that throughout the summer the grisly toll of deaths continued. For the media and supporters alike, the gruesome truth was that eventually the effect was similar to the later moon landings. It was impossible to get as emotional about the fifth as the first.

I felt this myself, until the beginning of August when I went to Belfast on a 'Troops Out' delegation. Every wall in a Catholic area was plastered in pictures of the hunger strikers. Every shop, office and public building was covered with details of that day's local protests. Dozens of men and women stood in a line in the middle of the road, each holding an enormous photo of a hunger striker, as almost every car tooted, with a special elongated toot to signify maximum defiance. Between a quarter and three-quarters of houses, depending on the area, displayed hunger strike posters. Every shop had a collection box. All around buzzed the partisan frenzy of a football crowd outside Wembley, and the public displays of support in the form of posters and graffiti made the place look like a giant version of a thirteen-year-old's bedroom.

A bulky bushy-haired representative from the H-Block committee greeted us in a hall in Andersonstown. 'Make sure you stay close to the rest of the group,' he insisted, in the style of a package holiday guide warning you not to wander off from the coach party while walking round Marrakech. He told us where to get the cheapest meals, what time to arrive for the specially laid on night of traditional local music, and in the one break from tour operator tradition, where to run if the march we were on was fired at by the army.

There were around 200 of us on the delegation and we slept in sleeping bags in a community hall on an estate, which lay at the top of a long winding lane. So the next morning, as we queued for bacon butties being served from a van, we were treated to the advantages of this terrain. 'Saracen,' screamed a boy of about eleven, who'd been sat on a muddy bank opposite for some time looking wonderfully eleven, with skinny arms, food across his face and mud caked on to his knees. And as we gazed down the lane, away in the distance there was indeed a British Army Saracen, creeping around the bends which would eventually lead past our hall. It was a thin lane and I remember hoping that it came across a little old man in a Ford Anglia going the opposite way. As we'd have been treated to the comedy of an armoured military vehicle reversing into a gap in the hedge, while the sniper poking his head through the roof called out 'back, back, you've got a couple of feet before you hit the gate'.

Instead, within seconds of the lad raising the alarm, around a hundred people of all ages had gathered, armed with stones, rubble, any dispensable and throwable object, and petrol bombs made from milk bottles, a rag and, importantly, petrol.

As the Saracen approached, each person in the crowd hurriedly shuffled and dodged backwards and forwards, like footballers in the moments before the taking of a corner. Then, in a sudden flurry, missiles rained down on the army truck, one or two exploding into miniature fireballs, and in return a hail of bullets came ricocheting at all angles around the area. I can honestly say I wasn't scared, not out of bravery, but because until I inspected the three-inch long rock-hard plastic bullets, which looked like off-white giant batteries scattered around us, I didn't register that we'd been shot at.

The process in my mind during those short moments must have been a) my eyes are telling me there's a sniper poking out of an army vehicle with a gun, and he's firing and bullets are flying, and b) but they can't be shooting; that's ridiculous.

The moment the Saracen had passed, every kid scurried around to collect a souvenir plastic bullet. Over the next few years fourteen people kept a more lasting momento of their plastic bullet experience, being killed by the things.

That afternoon we travelled to the centre of Belfast to attend a meeting, and as we hovered outside afterwards, an eerie mournful noise began to rumble. It was the sound of dustbin lids being clattered on to doorsteps in gradually increasing numbers. Within a few seconds every house in the vicinity had its front door open, while outside a woman knelt and thwacked a dustbin lid. It was like no other noise I'd ever encountered, in that it was both nearby and distant at the same time. Your ears would sometimes stop picking up the piercing ringing of adjacent dustbin lids and tune in on another wavelength to the musical reverberations of dustbin lids several roads away.

The chilling drama of the sound relayed an obvious message: the death of a hunger striker. Today it was the ninth, Tom McElwee, a farmer's son from County Derry. Some of us went to the funeral, a gathering of tens of thousands in the rural town of Bellaghy. Why so many, if he was just a thug? What made entire communities paint murals, spray graffiti, hold collections, display posters, allow their kids to lob petrol bombs, bang dustbin lids, in the name of psychopaths? And could anyone without the deepest conviction, born of tradition and intellect, however flawed, put themselves through the unimaginably harrowing process that led to that funeral taking place?

A few days later, I went for a lunchtime drink in a Bogside pub in Derry, which appeared as any other pub in a poor area during a weekday lunchtime session. A couple of lads had cashed their giros. Two old men in caps slurped Guinness. A mechanic bolted down a pint while looking at his watch. And an old woman sat proud and upright on her own, in her buttoned-up coat, supping a glass of Mackeson. But the atmosphere was chilled somewhat by the crashing open of the door and the appearance of an army patrol.

'What's in there?' demanded the corporal, pointing his rifle at my rucksack. And he told me to open it up, hold it upside-down and tip out the contents on the floor. 'Leave him alone,' said an old woman.

'It's nothing to do with you Mrs Mulligan,' said the soldier.

'How the devil are you knowing my name?' she asked.

'We know everyone's name, you ought to know that by now Mrs Mulligan,' he said, and took delight in telling the other four people in the bar what their name was.

But he didn't know my name. So to make amends, he hooked a pair of my underpants, by now scattered across the floor, on to the end of his gun. Waving them about he made 'woooor, what a smell' jokes, the way you might when someone takes their shoes off when you're seven.

The squaddies chortled. 'You're a very tall man,' Mrs Mulligan said to the corporal, 'you'd look awfully nice in a coffin.'

An hour or so later, I wandered across to the bus station and was intercepted by another unit, who helped me into a van and took me to Waterside police station. 'We have reason to believe you attended an illegal march,' they told me, and to prove it displayed an armful of photos of demonstrators, taken from a helicopter. But I hadn't been on this march, as it had taken place at the same time as the funeral.

Then they showed me the photos one by one, with the enthusiasm of a relative handing you their holiday snaps. It would have seemed natural if they'd said things like 'And this is one of the commander of the IRA No.6 unit in Ardoyne, marching past Woolworths. My, doesn't he look chubby?'

They established that I hadn't taken part and then spoke to me for an hour about the evil nature of the IRA and how I shouldn't be taken in by the wicked people I'd been mixing with, before they eventually let me go.

But who was really taken in? The Republican strategy led to atrocious events but the root cause was the conditions that bred such hatred. Furthermore, when those of us who'd considered why people became Republicans described their bombs as disgraceful, we meant it much more than the pious politicians, who chose their word of the week, but cared nothing for the victims of official terrorism in Vietnam or Nicaragua.

Who was really taken in? I've no idea what became of Johnny. He may well have ended up killing, or being killed. He probably went to jail. Maybe he supports the peace process, or has been interviewed on the news denouncing it. But the one thing I'd put money on is, he's still skint.

There's one final irony in all this. One of the most common recollections of the politics of 1981 involves the state of the Labour Party. That was the time when Labour became so left-wing that it made itself outrageously hideously grotesquely unelectable.

So what did they say about the hunger strikes? On 1 May, four days before Bobby Sands died, Don Concannon, Labour's spokesman for Northern Ireland, flew especially to Belfast and travelled to the H-Blocks to visit him. As Sands lay blind,

Concannon told him the Labour Party firmly supported Thatcher on the issue of political status, and he'd come to tell him personally so there could be no doubt in any prisoner's mind where Labour stood.

Across the world the name of Bobby Sands is remembered. Does anyone remember the name of Don Concannon? I had to look it up myself to check I'd remembered it correctly. How many will go to his funeral? A hundred thousand? A hundred? Maybe it's already happened. Does anybody know?

Chapter 11

In the early eighties then, almost everyone is now agreed, Labour was too left-wing to win an election and nearly collapsed under the weight of its own left-wingness. For example, Roy Hattersley has written: 'Trotskyists, one-subject campaigners, Marxists who had never read Marx, Maoists, pathological dissidents . . . played a major part in keeping the Conservatives in power for almost twenty years.'

But the first of Labour's defeats came after five years of being in government. Surely, the Prime Minister and Chancellor in that government had *some* responsibility for losing that one. Unless Hattersley means that Jim Callaghan and Denis Healey were closet Maoists. In which case it's no wonder they got in a mess. The governor of the Bank of England would ask them what they were going to do about inflation, and Healey would suggest a long march into the forest.

Every establishment figure in the Labour Party, and most who were on the left at the time, agree that they were gripped by a collective madness, which resulted in outlandish policies, conference delegates yelling from the floor and Michael Foot in a donkey jacket. Yet the main success of the left was to change the rules, so that Labour MPs had to stand for reselection by their local parties before each General Election. Is that Trotskyist or Maoist? Could a social worker classify someone as 'pathologically dissident' for that? The other demand was that the conference should select the party's leader and manifesto, rather than the MPs and the union block vote.

I had always been puzzled by Labour conferences, especially the block vote. Someone in a slightly too tight waistcoat would announce 'For the motion, 6.9 million, against 6.5 million'. Then hundreds of enthusiastic young members in denim jackets would jump up and down, clapping and cheering like ice skaters when the board flashes '6.0 – 6.0 – 6.0'. Who were these 6.9 million? It clearly didn't relate to a number of *people*. That's roughly the population of Belgium. Was it an unfathomable points system, like the scoring on a pinball machine? Maybe it had started out with sensible numbers, but sped out of control, like the Italian lira.

Even then, the result would mean Labour now had a policy of curbing police powers or cutting arms spending, but everyone knew they weren't going to do it. So why did they bother having the conference at all? It had no more bearing on what actually happened than my old school council. At least we decided on the venue for the Christmas outing.

The left were attempting to make the leadership of their party more accountable to the members, against objections from the leadership. Then Benn stood to replace Denis Healey as deputy leader, and a layer of Labour members left to form the SDP. Not because Benn was imposed on them, or even elected, but because he stood at all. Huge meetings took place to support Benn's campaign, thousands wore 'Benn for Deputy' badges and there was a sense among that number that they were changing the world, by making the Labour Party the property of its members, so the dis-appointments of the last Labour government could never be repeated.

These were honourable aspirations but seemed to be based on a condition common on the left – self-delusion. This is the state that results in rallies and public meetings in cavernous halls, beginning with the chairperson announcing through an echoey and slightly squeaky PA, 'I'd like to thank everyone for coming to this wonderful event, and what a *magnificent* turnout we've got today.' And you're stood in the audience thinking, 'But there's only fifty of us. The place is fucking empty.'

Worse are the local union officials who introduce themselves at Trades Council meetings, at which there are seven people, by saying 'Ted Braithwaite, deputy divisional secretary of the regional sub-branch of the Finance and General Purposes Committee of the GMWU, and as such representing 130,000 members'.

The campaign to reform Labour seemed afflicted by this virus.

I'd become a socialist with the aim of getting working-class people to oppose the unfairness of the world. Not many of them seemed to be taking much notice. But the worst thing was to imagine you were succeeding because you'd won a vote in a room of thirty activists.

Tony Benn did exceptionally well, winning 49.6 per cent of the Electoral College, to Healey's 50.4 per cent. If those figures had represented the real level of support for Benn's ideas, what an exciting time it would have been. But whenever there was a ballot amongst all union members, it went overwhelmingly to Healey. In opinion polls, Healey led Benn by 72 per cent to 20 per cent. By the end of 1981, the SDP were winning by-elections and leaving Labour's poll rating at its lowest level for fifty years.

Thatcher had beaten almost every strike, a Labour government and some of the strongest unions in the country, and now there were three million on the dole. The effect was to drag people away from the notion you could win by using the collective strength of the masses. It was a period summed up by Paul Weller, who gave up his belligerent Jam for the easy-listening Style Council. Now he was singing 'the walls come tumbling down', but in a genteel cabaret style that would make hardened Mexican guerrillas snuggle under a poncho with a hot water bottle.

I had spent the last few years as the optimist amongst pessimists. Now, when I met people campaigning for a revitalized Labour Party, I was a pessimist amongst optimists. A few thousand was a healthy number to be participating in a campaign but they were acting as if they represented millions. Yet what did it mean to most people, this talk of electoral colleges, manifestos and mandatory reselection?

Far-left groups who'd spent years handing out smudgy close-typed unreadable documents accusing Labour of being worse than the Tories, joined Labour to make it more socialist. Remaining outside Labour felt like being old men in a Californian barn, shaking our heads while everyone else grabbed their shovel to rush off for gold that we knew didn't exist.

Part of the SWP response was to insist it would be difficult to withstand this stampede without becoming acquainted with the details of Marxist theory. Power in society, Marx claimed, rested with those in control of the means of production. In the modern world that means the multinationals, food empires that hoard grain to keep the price up, drugs companies that spend more on advertising than on research, arms dealers, oil barons and bankers whose money financed regimes in Chile and El Salvador and South Africa.

Would these people surrender a fraction of their power because of a ruling from parliament? Would the head of Hawker-Siddeley issue a memo that none of his plants were to sell weapons to Saudi Arabia because the Labour conference had passed a motion by 6.9 million votes to 6.5 million not to trade weapons with them? Would they care that it was now in Labour's constitution that the manifesto was binding? And what if the multinationals refused to do as they were told? Would the police surround the boardrooms of Britain and march in carrying riot shields, shouting 'we've got you, you shareholding bastards'?

Who ruled the army? And the press? And the judiciary? Surely, no fundamentally anti-establishment measures could pass through the formality of parliament, with its equerries and maces and Black Rod. You could hardly imagine the Queen reading 'my government – will introduce a bill – to abolish my husband and I'.

The threat to their power, it seemed to me, came not from parliament but from the mass action of working-class people. The dictators of Poland had made more concessions in a month than the multinationals had ever made under a Labour government. The reason, it had to be assumed, was eleven million people on strike. The problem in Britain in the early eighties was getting eleven million people to see it like that. But facing that problem, however unpalatable, was preferable to capturing a selection of committees and pretending they *represented* eleven million.

That's why, to sustain the idea that mass action was still the means by which working people could change the world, required an understanding of theory. And that meant books. One of the first things I had noticed about people on the left was their books. Everyone had books. Bookcases crammed with them, and not padded out with ashtrays from Devon. Extra shelves specially fitted and laden with books in alphabetical order. Odd ones half-read and scattered across the settee. A book by the telephone, a book on the arm of a chair, a book on the cistern. It wasn't like this when I was growing up. We had one bookcase, with a glass panel door that jammed, rattled and if you were determined to open it, came out altogether.

There were four shelves in the bookcase. The top one was empty. On the second were a wooden antelope, a porcelain zebra and a china milk-jug that was too posh to put milk in. Then came the shelf for the week-by-week easy-to-collect leather-bound *A-to-Z Encyclopaedia of Gardening*. And on the bottom was a set of hardback novels, with identical patterns on the jackets, which looked like the books that sit on the walls of pubs trying to create a musty theme. Nobody could remember where they'd come from. If someone had suggested reading one of them, it would have provoked a similar reaction as taking the ornamental teapot, used for holding sticking plasters and paper clips, and using it to make a pot of tea.

Whenever I wandered into a fellow activist's house for the first time, I'd see the array of books, proud and categorized, lining every room, and be mightily impressed and equally baffled. I'd never considered that you could have more than about twenty books. It was quaint and charmingly eccentric, but you just didn't need that many books. Having 300 books was like having fifty kettles. And how would you ever read them all? It took me three months to read a book and then three months to work up to the next one. Three hundred books would last me 150 years. These people were wasting their money.

As well as books, we were encouraged to hold weekly meetings in which speakers read long quotes from books. There were talks on economics, culture, and mostly on revolutions that had gone wrong. There seemed to be a template for these talks, which meant that every week the meeting would go something like:

CHAIR: 'I'd like to welcome everyone to this week's meeting. This week John has come to speak to us about the Meblibian Revolution. John.'
SPEAKER: 'Thank you. Now in Meblibia there was a small but fantastically significant working class and quite a lot of peasants. It started off with a small strike, grew into a fantastically massive

strike, then the reformists told them to go home which mucked it up, so the army came along and shot everyone, and the lesson we have to learn is you've got to have a revolutionary hardened Bolshevik party. Any questions?'
CHAIR: 'Well thank you very much John, you covered an enormous amount there, which I'm sure is going to stimulate a lot of questions and contributions. So anyone with anything they'd like to add – or any questions you'd like to ask, just raise your hand. Any question at all, it doesn't matter how simple. Anyone at all. Anyone. Doesn't have to be a big point. Were you going to say something, Tim? Go on. GO ON. Why not? Hmmmm. Ahem. Hmmmm. Weeeeell, *I've* got a question I'd quite like to ask, John.'

Nonetheless there was usually a sense of anticipation before each meeting. One week in three, this would be shattered when the speaker began and it became instantly clear he was an academic lecturer, with the flair of a maths professor on the Open University. There would follow an account of the most extraordinary events of the Russian Revolution, delivered as if it was part six of a course on plumbing to young offenders. 'At this, er, point, there was a situation, er which, cough, a situation, which er er er er er er, situation which Lenin described, described as er er, which Lenin described, cough, described as the festival of the oppressed, er, oppressed.'

After one such lecture on Trotsky, I put my hand up and said that if Trotsky was as dull as he'd just been depicted, you couldn't blame Stalin for wiping him out.

I was more sympathetic to the speakers who were obviously novices and had fallen into the trap of thinking they'd make no sense unless they included every relevant fact in the world. They'd set off on their epic account of the military coup in Chile in 1973. Thirty-five minutes later, the chair would be frantically thrusting in front of them a sheet of paper, on which was scrawled a two-inch thick 'WIND UP NOW!', and the poor speaker would gaze forlornly at the eight remaining pages of notes and lament that they were only up to 1965.

The intellectual turn led to other habits. One was the Marxist puzzle. Supping tins of beer on a settee late at night, someone would come up with an implausible scenario and ask what the correct Marxist line would be if this was to happen. 'Suppose an independent state was established in Corsica, and it launched an invasion into Sardinia, would that be imperialist?' Or 'What would we say if we were peasants in Ancient Rome at the time of the attacks of the Barbarians?' Then there would be an argument about this, which would go on for weeks.

Worse were the contemporary rows, which not only could nobody else understand, but nobody else could even see where there was an argument. It would start with a comment like: 'We need to view the cadre as a layer that can develop independently, and not see education as a panacea that can substitute for wider debate.' Then someone would snap back with, 'It's all very well saying that, but how do we ensure that's carried out in practice?' Then the argument would go back and forth, with lots of huffing and interjections of 'that's ridiculous and you know it'. On one occasion, a protagonist in one of these debates yelled, 'It's like the issue of whether we should have a break half-way through the meeting. You didn't think we should have one, but I knew that people needed to go to the toilet. And that's why I had no choice but to resign from the branch committee.'

The theoretical bent didn't mean abandoning the ritual of yelling '*Socialist Worker*' at local shoppers. The art to this task was to tread the delicate balance between coyness and madness. The temptation was to slink up against a lamppost, papers draped over one arm like a waiter's cloth, occasionally muttering 'sushelawukka'. That way, no one could think you're a weirdo, but your only chance of selling one was if someone came up and said, 'Is there any chance I could buy one of your papers, in spite of the fact I have no idea what it is?'

At the other extreme was the overenthusiastic market-stall type, who'd stride briskly into the pedestrianized section of the Arndale Centre and bellow, '*SuuuOOWWsherlist Worker*!!! Only twenty pence, if you HAAATE the Tories and HAAATE Margaret Thatcher get yer copy of *SuuuOOWWsherlist Worker*!' The barrage would be broken only when he singled out one woman in particular: 'Would *you* like a copy of *SuOWsherlist Worker*, only twenty pence, paper for anyone who HATES the Tories and HATES Margaret Thatcher?' The woman would respond with a nervous smile, a polite 'no thank you', looking as if she'd been picked out of the audience by a unicyclist in Covent Garden. But it didn't matter, because before she'd even started saying 'no', the seller was on to the next '*SuuuOOWWsherlist Worker*'.

Most of us hovered between these outer limits, usually earning a couple of sales and one passing comment of abuse. Most common was the predictable 'Get back to Russia', to which someone would reply by yelling, 'We're not supporters of Russia actually, we believe that Russia is state capitalist and owned by a ruling class clique actually if you bothered to find out mate.' After which bemused shoppers would peer across, wondering whether this dispute about the class nature of Russia might end up in a bundle.

But the greatest delight of selling papers at that time was the response from some of the old people. Much of that generation that had been through the thirties, and thought the degradation of those days would never return, held a special hatred for Thatcher. It was common for an old woman of about eighty to come up and say, 'Kick her out? You don't want to kick her out, you want to kick her teeth in, that's what you want to do.'

The first time this happened, I made the mistake of egging this particular woman on, with a patronizing 'you're right dear'. Then she was away. 'Kick her teeth in and poke her in the eyes. She's evil. Evil. She's the devil.' If you weren't careful, you could end up selling no papers all morning, as you stood vaguely nodding while a pensioner waved his umbrella snarling, 'Boiling oil, that's what they want to put her in. Then they want to smother her in jam and stick her in a nest of wasps. That'd sort her out.'

There were wonderful moments when the theory connected with the practice. During a national rail drivers' strike, a few of us arranged for local pickets to speak at trade union meetings. At one hospital, about one hundred nurses came to cheer the strikers and hand over a donation. Every strike is an education, and this one reaffirmed that when people are drawn into confrontation with the government, they become open to socialist ideas. I also learned that the local train-driving fraternity included a huge gay circle, most prominently a gloriously camp Northerner called Alex who was undivertable from his twin obsessions of trains and men's bodies. At the age of twenty-two I had a level of confidence I could only dream of at eighteen, and was sure I could no longer be surprised by picket-line banter, until this new phenomenon of *gay* picket-line banter. 'What does everyone want?' asked a picket who was heading to the cafe for some teas, at about half past six one morning. 'I fancy eight inches of steaming hot cock,' replied Alex.

And he would keep this up, as it were, all day. On the one hand, I was impressed by his openly gay stance. But every time he spoke at a union meeting, I was terrified he'd point at the union rep and say something like 'I tell you what my main demand is – to be let loose with you and a pound of butter – oooooo'. My wish was that he got a transfer to making the tannoy announcements. 'The 8.14 to London Bridge will be coming in another three minutes. Mind you if it's anything like my night last night, that's a promise that won't be kept and it will be here in ten seconds – haaaaaaa oooooooooo I shouldn't.'

My proudest moment concerning that strike came a few months after it ended, as I walked along a platform at Victoria Station. A driver recognized me from the picket line, opened his cab door and I travelled home in the front of the train. In the front of a train with a militant trade unionist on account of helping out on his picket line! That was my childhood and adult dreams rolled into one.

I helped write strike leaflets for local journalists, who won the reinstatement of their sacked union rep. The reinstated woman came to the local SWP meeting to thank us, but was so drunk she spent the whole meeting blowing bubbles through a kiddies' bubble wand, until it was almost impossible to see the beleaguered speaker as he persevered with his account of the Vietnam War.

I was coming to understand the importance of small victories as the engines that keep people going. A civil servant told me how he'd once succeeded in getting the staff of the British Museum to walk out on the day it received a visit from General Caetano, the military ruler of Portugal. And there was the celebrated tale of the Tilbury dockers who, as General Franco lay on his deathbed, won a vote to send him a telegram that said, 'Die, you bastard, die.'

Then things got even better, when I started going out with my first socialist girlfriend. This would be brilliant. We could go on demonstrations together and moan about the Labour Party together; normal women didn't appreciate it if they asked where you fancied going tonight and you suggested the picket of Lambeth Town Hall.

I still wasn't certain about the rules in left-wing relationships. So I wasn't entirely sure how to react when, from time to time, she'd tell me over a pint of lager how she'd got off with that bloke in her office at the weekend. 'You know, the one I told you about, the Spanish one, anyway, do you fancy some crisps?' Was I unfair in wanting to say, 'Look, I don't mean to be possessive or anything, but can you not do that please?' Though considering I was skint, unkempt and had a diagonal toilet, I should have considered myself lucky. Eventually she packed me in to become gay, the day before the start of the Falklands War.

By the start of 1982, Labour was on the way to being back to its old self. An investigation was set up which would lead to the first expulsions of Militant supporters. Michael Foot didn't turn up to the launch of Labour's 1982 programme, deciding to go to parliament instead, as the Commons was sending official congratulations on the birth of the royal baby.

Then came the Falklands. At first, there was confusion. What did it all mean, flags being taken down in Port Stanley and ships heading off for this place that few people had heard of? Would there be war? Would we all have to go? Were they anywhere near Denmark? One of Thatcher's main justifications for the war was that the Argentine regime was a brutal military dictatorship. Which it was. But this had never bothered her before and it didn't bother her 17 years later, when she campaigned for the release of brutal military dictator Pinochet because he'd been a crucial ally to Britain during the war.

As Margaret Thatcher prepared one of her most appalling acts, what was the demand of the leader of the Trotskyite, Maoist and pathologically dissident party? Foot said, 'We demand that she carry out in deeds what she has said in words.' That was how to sort out Thatcher. Shout 'go on Maggie, I dare you'. What did he think she would do? Did he think she would break down and cry, blubbering, 'You're right Michael, I'm just a silly girly and I'm not up to it.'

This was the first example I came across of what proved to be a recurring theme, of liberals being honourable opponents of unjust wars, on the condition that they ended 15 years ago. But at the time they fall for all the bogus humanitarian justifications. Almost everyone now refers to the First World War as a tragic waste, but how was it justified at the time? Do they think Asquith said, 'We're going to war with Germany in order to protect profits and waste half a generation in a futile battle for an acre of mud?' The Kaiser was evil, the Germans were bayoneting babies, brave little Belgium, it was all the same tosh.

By the time the Task Force arrived in the South Atlantic, half the country were experts on naval warfare. Union Jacks appeared in windows and debates raged about the best way to smash the Argies, with no space for a view that they shouldn't be smashed, or drowned or burned to death or bayonetted for a forgotten piece of rock. One Sunday lunchtime, as I sat in a local pub, the landlady announced through a microphone there would now be a singsong for our brave boys. And within seconds, the whole pub was raising its glasses to 'There'll Always Be an England'.

On Friday nights, a few of us often went to a sleazy drinking club hidden under a kebab shop in Tulse Hill. One night, as the torpedoes fizzed 8,000 miles away, a transsexual stood on a table and danced to musical numbers until, during an animated 'whip crack-away whip crack-away', his top fell off to reveal his hormone-induced breasts. At which point he declared that in honour of our boys he would perform a rendition of 'Rule Britannia'. A gay friend I was with objected, the transsexual yelled that this was unpatriotic, and the two of them started shoving each other across the floor until a manager appeared and threw us out. At least if my son ever asks me 'What did you do in the war daddy?' I can say I was ejected from an illegal bar because my mate was fighting a jingoistic topless transsexual.

Then the General Belgrano was torpedoed, 340 Argentine sailors were drowned, and the nation rejoiced. Gotcha. You sick bastards. All these years of outrage from press and politicians about violent demonstrators, unruly pickets and the psychopathic IRA, and now not only had Thatcher committed the most violent act for a generation, but she and her followers saw it as a cause for celebration.

In one sense, it was the most ineffective I have ever felt. Not only had this monstrosity taken place, but most people supported it, even welcomed it. But in another sense I was grateful to be part of a group that unequivocally opposed it, in whatever ineffective way we could. It wasn't going to stop the war or revive the dead, but it was invaluable for peace of mind to stand in public handing out anti-war leaflets and selling anti-war papers.

At the council depot, where I did a weekly paper sale, I arrived to find the biggest Union Jack of all time draped across the back wall of the rubbish-tipping yard. Ever so politely, a dustman approached me, placed his hand warmly on my shoulder and said, 'Not today mate.'

'I'm sure some of your workmates are against the war,' I blustered.

He nodded his head and very paternally repeated 'Not today'. Then very quietly, 'I'd go home if I was you.'

I felt like a naive ice-cream man who'd inadvertently put his van on a spot controlled by the mafia.

'All right mate,' I said.

'Cheers,' he said and patted me on the shoulder as I left.

Then the military victories started. South Georgia, an uninhabited island near the Antarctic, was recaptured by the Task Force and a Union Jack was rammed into the ice. Banner headlines squawked this glorious news at the nation and TV newsreaders adopted that 'trying hard not to smile' expression they reserve for heartwarming stories. The next day at work, while chatting to a couple of clock repairers I'd become friendly with in the depot, a bulky engineer came bounding past the machinery, puffing with excitement. 'It's fantastic isn't it,' he wheezed, 'South Georgia, it's fantastic.'

What fascinated me was that he knew the three of us were opposed to the war. But he was so delirious he assumed that even *we* would be delighted by this great event. 'But it's rubbish,' we all said, 'It's an uninhabited block of ice.' And he looked so deflated that we weren't joining in that I almost felt sorry for him. It was if he'd run in shouting that his wife had just given birth and we'd all muttered 'so what?' I asked him why he was so pleased. 'Why? Why? Because we've got deep sea anchorage, that's why.' How could we have forgotten?

He wasn't an unpleasant man, this engineer. If he saw someone drowning in a lake, I dare say he'd go to great lengths to rescue them. But surrounded by exhortations to celebrate the drowning of hundreds of young men, whose families he would never have to look in the eye, he grabbed the rare opportunity to feel proud. Over the last few years, the certainties he'd been brought up with had been dragged from under his feet. No longer could he be sure that his skills would be required all his working life. The hard-working but secure future he'd expected looked increasingly precarious. But here was something he could be proud of. We had our deep sea anchorage back.

Maybe, at the beginning of the war, he could have been dissuaded from supporting it. We'll never know. Because what did the leader of the party he'd voted for all his life say? 'We demand that she carry out in deeds what she has said in words.' If Foot's tactic was to pose as the chief flag waver, he was living in fairyland. There was only ever going to be one beneficiary from the eruption of patriotism and she milked it for all it was worth. For months after the war, there seemed to be a victory parade every week, including welcoming receptions for returning sailors, comprising mostly of women getting their tits out for the lads. Where was the Tulse Hill transsexual when he could have been of some use?

Anyone who claims that the Labour Party of the time was a chronic mass of unelectable extremism should be made to explain how that fits in with their gung-ho record during the Falklands War. Then they could explain the next fiasco, in Bermondsey. The episode is often cited as the zenith of the party's self-destructive tendencies, when leftie-madman Peter Tatchell became a Labour candidate in the by-election and was duly thrashed in an erstwhile safe Labour seat.

The modern wise men who shake their heads at Labour's extremist habits of the time would presumably have been happier if the party had stuck with the old candidate, dependable moderate Bob Mellish. Mellish was ahead of his time as a Labour man, in that he was extremely business-friendly and would have nothing to do with the loony left image of the time. He opened one speech with the words, 'As I come to this platform, many of you will know that

I have never been an anti-racialist.' Tatchell and his colleagues doubled the local membership and won a vote to make Tatchell the candidate. Mellish resigned and forced a by-election, putting up his sidekick John O'Grady as an independent candidate.

Tatchell had fled Australia rather than fight in Vietnam and was a left-wing gay cyclist. Bingo. Mellish and O'Grady toured the area in a pony and trap, singing, 'Tatchell is an Aussie, he lives in a council flat. He wears his trousers back to front because he doesn't know this from that.' Six-feet high graffiti appeared throughout the area, on corrugated iron walls, the most succinct and to the point being 'Tatchell is a communist poof'. The Liberals toured the area wearing badges saying 'I've been kissed by Peter Tatchell', and someone distributed 10,000 leaflets headed 'Which Queen will you vote for?' Underneath was a picture of Her Majesty and a drawing of Tatchell covered in lipstick.

How did the pathologically dissident Labour Party resist this bigotry? Neil Kinnock, asked whether he thought there was a witch-hunt, replied, 'I don't know, but I know the difference between a witch and a fairy.' Roy Hattersley, at a press conference for a by-election a few weeks later in Darlington, opened his comments with the words, 'At least there are no poofs in this election.' And part of the deal whereby Tatchell eventually could stand was that he wasn't allowed to admit he was gay.

It was hard to know which was worse, the blanket of bigoted abuse thrown at him or the way that Labour's cowardice left him unable to respond. It was like watching someone being attacked by a bully and then for the victim's mates to join in with the abuse in an attempt to make themselves popular. As a set of principles it was shameful. But it was also pathetic as an electoral strategy. Did Labour leaders think that the bigots would say 'well we might vote Labour after all, as they hate poofs as much as we do'?

Finally, the same cocktail of cowardice and incompetence dominated Labour's general election campaign. Healey and Callaghan both made speeches, declaring they didn't agree with the party policy on scrapping Polaris missiles. It was unbearable to watch, like seeing a hopeless couple trying to work an insurance scam without co-ordinating their stories first. Party policy seemed to be 'Yeah, that's right, we'll be, er, scrapping the missiles and er, . . .'

'No we're not.'

'Aren't we?'

'You said . . .'

'Shut up.'

While all the time they were kicking each other under the desk, as the Tories found it hard not to burst out laughing.

And Foot may have been a media liability but the biggest PR disaster was Healey, who said that Thatcher 'glories in the slaughter' that had taken place in the Falklands. The next day he went back on TV to say he was really sorry, hadn't meant it and it had just slipped out without thinking.

The election campaign was a farce, but half of the campaign management team was from the right of the party and several Labour right wingers made no secret of their wish for Labour to lose. And can it really be believed that Labour would have done any better under Healey? Do they think the Tories wouldn't have flashed up images of him appealing to the IMF across every billboard in the land? Or not reminded people every minute that he was the Chancellor in the disastrous government that had lost power in the first place?

By the time of Thatcher's celebrity-packed rally, shellshocked Labour supporters were shuffling through their days in frozen numbness. By the night of the election, the only saving grace was there was no possibility of disappointment, as throughout the campaign there hadn't been a single glimmer of isolated hope. A handful of us sat in my living room and watched the election programme, in the same way you would watch *Match of the Day* if your team was on and you knew they'd lost 6–0. And for the days afterwards, it almost seemed that most Tories weren't celebrating as much as you might expect, out of a sense of it having been so embarrassingly easy. The fault of the left lay not in their ambition, but in their belief eighteen months earlier they'd been on the point of transforming Britain towards socialism. Now it was clear that even if Labour had gone into the election with an unhindered radical socialist campaign, they'd still have been battered.

There was a route through this quagmire. The tradition of those at the bottom of society resisting attacks from those at the top had to be rebuilt. Striking train drivers and journalists, gays and the right of conscripted Argentine sailors not to be drowned, had to be defended, regardless of whether they were electorally popular or not. The tragedy of most of those who campaigned to change Labour was not that they weren't popular, but what happened to most of them once they *realized* they weren't popular.

The New Labour hierarchy is packed with figures like David Blunkett and Margaret Hodge, who were amongst the most passionate advocates of changing their party, in such a way that it could never again be led by the sort of people they've become. Peter Hain, Blair's right-hand man at the heart of New Labour, wrote an article in *Socialist Worker* that bellowed, 'Yes, that means supports for strikes and occupations, and the march on the Tory conference. But don't kid yourselves that this is enough.'

As the dust cleared on the debacle of the 1983 election, there was a feeling that the biggest test was yet to come. Almost unnoticed, the membership of one steadfastly confident union, in a mass ballot, had voted overwhelmingly for Tony Benn. And they'd voted for Arthur Scargill to be their new president. All right then, Thatcher, we all thought. You might have had it your own way up to now, but you know and we know there's one group you haven't dared go for. Come on then, you heartless bully, we're going to get our dad on to you. That's right – the miners. Then you'll know you've been in a fight.

Chapter 12

Around the age of twenty-three, everything changed. First, the squats were scheduled for demolition, following which the self-appointed squatters' committee invited a delegation of Conservative councillors to visit the area. This, the squatters' committee hoped, would bring about an offer of rehousing, at least for the squatters' committee. So they posted a note through every door telling us it was our duty to sweep the pavements and clean the windows in preparation for the esteemed visit.

Apart from the political objections, how could this work? It would be no use having a spotless kerbstone, while above it three blokes were shouting from a window that they were trying to find Oily as he's got all the acid.

It wasn't that I wanted to stay in the place. My co-squatting hippie slept in a hammock and was convinced that his sister's next-door neighbour was using a chicken to put a curse on him by making light bulbs go out. My neighbours had an adorable three-year-old son, who would lean over the collapsed fence as I emerged from the diagonal toilet and relate that today he was going to be a dragon or was thinking of going to the moon. But then I'd see his parents who were junkies and they'd tell me much the same thing. One night in the pub, around ten o'clock, the mother suddenly yelled 'Oh fuck, the kid' as she realized she'd forgotten to pick him up from the nursery six hours ago. They took to feeding their habit with petty thieving and selling the worthless objects that you only come across when minor criminals try to flog them round pubs, like lawnmower sharpeners and French–Swedish dictionaries. Their finest hour of criminal genius was to borrow a crowbar and use it to break into the house of the squatter they'd borrowed it from. Once in there, they stole a digital clock radio and the next day went down the street to find a buyer. But the first house they knocked at was the same house yet again, so the original owner punched the bloke on the nose and snatched his clock back. After a series of similar slip-ups in attention to detail, a squad load of police cars screeched to a Sweenyesque halt outside their house and battered the door down, while their prey jumped out of the window and over my back wall.

Then our pipes burst and the water was cut off. This left us dependent on our junky neighbours for water, and they responded with idyllic smalltown neighbourliness. They even gave us a key, so that twice a day we could march round with our buckets and negotiate a route across the syringes to replenish our supply, in scenes that were half *Trainspotting* and half *Fantasia*. 'Any time – what are neighbours for', we'd sometimes hear from a corner, said with the chirpiness of a housewife in Wimbledon handing over a cup of sugar. Except that this housewife was slumped on a cushion and gazing at something imaginary on the ceiling. Eventually the police were too smart for these criminal masterminds and they stuck the father in jail, which was bound to do him the world of good.

The council rehoused the locality into hard-to-let flats around Lambeth. I went with two others to an estate in Tulse Hill, but the hippie stayed behind in the hope of getting a place on his own. Due to a bureaucratic failing, the council assumed the squat was now empty and began demolishing it. So they were a little surprised, having destroyed an outer wall, when a hippie emerged from a hammock and asked them what they were doing.

I gazed at my new surroundings in awe, like an East End wartime evacuee in a countryside palace. There was a bath and a gas fire on the wall and floorboards in every room. The neighbours had jobs and cars and cats and got up in the morning and if they had kids, they remembered to collect them from the nursery.

Something else was changing, and I established contact with a different type of campaigner. Following the election of Ronald Reagan in 1980, an unease developed, evolving into abject fear, that the world's rulers were on course to blow up the planet. There were MX missiles, satellite missiles, ICBMs, and Cruise missiles were destined for Greenham Common. We needed to keep adding to these weapons presumably, because if we could wipe out the Earth fifty times over the Russians would leave us alone. But if we could only wipe it out thirty times, they'd be straight in and marching up Oxford Street. Reagan said, 'I see no reason why a nuclear war couldn't be won in Europe.' Then around once a month he'd say something like 'well no one would really miss Paris', until you weren't sure whether he was planning annihilation or having a laugh.

So a peace movement sprang up in response. Indecipherable murals with skeletons, doves, peace symbols and a mushroom cloud in the background appeared on walls in every inner-city area. Town councils declared themselves 'nuclear free zones', as if the radiation would stop at the borough boundary and offer a choice. The famous 'Gone With the Wind' poster was Blu-tacked to thousands of doors. The whole country mocked the laughable government pamphlet 'Protect and Survive', with its advice to withstand a nuclear attack by painting the windows and sitting under the stairs.

Huge marches took place all over Europe, including one of 250,000 in London. 'It's brilliant,' I said on the day. But I was saying it in the way you say a party is brilliant when everyone else is dancing and laughing, but you don't really feel it yourself. I knew I *should* feel brilliant, but wished I meant it. Why wasn't that massive throng of protesting people more inspiring than it was?

Perhaps it was because the ethos of the day, and the movement in general, was not to confront the world's rulers but to appeal to them. The demand we were making was enormous. Robbing governments of their arms race is virtually to deny them their right to rule at all. Yet the dominant sentiment was that we should reach out to their humanity.

It *was* brilliant that so many people felt committed to go on the march, and CND motivated countless vibrant students and campaigners. But anyone seeing the march as a confrontation with all that Reagan and Thatcher stood for ran counter to the general direction. The reason I don't feel that tingle of inspiration when I recall it, is that you could stand in Hyde Park and think 'oh isn't it lovely'. But you couldn't, in all honesty think 'yeah, this is fucking brilliant'.

Through the campaign I encountered a political type I'd had little contact with before, the self-congratulatory liberal middle class, summed up by that car sticker of the little sun saying 'nuclear power – no thanks'. It made me think 'really, well aren't you clever'. Can there be a more submissive slogan than 'no thanks'? Or, if you were really pompous, 'nein danke'. You couldn't imagine the Black Panthers coming up with 'racist police – no thanks'. If only the other side was as wimpish. And Margaret Thatcher's strategy for dealing with strikes had been to put a sticker on her car saying 'union power – no thanks'.

What troubled me wasn't that they had a different view about changing the world. Their aim wasn't to change the world at all, but to feel guilt-free. I saw a peace fair in Brixton around this time with a stall displaying 'tiles for peace', and there were all these tiles with doves on. So we couldn't blame them if the big one dropped: they had bathrooms decorated with tiles for peace. Blame him next door with plain brown tiles, an incitement to nuclear armageddon if ever there was one.

Many of the people behind this scene were ex-students, politicized by the events of 1968, and now academics, managers in local government or the media. But they wanted to retain a link to their radical past. So they created a social milieu which achieved that without them having to slum it with grubby poor people. For these types, the emphasis was on adjusting their own behaviour, especially their language. One of the results was it became almost impossible to call Margaret Thatcher a rude name. 'Witch' was sexist, 'bastard' offensive to bastards, 'bugger' was homophobic and 'cunt' was suicide.

Sometimes I would debate with these people but my heart was never in it. In arguments with normal people, it rarely felt hopeless. Even when that Swanley lad ripped up my paper in the pub, there was some point of contact, the way families know when they're getting a glimmer of a response from a relative in a coma. He was a builder on unsafe underpaid sites. It served his sense of pride to demonstrate he was doing fine by looking after himself and ripping up my paper. But at least we spoke the same language. This lot, with their sanctified lifestyles of non-oppressive syntax and anti-militaristic bathrooms, I found it impossible to connect with at all.

The irony was that without me realizing it, they were changing my life. As part of their quest to construct an alternative environment, some of that circle had set up and provided much of the audience for an alternative entertainment circuit around London. All I knew was I fancied doing comedy, and there were a few venues opening, so I gave in my notice at London Transport. And they all shook my hand and smiled and said they hoped it would work out. They were decent selfless people who had been compelled to bury their talents and copy numbers from a pink form to a blue form, dull only because they'd been forced to be dull.

The next change I noticed at 23 was a kind of second puberty, which affects most males in the modern world at that age. The simmering resentment that bubbles from early childhood onwards seems to evaporate. Around that age, it becomes possible to appreciate viewpoints other than your own. Gradually it made sense that Janis Joplin and Eddie Cochran meant as much to their generations as the Clash did to me. I bought Bob Dylan albums, which for a child of punk was like Ted Heath giving Margaret Thatcher a public snog. My parents' generation weren't the enemy, there were valid views other than my own, Dylan was as important as the Clash – this was a humbling process. And alongside came a change in the labour movement. Up until then, the staple diet of the activist was meetings. Labour movement meetings were usually about education or transport and made up of thirty people in a public hall. They would begin with a councillor or MP speaking for twenty minutes without once looking up from his notes, as he related every minor detail of a proposed White Paper.

After the main speaker, the first to speak from the floor would probably be an eager old person. They'd usually have something to read out, either an article from the local paper, or a poem they'd written that morning. Or it could have been a letter they'd written to Geoffrey Howe and the reply they'd received. Then it would finish with a question, such as 'This Tory council has put up our rent by another £8.70 a week from April the second. Now, it states in article forty-five of the United Nations charter on civil liberties "any unprovoked attack on elderly citizens will be deemed a transgression of international guidelines". So are you, councillor, going to apply UN sanctioned procedure by demanding that Croydon council is prosecuted under international law?'

One speaker would be concerned about privacy, furious that the recent letter from the education authority proved they had their name and address, finishing with 'What I want to know is what else are they using this information for?' A Labour Party activist would implore us not to forget their group, for example the Labour Party table tennis association, whose 'value to the spread of ideas locally shouldn't be underestimated'. An SWP member would point out the links between the threat to the local bus service and the defeat of the German revolution in 1923.

Finally, the evening would round off with a contribution from a group called the Revolutionary Communist Party. They would start calmly, but by the third sentence would be warming up like an old valve television until, in this cold church hall with thirty people in 150 seats and the murmuring and clumping of the judo club coming through from the next room, they'd be yelping like a Baptist preacher. 'The main enemy of the working class is not the Tories but the Labour Party,' they'd scream, and it would seem natural for them to continue, 'especially you lot. That's right, the worst twenty-eight people in the world are you people in this room. If it wasn't for you, everything would all be all right.' After about five minutes of this, people would be groaning for them to shut up and the chair would be trying to interject with 'Can you begin to wind down now please?' But that only made them worse. 'This is typical. Now you're denying my freedom of speech. You don't mind if petit-bourgeois reactionary elements from the imperialist trade union bureaucracy speak but you can't tolerate real socialists . . .' And finally, as a parting shot they'd shout at some bemused sixteen-year-old member of the SWP, 'And why weren't you on that Irish demo in Bournemouth in 1973?'

The Labour Party and unions responded to the despair that consumed most of their members after the election with two phrases. 'New realism', which was the view that trade unions could no longer combat employers or the government. And 'dream ticket', the Labour Party choice of Neil Kinnock as its new leader and Roy Hattersley his deputy. Pamphlets, focus groups and a flurry of essays established that strikes could never again have an impact on British society. Then the miners' strike started.

I arrived a few minutes late at a committee meeting of something or other and found everyone watching *Panorama*. The pictures were of hundreds of miners running down muddy banks to meet more miners. From that moment, for hundreds of thousands, possibly millions of people, for at least a year and maybe for life, everything changed.

The pit-closure programme had been announced, it was the final stage of the Ridley plan. It was like the last scene of a predictable Western. Along the way Thatcher had disposed of many casualties but now she stood face to face with her sworn enemy. Arthur Scargill is often blamed for calling the strike at the end of winter, when coal stocks were high. But the strike was in response to the closures. You can't call a strike in November on the off-chance that closures will be announced the following March. Nor can you announce in March a strike to start the following November.

The next point is, Scargill didn't call the strike. One of the pits due to close, Cortonwood in Yorkshire, walked out. They travelled to the next pit, where they ran down the muddy banks that led to the second group of miners, and from there it spread. The NUM could either back the strike or disown it. To say Scargill shouldn't have had a strike at that time is to argue he should have called off a strike that had started anyway.

Tory outrage exploded. The *Sun* called miners 'scum of the Earth'. Social security payments to miners' families were blocked. Ministers spewed disgust at pickets, adopting the slogan 'right to work'. And the police blockaded pits in Nottingham, put road-blocks across striking pit villages and turned back Kent miners heading into the Dartford Tunnel. This was it. It was how I imagine an army feels, having been camped on a hillside for months, when it hears it's going into battle. Our generation was having its very own miners' strike. Within days, most people I knew had miners sleeping on their settees and miners crammed into the backs of their cars under piles of placards and posters, on their way to speak at whatever meetings could be organized.

Two weeks into the strike it felt we were on the first bend of a

Formula One race, with the opening scramble over, able to assess who was winning. It had started with a roar but spluttered as it hit third gear. The first 80 per cent of miners had piled out but the other 20 per cent weren't budging. Around 15,000 were involved in pickets but that was nowhere near enough to shut down industry. Other patterns had emerged that would last all year. Coal Not Dole stickers, black on yellow, were appearing on every public object. *The Miner* was on sale in London markets and Croydon pubs, which a few weeks earlier would have seemed as peculiar as the *Tatler* on sale in the Rhondda. The news began every day with a report on how many miners were working today. It became a standard and soothing part of bulletins, like the FT index or gale warnings.

Then came the marches, the first national one taking place in Mansfield. There were the banners, enormous beautifully crafted high-quality cloth depicting winding wheels, crowds of miners peering proudly from beneath their helmets and a layer of coal dust, and a portrait of Scargill, or A.J. Cook, his counterpart in the general strike of 1926. And there were the brass bands that oompahed through every high and low of the strike for twelve months. Whether strolling through London surrounded by shirtless miners in July, or retreating across a sodden field at six o'clock on a freezing December morning, there, somewhere, was the reassuring pah pah pah of the perennial miner's trumpet. They were like an amateur performer desperate to get taken on by an agent, following them around at all times to do bits from their act. And there was the wonderfully simple refrain that rang through every day of that year, 'here we go, here we go, here we go'. Advertising executives would sit around varnished tables, smoking and frowning through sleepless frustrated nights before coming up with a slogan of such pithy contagious perfection. Everything about the feel of the strike was summed up in those eight letters. Here we go. We're here, there's more than one of us and we're on the move. Somewhere must sit a miner or supporter of the strike, who first shouted 'here we go', who wonders every day whether he could have legally established the copyright.

Along with camp Alex and other train drivers, I took my place in the Mansfield crowd, the first national display of support. But throughout the march lay an undercurrent of another trend; mass sexism. The slogan that dominated most marches of the time, 'Maggie Maggie Maggie, out out out', was already a little tiresome. But the miners chose a controversial alternative, 'get your tits out for the lads'. Oh dear. As it wound its way to the closing rally and the pubs of the shopping precinct, this demand grew in momentum. Up on to the tables went a group in the pub I was in and down came the trousers. Debating with the miner by my side whether it was sexist to call Thatcher a witch would have been a strange starting point, as he was waving his knob in the air screaming 'come here and get on the end of that'.

Many supporters of the strike, reasonably enough, wondered how this could happen. The most likely answer is it confirms that mass movements don't develop because people are rebels, but because they *become* rebels. As they do so, they carry with them the ideas from their pre-rebel days. The sexism was carried from their usual Friday night on to the Mansfield march. But here lay a chance of confronting it. The strike was opening thousands of eyes. The police weren't neutral; the press wasn't fair. The next thing they had to learn was that if you sing 'get yer tits out for the lads', you don't deserve the respect or support of women. Though another part of me was thinking 'just put your pants on, you filthy Northern animal'.

Then came another problem. A mass picket to stop a steelworks taking coal from the depot at Orgreave was beaten off by thousands of police, who arrested Scargill. From then on it was a war of attrition. Could the miners stay out long enough to deplete the nation's coal? For the rest of the year miners' supporters would calculate almost daily how long the stockpile could last, taking into account how much was coming from Poland, how much from Nottingham, aviation fuel from here, oil from there, and how if it got cold that would swallow it more quickly.

As well as high street collections and collections outside workplaces, there were collections at almost every gig and every event in a park. After every meeting about anything there was a collection. Every area had a miners' support group, my nearest being in Penge, and run by a strange couple who were lecturers and members of a secret group whose name they wouldn't divulge.

There were benefits piled upon benefits. When miners came to routine meetings, the meetings ceased to be routine. One night at a public meeting in Croydon, the main speaker finished, and we slowly put down our beers to offer the usual polite but tired and dutiful applause, the sort granted to a trad jazz band after a number in a pub on a Sunday lunchtime. But two Kent miners rose in the middle of the room and began vigorously clapping as if they were begging their favourite band for an encore. 'Listen,' one of them said, 'before you carry on, I want to say that I've been on strike for four months and everything that man said there is ABSOLUTELY TRUE. I hope you were all listening. Were you? WERE YOU?'

'Yeah,' we all said, perking up.

'Well I hope so, because that was THE TRUTH.'

By now I was speaking at meetings myself, one of my subjects being whether there was any such thing as human nature. At one meeting in Camden I finished, and without even raising his hand a Yorkshire miner said, 'Well if there's no such thing as human nature, how come whenever I see a copper I can't stop myself from naturally wanting to kick him int' bollocks?'

And the strike went on and on. Before the miners, it was unusual for a strike to last two months. Now benefits and meetings would be arranged two months into the future. Supporters talked about setting up monthly events. I wondered whether some people were under the impression the strike was an indefinite campaign, like the campaign against the arms trade, and had been set up in 1907 by a man who played 'here we go' on a banjo.

A trend developed that had as big an impact on society as the strike itself. Women from the pit villages founded 'women against pit closures' and began speaking at meetings and benefits. No one had ever heard of this before. Whoever heard of a striker, asked to speak to a car park full of dockers, saying he couldn't do it but that his wife could do it instead. It seemed as odd at first as ringing the fire brigade and being told that everyone was out, but the firemen's wives were available and would be round as soon as possible.

'I'd never spoken in public until last month,' one woman told me, 'but last week I went to a car plant in Belgium and spoke to a thousand car workers.' The women unleashed an untapped force that sustained the strike for another nine months. Holding families together in the midst of shiftworks, grime and blokes waving their knobs from pub tables, had sculpted amongst the miners' wives a formidable combination of unqualified warmth and uncompromising principle. They were humble and endearing enough to be terrified of speaking to a thousand Belgian car workers, but determined and unerringly tough enough to rattle the hearts of every one of them when they did it. Miners could make great speeches about why you should support them; miners' wives could *demand* you supported them, and if you already supported them, that you should support them more.

It wasn't always a cosy transition. Men who married women expecting them to honour and obey didn't all take to looking after the kids, while their wife went out to organize support for their own strike. But the movement of women was an enormous blow against the attitudes that had seemed so unshakeable a few months earlier. No march now could descend into a chorus of 'get yer tits out for the lads', as it was self-evident women deserved more respect. After all, no one would suggest their organization should be called 'Birds Against Pit Closures'. The *Yorkshire Miner* abandoned its practice of displaying its own page three models.

The strike came to symbolize the demise of an old Britain. Before it took place, the enclosed nature of the pit villages made them the clearest example of the nation's parochial ways. There were few foreigners, few students, few out gays, women had their place and no one ate foreign food.

It would be exaggerating to say that through this time the whole country embraced liberal values. But it was a time in which everyone became aware of the alternative to the old ways. The world of golliwogs and black and white minstrels, of 'oo ducky' comedians, and women marching into pubs on Sunday afternoons with their husband's burned dinner, was at the beginning of the end. Six years earlier, I'd become an active socialist, never having heard the word 'sexism'. Now it was an expression used in *EastEnders* and *Emmerdale Farm*. At the age of fifteen, I doubt whether I had tasted more than about seven different items of food; steak and kidney pie, fishfingers, potatoes, frozen peas, cucumber, lettuce and Heinz sponge pudding. In 1984 Swanley got its first curry house.

It was a national trend but nowhere more marked than amongst miners. Now they weren't just aware of students, they were sleeping on their cushions. They were living the most poignant example of the changing status of women. One forty-year-old miner I stayed with in Derbyshire was astonished that I hadn't brought any dope. He was under the impression that no one from London went out without their stash. 'I'd never tried it before strike,' he said, 'but now I look forward to a puff before bed.' And they had no choice but to eat foreign food, as they were relying on food parcels donated by supporters, the most generous of which seemed to be in Eastern Europe. A year earlier, the average miners' kitchen contained nothing more exotic than a beetroot. Now it was packed with tins of weird Romanian green things, thin and pointed with a red tip, that they weren't certain whether to boil, grill or distil and mainline into a vein.

Most spectacularly, the 1985 Gay Pride march was led by a contingent of miners. So on a glorious day in July, a procession wound through Central London that must have left onlookers startled. Round the corner came the banners, the winding wheels, the portraits of Scargill and A.J. Cook, the legions of miners and the ompah pah pah of the band. Then a jamboree of marchers holding hands, blowing whistles and waving their shirts in the air. Somewhere amidst that wonderful scene, I hope the campest most gregarious gay on the march went up to the conductor of the band and asked whether they knew 'Relax' by Frankie Goes to Hollywood. And that the reply wasn't 'Are you a poof then?'

Leaders of the labour movement did not share the boundless enthusiasm for the strike and its idiosyncrasies. Neil Kinnock refused to attend a picket line or events supporting the miners. And he pointedly said he 'condemned violence from WHEREVER it comes', while glaring at supporters of the strike. This was after six months, during which two miners had died on picket lines, states of siege had been set up in numerous villages and there had been thousands of arrests. Kinnock was like the teacher who marches up to a fifth-year battering a first-year, grabs both of them and yells 'the pair of you are as bad as each other'. One of his complaints, shared by many others, was the miners hadn't had a ballot, which would make the strike legitimate.

How I wished the leader of their side had a similar attitude. Imagine Thatcher refusing to support the closures unless the miners were balloted about them. Or announcing at a police conference, while glaring at the chief commissioner, 'I condemn violence from WHEREVER it comes.'

The effect of the leaders' distance from the dispute was noticeable at every level. Thousands of trade unionists held collections and invited miners to speak at their meetings.

But there were many more frustrating visits to union officials who would fob you off by agreeing with you. 'Yes yes, leave me the collection sheet and I'll take it round.' This is the worst answer of all. It's like ringing a shop that's supposed to be delivering a fridge and being told 'yes that should be round in the next few minutes' in such a way that you know they're lying. Because you can't say, 'No you won't. No you won't take it round you liar.' Teenagers trying this get shouted at – 'not later – NOW'. But that option wasn't likely to work with the south-east region area officer for SOGAT. So we'd have to go back a month later and be told 'oh this lot in here, they're not interested'. And it would turn out he'd pinned the collection sheet on a noticeboard under the sheet that tells you where to run if there's a fire.

It never occurs to them to give a lead. It's a good job they weren't in charge of the Allied forces during the war. We'd now be living under the Gestapo, while they said, 'I put that thing up somewhere about that landing in Normandy, but no one showed any interest as usual.'

One of the difficulties was that for many people, the strike seemed to be taking place in another land. The Tories ensured that relatively generous wage rises were paid to most other workforces, to ensure the unions couldn't open a second front. Nonetheless, at times it felt we might win. When the dockers struck in the summer; after the TUC formally backed the strike at the conference; and when the pit deputies announced their support, it all seemed possible. The orthodox view now is that the miners couldn't win. But the Tories were never that certain. Imagine being a coal board official, or Tory MP, seeing thousands of miners charging across country lanes to defy roadblocks after nine months on strike. Every study confirms they were anxious, uncertain and taken by surprise at the endurance of the miners. As we made our calculations, they made theirs. As rumours swept our side, so they swept theirs. Even Ian Macgregor, head of the Coal Board said, 'Thatcher panicked on more than one occasion.'

At Christmas, a group of us on the estate posted leaflets through every door, asking people to donate food for striking miners, ready for collection at the end of the week. On the day of the collection, almost every household was ready and waiting with carrier bags. From the most crumbling flats, families rolled out tins of tomatoes or rice pudding with one hand, while holding back the German Shepherd with the other. But the flat I remember most vividly is one where a couple, probably in their seventies, spent at least two minutes apologizing for not being able to get very much. Then they brought from behind the door two enormous boxes packed with food. From a glance, you could tell they were the sort of old people who had agonized over every ingredient of this hamper. They'll have spent several minutes worrying about whether miners were likely to prefer gherkins or pickled onions and whether the box of apple pies would be crushed in the van. They'll have stood in the grocers and infuriated the customer behind them as they discussed whether they could afford another fifty pence from the Christmas pension. When they were apologizing, they were apologizing in effect for being poor. Because the only way they could have given any more would have been if they were richer. For ten months the television, newspapers, government, police, civil service, judiciary and everyone important had been labelling the miners as scum, vandals and the enemy within. Everyone who contributed was defying the lot of them. Were the old couple from mining families? Were they old communists? Or did they just have a compassion that those aiming to starve the miners could never understand?

Just before Christmas, in my local pub, a van driver at the bar saw my badge and started talking about the strike. He was a classical South London van driver; huge, tattooed and carrying four pints of lager. The day before, he told me, he'd driven to a miners' welfare hall in Kent to deliver toys that had been collected around the sites. 'When I got in that hall,' he told me, 'and I saw this fucking massive heap of toys what had come from all over, I tell you, I bawled my fucking eyes out mate. Anyway, good luck.'

After the strike, Kinnock referred to it as 'Labour's wasted year'.

After Christmas, the activists from the pits were finding it hard to motivate the more inactive strikers. People can tolerate the most spectacular hardship for a cause, but what gets them is the feeling that you can't win. Some drifted back to work, and news broadcasts gleefully announced the numbers as if there was no one left on strike at all, though 63 per cent of miners stayed out to the end.

At a meeting of local supporters I attended in February, someone said that even the strike leaders had accepted the strike was now about securing the best possible terms on which they could return. The stockpiles were lasting, the waverers were drifting back to work, and it made no sense to claim the strike could still win. And I felt a chill, literally went cold inside. It wasn't the shock of bad news but the dull ache of having bad news confirmed. The end, like most deaths, was alarmingly mundane. A newsflash on a Sunday afternoon and it was over. The next night there was a special *Panorama*. I looked at the images, the masses of police, the demonstrations, Scargill's arrest, the bands, the exuberant mischievous shirtless marches of the summer, the windswept hand-rubbing picket lines of winter, the week of the dockers, Scargill's standing ovations at the TUC and Labour conferences, the stickers, the placards, the donkey jackets, Kinnock, the Brighton bomb, Ian Macgregor, the miners' wives, I didn't hear a word and I cried. 'What's the matter with you?' asked the not-very-political woman I was going out with at the time, looking puzzled and a little perturbed, and I knew that was finished as well.

The last speech I heard at a miners' support group was at a final rally in London, from a Nottingham miner who was one of the few to stay on strike at his pit for the whole year. 'I went back to work ont' day after strike ended,' he said, 'and walked to my old locker, still there as I'd left it twelve months ago. And all the others were getting changed, and when they saw me they all went silent. They looked at the floor, they looked in their locker, but they couldn't look me in the eye. I'd rather stay out another year, than have to be like that.'

There were families that never recovered from the financial blow of the strike. But plenty of them would also say the excitement, the confidence, the camaraderie, the new friends, the discoveries, the exhilaration and the love they experienced through that time, made it the best year of their lives. And thousands of their supporters would agree, as the miners provided an opportunity for a new, more promising and better way of looking at the world.

Many of them may now accept the New Labour mantra that those days are over, that we need to be 'realistic'. They should close their eyes, remember the excitement and the passion, and say 'go on, spoil yourself'.

Chapter 13

One of the finest political conversations I ever had took place in 1985 with a member of the group called the Militant. 'Socialism,' he said, 'is inevitable.'

'Well I don't know about inevitable,' I answered. 'Anything could happen. There might be a nuclear war.'

'Yes,' he said, 'but that would just be a setback.'

With the miners defeated, Neil Kinnock seemed to look upon the enhanced 'tough boy' image of Thatcher like a young boy watching a racing driver or skateboarding champion, thinking 'wow, I fancy a go at that'. The first thing he needed was an enemy. Thatcher had taken on the Argentine navy and 180,000 miners, so Kinnock would show the same ruthless leadership qualities by defeating the small group of Trotskyists loosely arranged around the Militant.

The Labour Party, it was decided, should be reserved for respectable socialists – like Robert Maxwell. The Militant's main success had been to gain a controlling influence on Liverpool Council, which had spent more money on services and council housing than legally permitted by the Tories. They were also the most exasperatingly impossible group of people to defend.

They were like an unruly flatmate who, just as you persuade everyone else in the flat to give them one more chance, runs naked through the kitchen and announces they've borrowed your car and lost it in the river. A typical argument was at Newcastle University, with the student union women's officer, on the night I was doing a gig there. She supported their expulsion, she told me, because of their sexism, while I pointed out that sexism wasn't the reason Kinnock was expelling them. Eventually I had to perform in this gloomy bar with its plastic glasses and sticky floor, which went fine until a group of eight blokes squashed around a table started singing rugby songs. One stood up with his t-shirt off and patted his vast stomach, while the others made 'aaaagh wooor hooor' noises, and did that arms out, beckoning of the three middle fingers on each hand gesture, accompanied by cries of 'come on then' to anyone who objected.

At the end of the pointless gig, I walked across to where the women's officer stood. 'That,' she said, with perfect timing, 'was your friends the Militant.' I felt as if I was in *Cabaret* and had been asked if I still thought I could control them.

'The "Round-London Jobs March" is coming near you', the Militant declared triumphantly one week, on posters and leaflets around South London. So four of us from the Croydon branch of the SWP went to join it as it passed nearby. But as it approached, we felt a similar disappointment to when your bus comes round the corner, but says 'Not in Service'. There were, it became apparent, six of them.

'We'd like to join your march,' we lied.

The one who seemed to be the leader pointed at the Socialist Worker banner. 'You can't come on this march with that,' he said. 'We've got widespread trade union backing for this march, so we're not going to jeopardize it by letting you bring that banner.'

'You may have widespread union backing,' I said, 'but I can't help noticing there are six of you.'

'I'm telling you,' he said, getting aggressive, and we folded the banner. Then I offered him a leaflet, and without looking, he screwed it up and threw it in my face. How I wish I'd said, 'No wonder you haven't got a job you ignorant tosser.' But instead, for the next half an hour, the ten of us marched along the side of the road, while the odd bemused motorist passed a puzzled glance in our direction. How much more puzzled they'd have been if they'd known that six of them were thinking 'this was all right until the other four turned up'.

And this was how they carried on, almost everywhere, almost all the time. Someone somewhere must have been instructing them to be like this, unless the 5,000 rudest people in the country happened to join the same left-wing group by coincidence. There was a house style, which made a Militant operation in the mid-eighties instantly recognizable, like a Stock-Aitken-Waterman single. A typical

Militant meeting was the one held in the Surrey village of Oxted that I went to with two friends, in which the speaker was advertised as Derek Hatton. It started with an apology that Derek Hatton couldn't be here, as he was 'unavoidably detained at an important meeting in Liverpool'. Of course he was. He'd sat all afternoon with the borough treasurers, urging them to hurry up with the audit report, so he could set off in time for his 500-mile round trip to a village hall in Oxted.

So the replacement speaker began speaking, to a creditable audience of about forty, half of which were local. The start was a series of grandiose pronouncements. 'Around the world we see capitalism in its final stages of decay. In Chile there have been marches against the dictatorship. In Paraguay, protests are rocking the government to its very knees. And I offer greetings to this meeting from the Brazilian metal workers, who have sent a message of support.' As if someone in São Paulo had sent a telegram saying, 'Our people are starving. Our shanty towns are under siege. Good luck with the meeting in Oxted.'

Then came the collection. Militant collections are superb. Like ITV wrestling in the seventies, the fact that everyone knows they're fixed doesn't detract from the entertainment. 'The struggle can not be waged without financial sacrifice, brothers and sisters, so who will be the first person in this room to offer me £200. Two hundred pounds comrades, a small price to pay for bringing an end to the system that has exploited us for thousands of years – and – is that a hand I see? Yes comrade, isn't that magnificent. A cheque for £200 from the comrade at the back. And now £100 . . .' And so this would go on, the effect being that everyone would put in a tenner and think they'd got off lightly.

Then came the speakers from the audience. So I said that I thought it was an excellent turnout and that everyone should support the Militant's right to stay inside the Labour Party, though as an SWP member I thought it was better to be outside the Labour Party anyway.

As the speaker replied, the bonhomie of the occasion evaporated. 'Let me tell you about this organization that this man here is a part of. For this is an organization . . .' The tone was becoming increasingly severe, the pointing more aggressive, and I was caught up in the growing tension myself. What was he going to say? It was like being singled out by the headmaster during assembly, when you didn't even know what you'd done wrong. 'An organization which . . .' He took a breath and prepared to let rip. 'WHICH IN 1967 CO-PRODUCED A PUBLICATION WHICH INCLUDED A SEXIST CARTOON – OF A WOMAN – IN A BIKINI!!!!' The words 'in a bikini' were roared with the unrestrained ferocity of a two-year-old in mid-tantrum.

There was a puzzled look around the room. All the questions raised by the flaws in this statement were being mulled over. Can this chap be blamed for a twenty-year-old cartoon? Is a cartoon of a woman in a bikini inherently sexist? Has anyone ever used the word 'sexist' in this village hall before? The speaker composed himself, the audience shuffled with forgiving embarrassment, muttering things like 'well he must be under a lot of stress', and my friends and I giggled like schoolgirls.

The Militant newspaper was packed with similar fare, the pinnacle being the celebrated letters page. Letters came in two categories, financial and political. The first would be an apology for the meagre amount the sender could afford to contribute, with a 'keep up the good work' to sign off. I longed to send in one of my own, saying, 'Dear Militant. I am an old-aged pensioner who has to struggle on the pitiful pension I receive from the gruesome Margaret Thatcher. So unfortunately I am unable to donate much money to your splendid fighting fund. However, please accept the floorboards to my house, which I have ripped out in the hope they may contribute towards your magnificent efforts. Keep up the good work.'

The second, political letter would be along the lines of, 'I am a welder and have never been interested in politics before. As far as I was concerned, they were all as bad as each other! But then I bought a saveloy and chips wrapped in a copy of *The Militant*. It was excellent! Now I've cancelled my wedding so I can spend the day selling *The Militant* in the Arndale Centre in Middlesborough instead.'

Meetings I'd attended, at which there had been fifty people, would be reported as having 300. Everything was in the tone of an ever-upward ascendancy towards glory, imminent, infallible – and inevitable. The fact they were being expelled in their hundreds from

the Labour Party and from several major unions with barely a
whimper from the rest of the movement, seemed to pass them by.
Instead, the way in which Kinnock's crusade had made them, and
especially Hatton, household names confirmed for their members
that they were storming the heavens. It was as if General Custer, as
he was routed at Little Big Horn, announced that this was
marvellous news as it was bound to get him in all the papers.

Militant-led Liverpool was one of forty-two councils that
originally pledged to defy the Tory law, known as ratecapping, that
prevented local councils from raising rates in order to maintain
services. One by one they backed down, but to their credit
Liverpool was the last to do so. To make things harder still, the
Labour leaders were desperate to make the party acceptable to
business. With the miners' strike defeated, a majority of party
members accepted this as the only way of getting rid of Thatcher.
At the 1985 conference Kinnock made his famous speech – 'a
Labour council, a *Labour* council'.

Kinnock's outburst was nothing to do with the undemocratic
nature of Militant. Liverpool council had been run for years by the
Braddock family, who were masters at packing meetings as and
when important votes required it. Liverpool council probably had
more supporters than almost any other. But Kinnock's strategy
needed their blood. By taking on Militant, he could pick a fight
with the left he was sure to win. A year earlier Scargill had received
a standing ovation. Now Kinnock got the ovation and Scargill was
isolated.

But none of the attacks permeated through to Militant's leaders.
Their crowning moment came with a rally at the Albert Hall, which
I went along to, partly out of fascination and partly because I knew
the comedians who'd been booked to do the entertainment. The
rally was due to start at one o'clock, and at exactly that time the
hall went dark, taking everyone slightly by surprise and making us
go 'wooooo', as if we were watching a fireworks display. Then
lasers shot across the hall, to Emerson, Lake and Palmer's 'Fanfare
for the Common Man'. A giant screen lit up, displaying the words
'1985 – Year of the Militant'. This was followed by an array of
images of Derek Hatton, then the lights came on and an almighty
cloud of dry ice exploded across the stage. For all the world I

expected Freddie Mercury to emerge, descending from the ceiling
in a harness on a pulley, with Hatton sat on his shoulders. Instead,
as the cloud began to clear, out walked Hatton and Ted Grant,
seventy-year-old founder of the party. What on Earth were they
doing? This was like a recording of *Gardener's Question Time*,
starting with the team rising into view on an elevated stage dressed
as the Village People.

What would be next? Would Ted Grant rap the executive's
pronouncement on possibilities of world revolution and announce
that two versions were on sale, the original and the 12″ club mix?

Grant began to speak. The only part I remember was his
prediction: the capitalist crisis will lead to socialist revolution in
this country in five to ten years, and across the world in ten to
fifteen years. And he repeated this, in case we misheard and wasted
our money on a pension plan. Even my calculations when I gave
out those leaflets at Gravesend dole office weren't as optimistic as
this. Why five to ten? Why not twelve? Was he reckoning on
capturing the cities in four, while remaining uncertain about areas
like Devon and Shropshire, which could take anything from one
more to another six? And the whole world? Even Afghanistan and
Easter Island?

After the speeches came the collection. An evangelical intro-
duction built up to the big moment. 'So who will open the
collection for me this afternoon? Who's going to offer a sum that
. . . what about this, I can announce I have a note here from a comrade who has recently sold his house. And he's handing over a
cheque for £10,000!'

'Where's the poor sod going to live,' I wondered aloud, but this
didn't fit the mood of the room.

But partly it saddened me. For the most part, these people were
motivated by all the fervour and more that had drawn me towards
being an activist. Most of them probably worked in places where
they sat bored and frustrated, as all around the conversation was
about the thickness of last night's gravy. And now they and their
comrades could fill the Albert Hall and watch their leaders cough
their way through dry ice to tell them the great day was coming, in
five to ten years. Of course they would throw my leaflet back in my
face. They were round the corner from world socialism, so why did

they need our silly banner on their march? Socialism, you see, is inevitable.

One of the hardest tasks on the left is to accept reality. The need to do so was the most fundamental point that Tony Cliff insisted on. If someone claimed to have won over a body or union branch, he would enquire how many were at the meeting where this was decided. If someone estimated there would be fifty at a meeting, he would ask who they were likely to be. If in reality there was going to be seven, better to admit it and see if it could be eight, rather than pretend. When someone informed him she was a member of the 'Pan-African Black Fellowship Society for Socialism', he said, 'My God, I hope you have as many members as you have words in your title.'

Even in the post-miners' strike eighties, there were sparks of mass defiance. There was a series of enormous demonstrations against apartheid, and every party lit up when the Specials' 'Free Nelson Mandela' came on. Public Enemy left a trail of fury wherever they went. The Redskins accomplished the extraordinary feat of getting into the top forty with a dance song about Russia being state capitalist. But every workplace and every pub had someone who'd bought Telecom shares and their council flat, and talked loudly about how well Thatcher had tamed the unions. It also had people who despised Thatcher but were generally reticent about speaking out. In the aftermath of the miners' strike her opponents were looking to Labour, not the left with its talk of striking and mass action, for a dash of hope.

Faced with these problems, all the far left went mad, it was just a question of degrees. We met in a pub called the Dog and Bull, a hostelry for an unusual mix of market stallholders, bald middle-aged rock-and-rollers with pony tails and junkies. Around twenty of us met there each week, in a room containing about sixty upside-down broken chairs and a disused pool table. The weekly speaker would be in full flow about the Paris Commune, when 'Blueberry Hill' would come on the jukebox, and the speech would be drowned out by dozens of people accompanying the piano bit with 'da da da da da da da da da da da da daaa'. This would set the dogs off who would whine as if they were auditioning for a horror film, and one week the singing stopped abruptly to give way to the sound of chairs being thrown, which ended when one went through a window. Next week, we thought, there'll be *seventy* upside-down broken chairs in this room.

Relating to the outside world became tricky. Speeches by SWP members almost invariably drifted into the details of the Russian revolution, whether the subject was Lenin, arthouse cinema or painting and decorating. Others would launch into a speech brimming with confidence but get hopelessly lost along the way. 'And if Kinnock gets away with this attack on Militant, I tell you what that means for every one of us. What it means, actually, is that, what it means, I tell you, what it means for everyone in places like Deptford, is that it's, it's, it's yet another attack he's got away with.'

And there were the ones who would knock on your door with an agenda they weren't going to be diverted from. The one concession to formalities would be a mumbled 'how are you' as you answered. But even if you said 'my entire family was wiped out this morning in a plane crash', they'd answer 'that's a shame, are you free for leafleting on Friday night because we need to cover the train station at 6.30'.

The odd behaviour, like much lunacy, was a result of isolation. So when someone new turned up, there was great anticipation. But this could lead to such disappointment. One night, as we drooled over a new person, he put his hand up. 'What I'd like to say,' he said earnestly, as we all hovered eagerly, 'is that on my way here tonight, I was shot.' Another night, around the end of 1985, I spoke to a new visitor for about half an hour, and then mentioned the questions raised by the miners' strike, that had ended nine months earlier. 'Yes,' he said thoughtfully, 'the miners' strike. Tell me, is that still going on?'

As I rounded twenty-five I felt the need to justify my activities to myself as adult behaviour. I could pass off smashing that greenhouse as the actions of a bored teenager but I wouldn't be able to excuse it at twenty-five. Similarly, I could tolerate being thought of as peculiar when I was an eighteen-year-old rebel. But now I wanted to be on friendly terms with neighbours and colleagues, and even members of my family. In particular I was a stand-up comic and wouldn't have much of a career if I provoked the same reaction as when I worked at the Post Office. Audiences everywhere would shuffle off to the bar muttering 'there's that nutty one who's always drivelling on about Ireland'. Whenever I met anyone for the first time I took great care to ensure they were aware I could have a pint and talk about sport and the telly. But then I came across the opposite problem. After a couple of months, it was difficult to say, 'Oh I haven't mentioned it before, but I believe in the working masses creating revolutionary institutions to take control of the means of production. Are you having another Guinness?'

My line to the world was 'I'm a Trotskyist, but I'm not mad, honest'. Which made it so depressing to turn up at a socialist event, especially if there were a few new people, and find the place swarming with a wide selection of bizarre Trotskyist groups. Up they would spring, with speeches full of phrases like 'we must construct a programme of transitional demands and take these to the working class'. I always wondered which bit of the working class they meant specifically. The Canadian lumberjacks of the Yukon? The blokes from the council who raced each other across the grass on sit-down lawnmowers? My Uncle Arthur? WHO?

If you say you convinced the woman you work with to stop buying South African oranges, that means something. But 'taking it to the working class' is meaningless. Were they honestly going to knock on their neighbours' door, and say, 'Ah, good afternoon, as this is a working-class area, we're going door to door with this programme of transitional demands. So here are yours. Sorry to bother you, bye.'

A typical phrase would be, 'The working class will not tolerate petit-bourgeois vacillations.' And do you know, that's exactly what stopped my mum from becoming a Trotskyist. 'Oo no dear,' she said, 'I would, but you put me off with your petit-bourgeois vacillations.'

They would dish out leaflets in close-typed tiny print, displaying the most extraordinary language. 'In this pre-revolutionary situation, parties that prevaricate and offer falsehoods will pay dearly for their procrastination.' And I would expect it to continue, 'Forsooth sire, methinks the betrayals of yonder Kinnock doth render him one unholy cur.'

At major events in London, all manner of colourful characters

would appear. There was one group called the RCPGB (M-L). And
the brilliant thing about them, is when they announced who they
were, they would actually say 'RCPGB – brackets – M-L'. I longed
to ask them whether they were a split from the 'RCPGB –
parentheses – M-L'. Or write to their paper saying I was a member
but as a protest against what I considered petit-bourgeois
vacillations I was leaving to form the RCPGB (*£).

Then there was the Revolutionary Communist Group. This lot
believed you could only be a socialist by identifying with the culture
of third world nations. Under their banner at the start of demonstrations, instead of selling papers, they would perform tribal
dances. So there would be these songs beckoning the peasants to
take up the armed struggle, which would be a stirring sight in the
villages of Tanzania but made less sense performed by six white
students on the concrete path outside the Royal Festival Hall.

Even they were trumped by the Maoist group whose slogan was
'dig tunnels and store grain' in preparation for a peasant war,
which presumably would be led by the staff of garden centres, the
nearest thing Britain has to a peasantry.

One day, at the beginning of 1986, I got a phone call from the
enigmatic couple who had been stalwarts of the local miners'
support group. I hadn't seen them for nearly a year, and they
wanted to speak to me. So two of us sat on their settee, as they told
us how they'd left the secret group they'd been members of. The
group had thirty members nationally but, through a strange quirk
of history, twenty of these happened to be in Penge. 'They were
mostly lecturers,' he said, 'so we were the token working-class
members, and they'd ask us to do their chores. I started thinking
they were strange when I was driving three of them back from East
London and we were stuck in the traffic coming out of the
Blackwall Tunnel. One of them suddenly said "have you seen these
cameras at the side of the road?" I said they were traffic cameras,
they'd been there for years. He said "yes – well that's what they
want you to think". Then he said "and watch that car, three
vehicles behind us, the Vauxhall Cresta". Five minutes later he
asked me if it was still there. I said of course it's still there, we're in
the middle of the rush hour coming out of the Blackwall Tunnel,
where else could it have gone? He said "there are three members of

our Central Committee sat in here, don't you think they're keeping an eye on us. Now just act natural".'

My friend and I were cackling and clapping and could barely drink our tins of beer. 'Don't laugh,' he said, 'this has been a really trying time for us, we were serious about this group.'

'Then,' he said, 'there was the merger. Our group resolved to merge with a different group, which had a national membership of twenty. So we produced these documents that went on for dozens of pages, about how the working class would forever commemorate the grand historic merger of the mighty forces of proletarian struggle and all that. But privately, our group of thirty still hated the group of twenty, and we thought by merging we could nick a couple of their members. Then the central committee became concerned about our printing press. The other lot might sneakily use it to produce documents denouncing our group. We could hide it, but then we'd never be certain they wouldn't find it. So one Sunday morning I was asked to go round this house with a shovel. And four of us stood in this garden digging a hole, until it was deep enough to bury the printing machine. Then, to make absolutely sure, we concreted it in so no one would ever be able to use it again.'

And the two of us were rocking backwards and forwards, tears rolling down both cheeks, aware that as long as we found this funny, at least we were in touch with our own sanity.

Chapter 14

The middle of the 1980s, according to many accounts, gave birth to a new tyranny, the jackboot of the loony left and their wicked creed, political correctness. One Conservative academic referred to this trend as a 'new McCarthyite order'. As if comedians like Frank Carson were forced to provide lists of names to the House Un-politically Correct Activities Commission, of other comedians who'd once told a joke that started 'this Jew goes into a pub'. Presumably, in sweaty intimidating courtrooms, PC officials banged mallets and boomed into the microphone, 'Do you or have you ever referred to a chairperson as a chairman?'

Any hint of liberalism, such as naming a student union bar the 'Nelson Mandela Room', or awarding a grant to a group with 'Afro-Caribbean' in their title, was evidence of loony leftness. When objections were raised to the British army buying a weapon which shone a beam blinding the intended victim for life by burning a hole in their retina, the junior defence minister replied, 'Are our defences to be sacrificed at the altar of political correctness?' When you can't even melt the odd retina, it makes you wonder what you *are* allowed to do.

Much of the press got addicted from the fix of these stories, and like any addict, when the supply ran dry, they got desperate and made stuff up. The most famous loony left stories of the time – the council workers who couldn't say 'black bin liners' and the kids who had to sing 'Baa Baa Green Sheep' – were entirely fictitious. In any case, how was it that Thatcher had battered the unions, the miners and the Argentinian navy, but was powerless before the unstoppable might of the Haringey council gay and lesbian helpline unit?

Local councils and liberal groups were in no position to impose their attitudes on people with power. Camden council could hardly force Margaret Thatcher to rewrite her speeches to read 'the *woman* is not for turning'. Or 'the British people will never surrender to the evil men/women/gays, lesbians and bisexuals of the IRA'.

Instead, the liberal behaviour and language was directed against other campaigners, who were the only people they could impose themselves on. So the irony was that the real stories were even more bizarre than the invented ones. The most surreal demonstration I ever attended was in Newbury, in support of women from the Greenham Common peace camp due to appear in court. On a freezing February afternoon, I got off a coach and walked into a crowd of peace women who were objecting to men supporting them. They stood in a circle around us and wailed, while patting their hands on their lips the way I used to as a kid when pretending to be a Red Indian. I wondered if there had been an argument at the planning meeting, with some saying it would be more effective if they all went 'burdip burdip' like a frog.

How are you supposed to reply to this? It would have been easier if they were real Cherokees; at least we could have offered them some cigarette lighters as a peace offering. Even without their unorthodox means of communication, their demand was confusing enough. They wanted us not to support them. If we'd said 'all right then, we'll go back to London to join a gun club and watch some strippers' presumably they'd have cheered and announced this as a victory. Instead we squeezed past, and the sound of 'wowowowowo' followed us across the Newbury ring road. Round the corner was another protest against men supporting their protest, this time involving a line of peace women tossing pancakes in frying pans. This was becoming like a dream. I was half-expecting to find myself on a boat sailing past the pyramids, or for Jimmy Saville to arrive and announce he was my brother. No one ever explained the significance of the pancake women. But there they were, flipping with the confidence of women demonstrating non-stick pans for Debenhams in the shopping centre. But without the make-up.

To get to the demonstration involved finding a way past a series of these obstacles, as if it was a computer game or a test for Indiana

Jones. After the pancakes came the more conventional haranguing
and screaming to 'get out, this isn't for you' and yells of 'take the
toys from the boys'. There didn't seem a lot of point in shouting
anti-missile slogans at me, as a) I didn't have any missiles, and b) I
was already demonstrating against the bloody things. Or trying to.
And it wasn't just men who were objected to, it was women who
were with the men, or more accurately, men in drag. But like a
special unit negotiating with a team of hijackers, to be on the end
of a tirade of abuse was a major step forward, as at least this
established a line of communication.

'We're trying to support you,' I pleaded with one peace woman
in exasperation. So she started the Red Indian noise again. To be
fair, as a tactic for infuriating your opponent in a debate, it works
a treat. Politicians should try it for television interviews. Every time
the presenter catches them with an embarrassing question, just lean
towards him and squeal 'wowowowowowowowowo'. Within five
minutes even Paxman would be banging the table and yelling, 'Stop
making that bloody noise!' I turned around and walked into the
town, finding a café to sit in until it was time to get back on the
coach.

A tactic was developed on peace demonstrations of standing in
circles and holding up mirrors to reflect the evil of the missiles back
into the base. I was always sceptical as to whether this would work,
though I would have loved to have been proved wrong. What a
moment, if rectangular American officers suddenly knelt on the
grass, holding their head and screaming 'no no no, aaaagh', like a
baddie being swallowed by their own evil force at the end of an
episode of *Star Trek*.

I forced myself to overcome my cynicism and went to a
demonstration at the missile base in Molesworth. The aim, it
transpired upon arriving, was to hold hands around the outside of
the base. To get there required a two-mile walk across the
squelching muddy fields that surrounded the place. Then we all got
in a line and I just couldn't do it. Maybe the radical feminist
pancake women were right: there was something inherently macho
in me that couldn't bring myself to hold hands as part of a chain of
people as a symbol of anti-militarism. It was as if I was at an actor's
workshop and was being asked to streeetch like a tree, or mouth

'ma me my mo moo' as a voice exercise. My only thought was 'I'm not doing that, I feel STUPID'. So I stood in a puddle and watched. These people who wrote to the *Daily Telegraph* complaining about loony left councils never had to go through *that*.

The press knew that to discredit Labour, their main target had to be local councils, and to a degree this strategy worked. Partly this was because the controversial policies were dispensed with the air of a pompous headmistress. An advertising campaign began in my area with posters and billboards that said, 'Are you a racist? You'd be a nicer person if you weren't.' Did anyone imagine this would have any impact on racists? To start with, it could only work if it was a concern of your average racist to be thought of as nice. Then they might see this poster and think, 'Oh that's why I can't seem to establish a rapport with the Asian shopkeeper. It's because I yelled abuse at his mother and daubed a swastika on his car.' When I first saw this, I thought they might as well put up a series of posters saying, 'Are you a cunt? You'd be a nicer person if you weren't.'

At this time I was going out with a woman who worked for a homeless persons' unit, a trust run by Camden council. One week, the staff had to attend a race awareness course. So an instructor began the first day's session by splitting the workforce into two groups, and everyone was handed a selection of coloured pieces of paper. They were told to go up to people from the other group, who also had coloured pieces of paper, and ask if they could exchange them, until they had a complete set of all one colour. But they could only communicate by making animal noises. For example, to ask for orange paper you had to oink like a pig, or for blue you had to make a cock-a-doodle-do cockerel noise. This is the sort of thing drama teachers try to get you to do at school and it resulted in the same outcome: a room of people falling about laughing and making farting noises while an exasperated instructor yelled 'IF YOU'RE NOT GOING TO TAKE IT SERIOUSLY THERE REALLY IS NO POINT AT ALL'.

The aim, she said, was to enable everyone to experience life as the outsider. This would help them to understand the experience of being a foreigner in Britain. Which it would, as long as the foreigner in question had a job playing Happy Families with a

selection of farmyard animals. Her fee for the week's course was
£2000.

Despite the press abuse, Labour councils who pursued these
policies were broadly tolerated while they funded services, festivals
and cheap fares. But once the councils surrendered and agreed,
however reluctantly, to impose cuts, there was nothing left of their
early eighties radicalism except race/sexuality/gender awareness.

Now, Labour councillors were seen as another bunch of officials
closing libraries and taking four months to process your housing
benefit. When the lift in my block broke down, it remained out of
action for two years. There must have been kids who listened to
stories of the old days, when that smelly tin box went up and down
to different floors, and thought it was granddad rambling again.
One day, a group of us took on the laborious task of contacting the
housing office, because the water for the whole block had been
suddenly cut off. After a morning of getting nowhere, I got on a bus
travelling down Tulse Hill and saw a huge banner had been erected,
saying 'Lambeth Council – well worth defending'.

The only difference now between them and other faceless
officials was they named clumps of wasteground after African
leaders and made people trumpet like an elephant on surreal
courses. The policies on language and awareness derived not from
their power, but their lack of power. It was as if the councillors
worked out they couldn't change the world, or even the borough,
so the one thing they could change was the language, or whether
the person carrying out the cuts was a man or a woman. This logic
played an even bigger part in some of the socialist meetings of the
time.

I spent one weekend at an event called the 'Socialist Conference'
in Chesterfield, and for the last session we divided into groups
according to our local areas. Around 120 people were in the South
London section and the first task was to elect a secretary and
treasurer. 'Obviously one of them has to be a woman,' about ten
people shouted immediately. 'If we're to be seen as taking race
seriously, one has to be black,' someone else called out. This was
agreed, but there was only one black person there and he didn't
want to do it. So a group surrounded the poor sod to tell him he
had to, otherwise we wouldn't be taking race seriously. I was

longing for someone to object that one of them should be gay, as this would produce a wonderful mathematical conundrum, like the sort you get in school tests. The obvious answer would be to select a lesbian, or to tell the black bloke that not only did he have to be the treasurer, he also had to become gay, otherwise we wouldn't be taking gays seriously.

Next came a debate about voting procedure. 'Surely the men can't be allowed to vote on the women's post,' yelled someone. I was hoping the black bloke would demand the same criteria was followed for the black post. Then he'd have the only vote and could abstain, ridding himself of this job he didn't want. Eventually it was agreed that men couldn't vote on the women's post, but then came the demand that men shouldn't even be in the room while the vote was taking place. Our presence, it was argued, would be intimidating. How I longed to say that I agreed, and add 'so come on lads, we might as well nip down the pub for a few beers and leave the cackling to the women'. On and on raged the debate until, after two and a half hours, the caretaker was hovering, ready to close the building, and item one on the agenda hadn't begun to be resolved. 'Well it doesn't really matter,' said the self-appointed chair, 'as we only needed to fill these posts so we've got names to give the Post Office for our PO box address.'

As well as 'loony left', the times were dominated by another phrase: 'yuppies'. Everyone could make money, the boom would go on forever, just get on the property ladder and live your dreams. In the seventies, the Strawbs' satirical anti-union song had backfired to become a trade unionist anthem. In the eighties, the satirical anti-yuppie film *Wall Street* backfired, and the Gordon Gecko remark that 'greed is good' became a yuppie catchphrase. City brokers and property developers made their fortune, but many more believed they had a finger in the same trough, having bought a folderful of bonds or Sid's gas shares.

With the financial boom came a property boom. But when people I knew started buying a fourteenth of a house that had been converted into a flat, I underwent a dual shock. First, that I was old enough for mates of my own age to be buying houses. The second came when I went round to see the thing. A friend bought a flat in North London, for which the mortgage swallowed over half his income, and as I glanced around it was difficult not to splutter 'Is that it?' It was like going to the cinema and seeing the credits roll up after twenty minutes. It would be impossible for two people to move around at the same time without planning in advance which route you were intending to take. Whenever there was a gap in a high street, an estate agents would suddenly appear, as if it had landed in the night. And pubs were full of conversations along the lines of 'well we bought ours last Wednesday for sixty-five thousand, and the one across the landing from us, which is smaller than ours, went yesterday for half a million'.

The yuppie era was built almost entirely on credit. House-buyers saddled themselves with suffocating mortgages and small businesses with ridiculous loans. It was the first time that almost everyone had a credit card. Which was a disaster for people like me, as the credit card had the power to lead me into a curry house, where I'd see the sign saying 'we accept Access' and read it as 'today everything is free'. And it boomed on the basis that the boom would go on forever. Banks fell over themselves to loan billions to speculators and developers, because if they didn't their rivals would.

But the most obvious hole in the theory that Britain was floating away on a cloud of prosperity, was that millions of people were poor, even in the districts known as 'yuppie areas'. True, some high streets were full of estate agents where couples sat on red leather sofas, or delicatessens selling fifty varieties of olive oil, or hair-dressers that brought over a bowl of olives while you waited. But behind this façade, areas like Battersea were home to as many neglected dark-red-brick council estates as ever. If anything, the new trend made things worse for most people, as wealth and decadence was flaunted in front of them. Stories about city dealers in their twenties pocketing half-a-million bonuses flowed almost daily. Porsches would glide through inner-city areas with an arrogant grunt on their way to the city. Whole populations were decanted from council estates, so that developers could stick a swimming pool and gym in the basement and flog them off as luxury flats.

Suddenly there was a new breed of homeless. In the seventies they'd been tramps, with long matted beards and green coats, shuffling around the parks of London as if they were an institution, dressed up specially by the tourist board. By the middle of the yuppie era, every subway in central London was home to long lines of sleeping bags, from which twenty-year-old heads poked out to ask if you'd any change. Huddles of what appeared to be rubbish would suddenly shuffle in a shop doorway and ask for a few pence in a Scouse or Glaswegian accent. Then, to show they were responding to the ethos of the day, they started expanding into new areas until, as with Our Price and the Body Shop, every high street in London could boast their own handful of freezing waifs.

On my estate, a seven-year-old lad was often outside my block, merrily hopping aimlessly along the pavement. Everything about him was cheerfully seven; the way he'd strike up a conversation about dinosaurs with a complete stranger, or ask questions like 'Who invented cheese?' and 'How much does the moon weigh?'. Sometimes he would come indoors, and joyfully leave with no apparent concern that his parents might be wondering where he was. Then I worked out that his parents were my junky neighbours from the squat. His dad had come out of jail and the family had been rehoused on the same estate as me, the prison system having enjoyed its usual success rate at getting people off drugs. I told him we'd once been neighbours, and one day, as he bounded alongside me on the way back from the shop, I asked how his mum was doing. 'Well this week,' he said perkily, as if he was about to tell me she'd bought him a fire engine, 'my mummy's gone to heaven.'

Some of the most dynamic trade unionists from the seventies were found in dark corners of dingy pubs, reeling from the apparent hegemony of the Thatcherite creed. They were victims of the notion that 'something' had to be done about the unions. Now something else was being done about them in the print industry, by Rupert Murdoch. He sacked his old workforce, banned unions and moved his operation to Wapping.

For over a year, Saturday night was mass picket night. Friends would ask if you were going up Wapping this Saturday, as if it was the nightclub in a small town. For the printers it was even more like that, as they dressed in shiny leather jackets and gleaming shoes, as if they were expecting bouncers at each end, refusing to let people link arms if they were wearing jeans. Every week thousands would gather, push, sing and chant. Then Tony Dubbins, secretary of the main printers' union, would appear on a box and make a speech that we'd all done very well but it was time to go home. The sight of Dubbins was like the smoochy record being played, and when he finished it was as if the lights had been put on and the staff were urging you to finish your drinks quickly, please. At around 1.30 in the morning this enormous crowd would saunter up Wapping High Street, chatting about how it had gone, like a horde of football supporters leaving the ground after a match. Finally we'd hear a clunk and a roar, and turn round to see a procession of TNT lorries piling into the plant past the spot where we'd been. Occasionally this routine was broken, most notably on the first anniversary of the strike, when the police led a charge and scattered people in their normal way.

The Thatcher-inspired yuppie-led onslaught marched on, but didn't have universal backing. Ben Elton's anti-Thatcher rants on *Saturday Night Live* became hugely popular, though few people said they enjoyed them because they were funny, more because 'at least someone's having a go at the Tories'. There was outrage after the Chernobyl disaster and when Reagan used Britain as a base from which to bomb Libya. But it was a frustrated, despairing opposition, which led not to protest but to hope for anything, someone, anyone who could please bring an end to that bloody woman. The man who appeared to be in the position to do that was Neil Kinnock.

So many people so desperately wanted Kinnock to beat Thatcher. So much so that it blinded many of them to the fact that he was spectacularly useless. His first problem was he was incoherent. His speeches blurred into a lucky dip of long words that sounded like a spelling contest. In the House of Commons, they all seemed to go, 'Mr Speaker, is it not the case, that the proposals proposed by the party opposite, are a recipe not for conciliation but for confrontation, not for diversity but for dichotomy, not for oregano but for origami. And Mr Speaker is it notwithstanding the aforementioned case, that this country requires the providing, or provisions with which to provide a policy which is delicate, profligate and polyunsaturate.' Unlike most incoherent people, all his words were real words. The problem came with the order. It was as if he had one of these rare conditions, like the bloke who mistook his wife for a hat, and couldn't help but stick nine unnecessary long words into every sentence. Then he would turn to his own side and wink, as if he'd caught Thatcher out with some incredible piece of wit.

His most hopeless performance came when the Tories seemed to be in trouble, after Thatcher was accused of misleading parliament in a row about Westland helicopter company. Michael Heseltine and Leon Brittan resigned, and amongst the anti-Thatcher population there was a sudden spirit of hope. Thatcher, speaking later about the day of the debate in parliament, said, 'I didn't know whether I would still be Prime Minister in the evening.' I put the radio on early and waited eagerly, in the way you imagine people doing in the 1950s for a championship boxing fight. Eventually the speaker called 'Mr Neil Kinnock' and Kinnock began. He started by commiserating with Heseltine, then thanked him for his service to the country, then sympathised with the plight of the government. I was thinking, 'Come on. Get on with it. Go on. Tear her apart.' But he drifted off into 'obviation not obfuscation' mode and anyone who didn't know who he was would not have known whether he was supposed to be criticizing the government or defending it. It was like getting ready to cheer on an Olympic runner, but as the starting pistol is fired, seeing him walk over to the long-jump sandpit and taking a nap. In the evening, Thatcher was still the Prime Minister.

Yet in the 1970s he'd been one of the most popular speakers in the Labour Party, full of fire and Welsh passion and ideals. But as leader, Kinnock was on a mission to make Labour business-friendly, while retaining its working-class base. As he did so, he came to comprise the worst elements of the British working class combined with the worst elements of the British middle class. He mixed the snobbery of the rowing club with the Friday night chapati-throwing attitudes in a small-town curry house. He disliked people of status for looking down on him, but desperately wanted to be up there with them. He loved winking and waving and joshing like one of the lads, but was never happier than when he was accepted into company that would call security if any of the lads came near. He supported nuclear disarmament, but supported the Pentagon. He supported the workforce, but supported the board. So he tried to please both at the same time, and the result was that no one could understand a bloody word he was saying.

One of the finest things about being twenty-six, was to have so much time. If someone suggested a party that night, I could go. Or even have the party at my place. A visit to the pub would always end by dragging a bag of carry-outs to someone's flat for another session. At fifteen you act irresponsibly, out of ignorance, frustration and boredom. At twenty-six you can act irresponsibly on purpose. Instead of nihilistically demolishing an innocent greenhouse, a few of us would regularly try breaking a window in the Brixton Conservative Club. It was quite tricky, as metal grilles covered all the windows below the second floor, and even the top ones were small and divided into squares. But we would stand there, firing away like Palestinians on the West Bank, until someone struck home to enjoy that satisfying ripple of shattering Tory glass.

At Christmas 1986, after protracted negotiations with the hospital management, my dad was allowed to spend two days with my girlfriend and I at our flat. As I arrived to collect him, I was taken into an office and given a lecture on the essential medication he would need during his stay. They were still uneasy about him leaving at all, and as a parting shot, I was told, 'He doesn't get up until noon and he's back in bed at seven.'

On this day, Christmas Day, he was dressed as smart as is possible with one set of clothes in a withering mental home, albeit one with three lines of twenty-year-old paper chains sellotaped across the landing. Tie knotted perfectly, closely shaved, he stood up urgently as he saw me, the way you do when you've been eagerly awaiting someone since an hour before they were due to arrive. Over the next two days, whenever a friend came round, my dad would get up to shake their hand and say 'pleased to meet you' self-consciously making every effort to be on his best behaviour. He wore his tie all day, and offered to wipe up if I washed. When I made the dinner on Boxing Day, he watched me quizzically, as if he was watching a strange foreign game and couldn't work out the rules, and finally said, 'Bloody hell, she's got you under the thumb hasn't she.' He went to bed at eleven and got up at seven. He shaved, came for a walk, didn't take his tablets but did come to the pub for a lengthy session in which he apologized for not being able to buy a round as he didn't have much money on him at the moment. Occasionally he would say something that betrayed a loss of memory or logic, on matters such as whether we'd ever owned a cat. But it was obvious the main part of his illness was simply that he needed to be looked after, which was just a stronger strain of the virus that afflicted almost every man of his generation. After two days I returned him to the normality of the home. Across the broken snooker table and fraying carpets, the gibbering Polish man and the paper chains, one of which had come unstuck and was now dangling by the ripped armchair, jangled a tinny chorus of 'Jingle Bells'. And there I left my dad to spend the last few days of the year of the yuppie.

Countless people underwent their personal versions of the irony at the heart of the boom. For many people, Thatcher seemed invincible. But were Tory values as overwhelming as it seemed? Around my estate were people who had bought a few shares and applied to buy their flat, earning a slot in the statistics of those who had been bought off by the Tories. But as they wondered who to call when their water was cut off, what resemblance did they bear to the champagne-swilling opulence of the city? Had the hordes that punched the air to the Pogues, or peered through their Gothic powder at the Sisters of Mercy or Jesus and Mary Chain, succumbed to the lure of Douglas Hurd and Norman Fowler? The majority of those who believed that, because they'd bought a few gas shares, the Tories were acting in their interests, had not been lost forever to Thatcher. And I was 26. It wasn't all bad. But first we had to grit our teeth through Thatcher winning another election.

And on the first Sunday of the election campaign my dad died. There was a phone call late at night, followed by the tone that tells you what's happened before the words are spoken. Somewhere in that grimy fraying box of a building, two bus rides from his home, he'd had a heart attack and died. At my Mum's house before the funeral, we stood in the living room and waited in the manner that only people waiting for a hearse can. Every few seconds someone said 'tut' or did a long 'phoooo', and once a minute someone asked a question such as whether there'd been a lot of traffic coming down from Dartford. Then the vicar cleared his throat and made a speech. Who the fuck was this bloke? He didn't know my dad. He wasn't upset; he hadn't had him at his vicarage over Christmas; Dad never went to church. The vicar started speaking. 'And when we see Ernie depart for the final time, I want us all, at that moment, to feel God's presence.' What a cheek! You wait for people to be at their most vulnerable and choose that moment to pounce on them to peddle your creed. It was as crude as if I'd got up and said, 'And when we see my dad depart, why not choose that moment to buy this week's copy of *Socialist Worker*?'

Now instead of the grieving process for which funerals are designed, I was seething. After the vicar, the silence and phooing continued as before. Then someone remembered that my Uncle Frank was from Birmingham. Over the weekend there had been a fight at Edgbaston cricket ground in Birmingham, in which racists had stabbed a young Asian. So as part of the pre-funeral twittering, someone said to Frank, 'Wasn't that terrible, that incident round your way. I mean, you don't expect that sort of thing to happen at the cricket.' So Frank said, 'Well the trouble in Birmingham is that everyone these days is told they have to do everything the Pakistani way. So it's not surprising when some people get annoyed really.'

My girlfriend and I looked at each other, and through a series of facial twitches came to a decision that this was not the place for a bust-up. And that's the disadvantage of being twenty-six. If I'd been nineteen I'd have exploded in a fit of anger. If I'd been thirty-six I'd have composed myself and with an air of authority taken Frank to task at using this occasion to air his nonsense, and then turned to the vicar and told him he wasn't much better. Instead I decided to say nothing, though I'd have been a much nicer person if I hadn't. Then we stood in a chapel and listened to the vicar again, and afterwards everyone said 'lovely service'. And lots of people said that maybe it was a blessing, with him being the way he was. But they didn't know the way he was. The reason he spent his last few years shuffling across threadbare carpets in a semi-trance, robbed of dignity and purpose, was not because of his illness, but because he wasn't a priority. He could have led a decent life in his last years, my old man, but the will and the resources to make it happen went elsewhere. And on top of that, the Tories were 12 per cent ahead in the polls.

In many ways the 1987 election was nowhere near as gruelling as 1983. Instead of a resigned hopelessness, there was an enthusiasm amongst opponents of Thatcher to get as many Labour votes as possible. I took part in a Red Wedge comedy tour that visited marginal constituencies, at which the dates were all sold out and buzzing with a sense that there were more of us than we realized. Now, when people argued to vote Labour, the defensiveness of the last two elections was replaced with a sense of urgency.

The Labour campaign wasn't aimed at this mood. Instead it was a parade of cascading balloons, and Neil and his wife waving to 'We Are the Champions'. His election broadcast, hailed as an artistic masterpiece, tried to project him as a tough leader by highlighting his speech against the Militant, which would have been fine if Kinnock was standing against Derek Hatton, but not so effective as his opponent was Thatcher. It did him no good, although in the final days of the campaign a cruel slither of hope grew, that maybe Labour could wipe out the Tory majority. This time it *was* worth getting some drinks in and watching the results. The consequence was that on the morning after the election, not only did I have the sickeningly familiar depression that follows an election victory for Margaret Thatcher, but the pulping, blinding, rasping sickness that follows eight pints and half a bottle of whisky.

In the following week I met a friend's grandfather, a Welsh man who lived in a council house in Dagenham. Like many people of his generation, he was exasperatingly generous. 'Would you like a sandwich? Are you sure? Would you like some fruit cake? Are you sure? There's plenty there. Are you warm enough? Would you like a drink? Are you sure you wouldn't like a sandwich?' Then I saw a photo of him as a young man and he said it was taken when he was a miner. So I made a calculation, and asked if he'd ever seen A.J. Cook, the miners' leader in 1926, whose image I'd seen on so many of those miners' banners.

He put down the plate of sandwiches and stood upright, proving himself several inches taller than I'd imagined. He took a breath, allowed himself a semi-smile and said in a thrusting baritone voice, 'A.J. Cook. A.J. Cook. That man was the greatest speaker that anyone ever saw. And he was the finest leader that anyone ever had.'

Occasionally an event takes place, like the general strike, which sweeps with it millions of people who never thought of themselves as political. For most of his life, this man had been passed from one workplace to another, one dole office to another, lived in one area or another, with or without the repairs being carried out, depending on what was convenient for those at the top of society at the time. But one time he'd felt powerful. One time in his life he could proudly say to himself, and believe it and feel it, 'We're as good as they are.' And so powerful was that time that sixty years later, the mere mention of it relieved him from the tittle-tattle of everyday life and transformed him into a majestic character, remembering the time when he mattered.

Thatcher had had a good run. But had she crushed all of that? She reeled off her next list of reforms: more privatization, more laws against unions, and the community charge, whatever that was.

Chapter 15

I performed one night to a party of commercial designers, and after the show one of them asked where I lived. I told him, 'Near Brixton, on a council estate.' He said, 'Oh a council estate – that's trendy.' As if millions of council tenants met up once a week at cocktail parties, and said 'hasn't the piss in the lift been artistic of late'.

One of the tricks of my estate was that when anyone from an adjoining flat made a noise, it sounded louder in my flat than in theirs. Someone blowing their nose upstairs sounded like the dying splutters of Mr Orange in *Reservoir Dogs* downstairs. People from two up and one along would meet me in a shop and say, 'Hello dear, you've been sneezing a lot lately.' Occasionally, while piecing together the actions of a neighbour, using audio clues (he's running water into the sink for washing up – aha no chink of cutlery, he's leaving it to soak), I'd wonder how much my behaviour was affected by the knowledge that every move was public.

It was impossible to have a natural domestic row, as I'd be aware that every word was being followed by up to a dozen people. So during a squabble, a bit of me couldn't help but worry how the argument sounded to the audience in adjoining flats. A damning remark against me filled me with horror at the thought of No. 4 muttering 'well she's got a point there'. Whereas after a witty riposte I might think 'I wonder if that got a laugh at No. 6'.

Most difficult to come to terms with in these circumstances, is that this group of strangers is privy to every squeak, grunt and yeeaah of your sex life. So you try to forget that everyone can hear you. Except that, as with the arguing, it's impossible to blank out entirely. There remains a small corner of the mind which, during an especially frenetic period is thinking, 'What can the bloke next door

be making of this?' And yet a sense of polite decorum is maintained.
I never heard anyone on the estate, while chatting to a neighbour
say, 'Cor, you were giving it some this morning weren't you? You
started off in the bedroom and ended up in the kitchen! Anyway,
lovely weather.'

If the cynics who believe that human beings are naturally selfish
and tribal were to be believed, these conditions would result in a
constant state of warfare, with territorial boundaries and tactical
alliances being made and broken as if the place was a medieval
fiefdom. But most tenants were remarkably tolerant of their
neighbours' stereos, dogs, motor bikes, inept parking and sexual
activities.

There was a guarded side to this understanding nature. You'd
take a mug of milk round and swap stories about the rudeness of
the woman at the housing office, but rarely be invited into anyone
else's flat. It was as if the unofficial rule was 'you can hear us
bonking but you're not getting a look at our record collection'. So
all around were people I knew almost nothing about, except that
they sang in the mornings, how often they snored and they shouted
'Oh I don't believe it' during an orgasm.

My neighbour was a feisty Jamaican woman, who knocked one
afternoon, and as I answered, she screamed 'British Teleco-o-o-o-
om' in a magnificent vibrato, then went back indoors. Two floors
above were two amenable gay men in their twenties, who drove a
silver Audi which looked distinctly out of place amongst the rear-
lightless Escorts and Triumph Heralds on bricks which adorned the
rest of the road. 'They're a very respectable couple,' it would be
said. Until they had a row which ended with one of them locked out
and climbing naked on to the balcony below to ask if he could ring
the fire brigade.

No. 5 never spoke to anyone and always wore a string vest. And
the man at No. 9 coughed. At seven in the morning he coughed
coming down the stairs with a briefcase, and at eleven at night he'd
return and cough going up the stairs. Every morning the increasing
volume of his cough would signal the imminent arrival of his huge
frame at the bottom of the stairs, by which time there were enough
beads of sweat on his forehead for them to start connecting and
trickling on to his suit. He could have worn the finest Italian

designs and still looked scruffy. 'Good day,' he'd say between coughing, in a clipped Oxbridge accent. Then he'd disappear for sixteen hours before returning with his suit, briefcase, posh voice and gutteral unrestrained 19th-century miner's cough.

Putting all this in the shade though was that directly above me lived The Incredible Drilling Man. 'Eweeeeugh,' it would begin, with a preliminary second of noise more tortuous than the torture itself. Like a gangster's polite banter as he reveals his garotting wire, making the actual agony a welcome relief from the threat of it. Then a few seconds to respond. I'd groan, twist my head to see the time on the digital clock, groan again upon seeing it was twenty to seven and endure the awful moments of anticipation. A silence lasting slightly longer than expected, creating a cruel false hope that he'd just got up to do one quick hole in the night and go back to bed. Then the chinkle chinkle of bits being changed would provoke an audible gasp the way Winston Smith must have gulped when the rats went through the first of the trap doors.

Noise is a unique form of torture, in that the gaps when it stops make the terror more unbearable. The breaks between the clanging of a workman's kango, or pauses between an Alsatian's barking marathon, just as you've adjusted yourself to living with the racket for the rest of your life, add to the suffering.

Then, 'Veraaaaaaagh! Duggelduggelduggelvroom! Veraaaaaaaaaagh', each time a little throatier and at a slightly higher pitch, like a moped starting up. Then two or three more 'Veraaaaaaaaaagh's, before an infernal 'wzhzhzhzhzhzh' which after a few seconds becomes difficult to work out where it's coming from. Logically it must be upstairs, but it could be from outside, next door, under the bed or inside your own head. 'Wzhzhzhzhzh' with no respite except for an occasional 'babababababababababa' as the plaster surrenders and the drill bit moves on to the higher level of the brickwork, like a computer game taking the accomplished player to Level 2.

There's a phrase, 'So loud I couldn't hear myself think.' But no noise is so loud that you can't hear yourself think. It's just that all you can think about is the noise. You can think 'ah it's gone up half a tone there, maybe it's on a higher speed' or 'there's a bit of background "ungungung" been introduced there, I wonder if he's preparing to use two drills at once'. Eventually, I kept thinking, he will simply run out of space. His entire flat must already have been covered in tiny holes, like a giant dot-to-dot puzzle. During moments of drill-induced insanity, I wondered whether he'd exhausted every potential drilling region and had now started on random objects like tubes of toothpaste and potatoes.

St Martins had been built in the fifties, during the last days of ration books and national service. The bricks were a sandy orange in contrast to the dark estates of the thirties, and there were stretches of grass between each block. The look must have symbolized a Britain emerging from the grey of post-war austerity, and applications for flats had far exceeded supply.

Families granted a place were envied, the world of outside toilets and tin baths was in the past, and from such hope sprang a feeling of community. Volunteers staffed the youth club and Labour Party activists ran a healthy tenants' association. The state for which people had fought was giving a bit back and most of them were willing to help the process. But as boom turned to slump, cuts in maintenance, redundancies of council staff and gradual privatization, coupled with mass unemployment, snatched away the optimism of earlier years. By the end of the 1980s, where blocked drains and broken water tanks were once attended to within days, now they were left so long that those who could afford to paid someone to fix them privately. The alternative was to enter the exasperating world of the neighbourhood housing office. This required such obstinance and dedication that the government may have secretly had a rule that no one who succeeded in getting the council to repair something was entitled to unemployment benefit, as for the last six weeks they can't have been available for work.

'I'll go and see if he's in,' they'd say, on the odd occasion you got through on the phone. Then they'd disappear for ten minutes although the office was a Portakabin hut, not much bigger than a living room. Throughout this time could be heard distant giggles, half-conversations about someone's birthday and someone calling out 'Have you got a B18 on Mr Sullivan's CWR?', while you sat helplessly out of reach of their world. By the time someone returned I'd be dying to inquire whether Mr Oldfield was only three inches tall as only that would explain how it took so long to verify that he wasn't in the building. But instead it turned out you were now talking to an entirely new person, who would ask you to explain what it is you wanted repaired in the first place.

'But I made the original application a month ago,' you'd burp. 'I'm ringing today because someone was supposed to come round yesterday and they didn't turn up.' But no matter how far you'd travel along the process, you would always arrive back at the point of having to begin all over again, like a game of snakes and ladders which at one point has six squares in a row all leading back to the start.

For serious problems like long-term damp, the council's strategy was to send someone round with a clipboard. 'Oh dear' they'd mutter, as they waved a thing that looked as if it should be measuring earthquakes or radioactivity. 'Hmm' they'd say in an apparent trance and conclude that they couldn't be sure what it was, but had made a lot of notes on their clipboard. Finally they'd make a report which ensured a fortnight later two more people came round with a clipboard. Over forty of these visits were made to my flat in a period of two years, each time by people who'd say 'Oh dear' and 'Hmm', when anyone normal would have gone 'Fuck me, there's mushrooms growing out of your ceiling'.

There was still a tenants' group in name. At the one meeting I attended there were six of us. The deputy secretary spoke at length on the reasons for the chairs being set out in a circle rather than straight lines – it would be more conducive to discussion. It then became clear that a Chinese man who'd brought his poodle couldn't understand a word that was being said, and a huge man with a portable stereo found a socket to plug his machine in, put a heavy dub tape on and stood in the centre of the circle dancing. No one made any reference to this, and we continued the meeting, the other four having to lean heavily to one side to see each other around the dancing man.

Then the burglaries started. The first victim was the cougher at No. 9. As the burglars left, they tossed a suitcase over the balcony, which thudded on to the grass below, bursting open to reveal a library of hard porn magazines. Then one by one everyone in the block was burgled, before the process began all over again. Each time the police would pay a nonchalant visit three days later, during which they'd peer at the point of entry and do that 'Hoo hoo gaw dear' laugh you usually hear from a builder making an estimate.

Each time they would offer the same worthless advice: 'If you see anything suspicious let us know.' A sentence which fulfils the same purpose as a doctor's 'if it hasn't got better in a couple of weeks, come back'. A few days later my Jamaican neighbour caught a burglar as he emerged from an upstairs flat with a television. She telephoned the police, who arrived half an hour later, let the burglar go and arrested her instead, until persuaded to release her by the crowd that had gathered.

So we called a meeting. Councillors were invited, along with the local MP, a police spokesman and everyone from the flat. There were three attitudes being aired. One involved a call for more police. But the one time the police had arrived, they'd arrested the person being burgled. If we had more police, the burglars could end up with all day to rob us, as we'd all be in the slam. Another tactic was to wait on the stairs with a crowbar and give the burglars a good hiding. Which would solve nothing and probably land us in the tabloids for mistakenly breaking the legs of a team of charity workers collecting for a sick puppy unit.

There were two other SWP members in the block and we set ourselves the task of persuading the neighbours to make demands on the council, rather than on the police or a baseball bat. If the weedy doors and frames, which could be prised open in seconds with a screwdriver, were replaced by a structure which offered some resistance, this would probably be enough to deter the intruders.

So the meeting began, with full attendance. For years I'd been going to political meetings at which almost everyone present was a veteran of countless other meetings. Now here was a meeting with the neighbours. Instead of predictable speeches from seasoned activists, this could go anywhere. Would the gays start rowing? Would the Chinese man come in with his poodle? Would we get half-way through the meeting and hear drilling? Would we be able to hear anything at all above No. 9 coughing?

'Thank you,' began the community copper, with a smile. 'What you have to remember,' he continued, with the paternalistic smirk of a 1960s children's TV presenter, 'is that the police are here to help you.' And on the word 'you', he pointed around the room with both hands. At which point the words 'absolute rubbish' boomed out in a voice that would have sounded more in place at a meeting of the MCC. 'Are you asking us to believe, my good man, that the police see their role as assisting the likes of us,' continued the coughing man. 'Absolute rubbish,' he reiterated and then he started coughing.

'If I may continue,' said the copper, and one of the gays interrupted him. 'I'd like to support the previous speaker,' he said. 'I'm a salesman, and while visiting a client I had something stolen from my car. The police came round straight away and because I was in a suit and had a new car they were very polite and pursued my case. But as soon as I'm back on this estate you all see me as worthless.'

'There you are. There's one case in which we were able to help,' said the policeman, missing the point completely. 'See,' said the coughing man loudly.

Then the policeman defended the actions of his colleagues who had arrested my Jamaican neighbour, while she waited politely with her arm raised. 'I'm rather shy and not used to making speeches,' she said when her turn came and slowly repeated the details of that evening. As she progressed, she was reliving the humiliating way she'd been dealt with and for about a minute delivered a fiery, evocative Martin Luther King style oratory. Without pausing she slipped effortlessly into an equally magnificent speech about her broken water pipes, the dog round the corner that never stops barking, and British Teleco-o-o-om. So many times over the years she had screamed at officials trained not to listen. So many hours had been spent politely repeating the details of the repair she'd requested while internally fuming and choking. This was her chance to be heard. Because for once there was more of us than there was of them.

'I certainly appreciate the strength of feeling,' said the MP, and he collected his papers and made for the door. As he was leaving he said, 'So I'll make sure a report of this discussion is raised at the next meeting of the housing committee.'

'When's that?' I asked.

'Two months' time,' he said.

'Shall I write to the burglars and ask them to lay off for two months?' I asked, and we won a unanimous vote for a rent strike. Then we all noticed that the man in the string vest had his hand up.

There was a moment of dramatic uncertainty. He was the only one who hadn't spoken, not just in this meeting but for at least a year. Would he break the solidarity? He held his pause an extra moment. 'When,' he began, 'are the Council, this MP and the police [another, longer, pause for tension before increasing in volume to a crescendo] going to get your fingers out of your arseholes for ORDINARY BLOODY PEOPLE?' Then he turned around, went straight out of the door and I never heard him speak again.

On the way home the coughing man whispered to me, 'You haven't heard anything about an item of mine apparently thrown from a window, have you?'

We paid the rent into a separate account, having informed the council formally they wouldn't be getting it until we got our security door. A week later we met in someone's flat, and as the meeting ended someone asked me quietly, 'Do you reckon it would be all right to skin up?'

'I suppose so,' I said, which was the only rational answer. Except that these people were the neighbours. No one skins up in front of the neighbours. They're like your mum and dad, in that one of their functions is to be people you don't skin up in front of. 'Well,' said No. 6, in that forthright way people say 'well' before an important announcement, 'I'm going to roll a joint.'

'Then I'll go and get my dope,' said the son of the Jamaican woman. 'And I'll get mine,' said one of the gays, and the drilling man.

'So where do you work then?' everyone asked each other, to people they'd been living within inches of for five years or more. The Jamaican was a dance teacher, No. 10's husband had run off when the kids were born, one of the gays was in the Labour Party and the drilling man was an insurance man.

After a few weeks of the rent strike, the burglaries stopped, partly as a result of the new camaraderie leading to an efficient lookout system. The strange shadowy figures that snored and rowed and coughed and screwed and drilled had become people with lives and pasts and ideas and reasons for doing these things. Instead of disembodied noise, we were listening to the routine of people we knew. Instead of 'What are they rowing about?', you thought 'John and Sandra are going for it tonight', which is altogether more acceptable. A community spirit revived, not because of adversity but through opposition to adversity.

'Come in,' said John, which turned out to be the name of the drilling man, one afternoon as we chatted on his doorstep. 'This is it,' I thought. 'This is the moment when I get to see inside the place whose holes have caused me such anguish. I can work out how many more holes are needed before they all connect up and the whole place collapses.' But as I looked around, there wasn't a single piece of evidence of any drilling anywhere. No shelves, no picture hooks, no random holes for purely decorative purposes, nothing. I took a decision to remain puzzled and never asked what on earth he'd been drilling all these years. Maybe he'd drilled a secret passage to another world, where people spoke in drilling language.

That night it started as usual, and after an hour of especially vicious 'Veraaaaaagh's there was a barely audible knock at the door. I answered and saw Linda, the dance teacher, who shouted, 'What can he be drilling up theeeeeeere?' and without waiting for an answer went next door and back inside.

Chapter 16

As the decade neared its end, the world changed. All my life and more, it had been divided into two camps, East and West. It seemed this was a permanent fixture of the planet, built into its structure. It was round, it spun, and its East and West bits spied on each other, threatened to annihilate each other and gave each others' gymnasts low marks at the Olympics. Then suddenly the East had a leader, Gorbachev, whom it was all right to like in the West. 'Glasnost' and 'perestroika' became like 'black hole' and 'DNA', in that everyone knew the phrases but no one knew what they meant.

We were witnessing the process of the communist countries hurtling towards destruction. But as it happened, its defenders were like loyal dogs, ready to the end to bare their teeth and snap at anyone who laid a finger on their master. I had a typical experience one night after a local protest, talking amiably with a Communist Party member in a Wimpy Bar. After about an hour, he asked me at what point after the Russian revolution did I think Russia had ceased to be socialist. I said that Stalin starving millions of peasants to death was probably a turning point, and suddenly his fists were thumping the table, causing the plates to jangle into the air and the relish to fly in all directions. The peasants were petit-bourgeois and threatened the re-introduction of private property, and the figures were made up, as I'd know if I'd bothered to read the 1929 report from the Supreme Soviet for Rural, Agricultural and Vegetable-Related Matters. I suppose I shouldn't have been surprised, as I had just called his hero a mass murderer. I expect you would get the same reaction if you suggested to the president of the Barry Manilow fan club that before he became a singer Barry poisoned the entire population of Mexico.

For Soviet loyalists, it made no difference how much evidence

piled up that these states were the opposite of socialist: undemocratic, unequal, oppressive, and millions of people living there
wanted to leave. The inspired anarchist poet/songwriter Attila the
Stockbroker, once told me he'd just returned from East Germany.
It was a glorious revelation of a place, he said, enthusing that 'the
people staying at the hotel I stayed in – WERE ALL WORKERS'.
As if the only people who stay in hotels in the West are the landed
gentry.

People could return from a town with 20 per cent unemployment
and prisons packed with political dissidents, and say things like
'but the plumbing in the town hall is marvellous'. The condition
wasn't restricted to Communist Party members. Almost every level
of the labour movement enjoyed contact with East European party
officials. From Croydon Labour Club several regional officers went
on regular beanos to Eastern Europe. They didn't go because they
were corrupt. They went because they adored the 'socialist
countries', and their trips confirmed their instincts, because their
hosts took them in the morning to a factory that had trebled its
head gasket production and in the evening to a free piss-up.

The most obvious puzzle about this model society was that if it
was so splendid, why did they need a bloody great wall to keep
people in it. If you threw a party and found the guests secretly
constructing a hot air balloon in a desperate attempt to escape, you
wouldn't conclude that this proved the night was a success. There
was always a hastily concocted socialist answer. Those escaping
were the 'petit-bourgeoisie'. They were 'counter-revolutionaries'
seduced by 'capitalist trappings', like Sugar Puffs, ITV and Wimpy
Bars. A Communist Party member once relayed to me with
boundless energy an article he'd read in the *Morning Star*, about an
operation which Russian hospitals were the first to perform, to
remove cataracts. 'So how can you criticize the socialist countries?'
he asked. I said that assuming this were true, it didn't quite make
up for the invasion of Hungary, but his purpose hadn't been to
convince me, but to convince himself.

One of the driving forces of most Communist Party members
was hatred of Trotskyists. In Russia, following the civil war, Stalin
launched his campaign for 'socialism in one country', jailing and
murdering supporters of Trotsky who wished to encourage the

spread of the revolution internationally. Sixty years later, old men and women continued the feud by refusing to let Trotskyists speak at tiny meetings in church halls. In Croydon, Queenie Knight, who was almost eighty, went to every labour movement meeting imaginable. If she was chairing, and someone she suspected of being a Trotskyist had their hand up, she would ignore them. If no one else had their hand up, she would wait. This could go on for five minutes, while several people called out 'over here Queenie', to no avail. Then her friend would raise a hand and she'd say 'Arthur', and Arthur would speak very slowly for fifteen minutes.

If she wasn't chairing, she would wait until someone she suspected of being a Trotskyist made a proposal. Then she'd say, 'Well I'm just a pensioner and don't know much about politics. But it seems to me if we do as the young woman said, we'd confuse a lot of people and drive the pensioners away. And the last thing we need is to split the movement. But as I say, I don't know much about politics.' And the whole room would be won over by this sweet old woman, who didn't know anything about politics, except for the collected works of Stalin off by heart.

Gorbachev's reforms presented a problem for the Communist Party. Some thought he was dealing with new challenges in a modern world but some thought he was a traitor. So there was a split, with some leaving to form the *New* Communist Party, which was a glorious title as almost all their members were over eighty. But the tensions in the communist countries were growing deeper, and the first to explode was China.

As Gorbachev visited China, students began demonstrating in a demand for democracy. Within days thousands of students occupied Tiananmen Square, and marches of hundreds of thousands swept through the main towns. On the news we saw endless crowds of steelworkers, miners, nurses, teachers and students, many of them in uniform, chanting, striding forcefully, defiantly through a country that few people imagined could be consumed by urban revolt. Some on the left were unsure as to what attitude to take. Weren't these marchers supporting the West? Weren't they opposing communism? But if you singled out an individual amongst that crowd, you could see him or her pulsating as they yelled their slogans. I'd said 'Maggie Maggie Maggie, out out out' thousands of times. Most times I'd half-shouted it out of duty, the way you recite your address when asked to by a bank clerk for security reasons. These people were swallowing lungfuls of air, stretching their mouths and *screaming*. They were feeling each syllable. I had no idea what they were shouting, but every word was the culmination of years of frustration. Every contingent represented a swirling debate that must have taken place in the hours before. On every shift in every steelworks, someone will have agreed with the aims of the march, but said it was playing into the government's hands. Someone will have called for conciliation. Someone will have said something superbly ridiculous, such as 'can't we have the march on Friday instead of Thursday, as I'm supposed to be taking my sister to the theatre on Thursday'.

As they agreed to add their numbers to the masses, none will have been able to answer where this movement was going. But they'll all have felt a stirring, that it was better to do something than nothing. That after years of putting up with petty injustices, bullying foremen, uncertainty, fear and arrogant Communist Party officials adorned with wealth pleading for the poorest to tighten their belts, now was the time. As they did so, they were, at the same time, the people they'd always been, and entirely different people. No one will have been more surprised at the action they were taking than those in the middle of it. Many of the protestors will have wondered how on Monday morning they had been resigned to another weary week, and now they were the main item on CNN, making people who were thousands of miles away gasp.

Among the crowd at the square were builders who'd ripped up oppositional papers, office clerks who'd asked 'Are you a poof then?', and women whose previous political statements had been 'don't get in any trouble dear'. Of course some of them believed the West provided their model. They were like the miners but more so. They weren't protesting because they were revolutionary, but because they were *becoming* revolutionary.

One Sunday there was a vibrant march through Chinatown in London in support of the demonstrators, and a further march was called for the following Sunday. On the Friday night in between, I went to Nottingham to do a fundraising gig, and was met by a stony-faced man who said reports were coming over the radio that the Chinese army was firing into the square. The first attempt to crush the revolt had failed, as soldiers had refused to carry out their orders. But rural battalions from areas that hadn't been involved in the protests were sent in to do the job instead. The government was relying on agitators from outside the area. I'd been in situations in which peaceful protest had turned to violence and confusion, but what would that be like? What's that rumbling? Why are there tanks? Are they here to support us? My God, they're firing. Surely the government will stop them. Someone says they *are* the government. Through such unimaginable emotion was fought a battle of incalculable bravery, symbolized by the lone student stood before a legion of tanks.

The march the following Sunday was sombre and seemed hopelessly inadequate to the task. It felt even more hopeless when we arrived at the Chinese embassy, and on a sweltering hot day, the leaders of the march announced we would create a symbolic gesture by all turning our backs on the ambassador. Jeremy Hardy, who stood next to me, said, 'I suppose this is so we get an all-over tan.'

The world had seen and studied these events, and in the autumn of 1989, following mass demonstrations in Hungary and East Germany, the borders to the West were relaxed and then the Berlin Wall was knocked down. The Berlin Wall. It was like hearing that someone had dismantled Mount Everest or filled in the Pacific Ocean. Revolution swept through the region, until a huge crowd assembled in Bucharest, where they'd been ordered to cheer the Romanian leader Nicolae Ceauşescu. As he waved to the crowd, a section booed. On the television, you could see Ceauşescu's shocked face. Within seconds the whole crowd was booing and the revolution was under way. The unanswerable question is 'Who started the booing?'. Someone must have been whispering to a friend, 'I'm thinking of booing. If I start, will you join in?' Maybe the whole crowd was alive with mutterings of 'you first'. But the underlying animosity towards the dictators, combined with the sense that as governments fell around them, anything was possible, meant that one boo was enough to spark a revolution. But if no one had been the one to start, they might have cheered and wandered home with their normal resentment, some of them thinking, 'If I'd have started, no one would have joined in. You know what they're like round here.'

I had a socialist friend in Munich, a doctor whom I visited at Christmas. German socialists have two stereotypes to overcome, both involving having no sense of humour. But they seem to play up to it deliberately. He would start early in the morning, rattling through the finer points of Marxist theory as he dumped sixty unrelated items of food on the table for a German breakfast. 'It is very important to link the economic struggle with the political struggle,' he'd insist earnestly, as he was making a space for the celery and mustard.

A Russian woman called Irene (pronounced Ear-reen-a) was staying there. She worked in an office and half her income went on rent for her tiny Leningrad flat, which was crawling with rats. While she chased the rats away, members of the Politburo owned mansions they only used for holidays. I wouldn't believe, she insisted, how the police will sometimes attack peaceful protests. The more she went on, the more obvious it became that the point was not to debate which system was better. The point was that the leaders of both systems had more in common with each than with their own populations. And the populations of each system had more in common with each other than with their own leaders.

On Christmas night a news report on the radio suggested demonstrators had captured Ceauşescu's palace and overthrown his police force the Securitate. Frantically we twiddled between stations, grabbing unconfirmed reports in a multitude of languages. Through a bout of prolonged crackling, it was reported that a people's militia had taken over. Then it was denied. Then reaffirmed, then denied again. And that was how I spent Christmas night in 1989, huddled over a radio in Munich. Suddenly everyone went 'shhhh' and there was an announcement. Ceauşescu was something, some Teutonic word that may mean captured or still in power. But the Germans were clapping and squealing. What? Ceauşescu was what, I begged them to tell me. Executed! Ceauşescu had been executed! One of the world's most brutal dictators had been brought down by the people he'd trampled on for forty years – and executed. Irene was a lone dismayed figure. 'No no, this is bad,' she called out. 'This is what happened in my country, revolution and then killing and much pain.' Squalor, shortages, fear and hypocrisy had surrounded her life, all justified in the name of revolution. The room went quiet, and a little embarrassed. 'They haven't killed him out of wanton violence,' I argued. 'While he was alive, his armies could fight for his restoration, but now the Securitate will crumble. His death will save many lives.'

She thought for a moment and said, 'Then yes, I see it is a good thing that he is executed.' And the cheering was resumed, even louder than before, until a student called Günter shouted 'And I hope that first they skinned him alive and tortured him in much agony.'

Television and radio companies spend the whole year desperately searching for the perfect feelgood programme to broadcast on Christmas evening. That year they found it, with help from someone whose name we will never know, who took a deep breath and booed.

A few days later I hired a car and drove to Prague where, just before Christmas, the Czech government had collapsed following a general strike. The playwright Václav Havel, jailed by the old regime, was emerging as the new leader. This was my first glimpse of revolution, in which two things were immediately striking. The first was how different from normality life was and the other was how similar to normality life was. A little old woman stopped as she walked up one side of Wenceslas Square and took a leaflet and paintbrush from a plastic bag. She dipped the brush into another bag, which was full of paste, and stuck the leaflet on to a door. As she walked away, crowds gathered to clamber over each others' shoulders, creating a sense that you were missing out if you weren't with them. There must have been tourists that week who rushed over to see what these crowds were watching, expecting to see a fire-eater or snake charmer, and walked away baffled as to why the whole street was studying a tatty leaflet.

There was an epidemic of ideas. Not that I could tell what they were, but the enthusiasm was unmistakeable. Students maintained a candlelit vigil at the top of the square and a continual line of well-wishers greeted them. Crowds walking through the streets, looking like any group shopping, or heading for a bar, would break into chants against the old government and for Havel. This would spark similar chants from other groups, the way a barking dog can set off every other dog in the neighbourhood, so that within seconds it felt like a mass demonstration. But people still queued for bread, sat in corners of bars and moaned about buses not arriving. Amidst the eye of this historic typhoon, plenty of people were worrying about the weather and fixing their Skodas.

On New Year's Eve an enormous crowd filled Wenceslas Square, for what was billed as New Year festivities, but became a show of strength and celebration for everyone glad to see the back of the old order. Around a quarter of a million people cheered singers who were draped in the colours and flags of the opposition. For the first time I was experiencing the mass euphoria of a movement that had overthrown its opponent. But amidst the joy and sense of liberation, I felt a twinge of foreboding. The direction this movement was heading in was the free market. Posters depicted a confident Czechoslovakia climbing into Western Europe. I didn't blame them for feeling that Western capitalism could cement their liberation from Eastern capitalism. But they were bound to be disappointed. Because the technique used to sell the free market to the East was the same as the methods used by any market. All the best stuff was at the front, so the Czechs looked over the border and saw West German prosperity. But as soon as they agreed to buy into it, the free market would be like any market and get the old rubbish from the back. The Czechs were sure to be told, 'Here you are mate, you can have Mexican poverty, Brazilian shanty towns and Australian soap operas. Next.'

As the dictatorships of the East collapsed, horrors were revealed that shocked even their harshest critics. The head-shaking and tutting of Western leaders who had befriended the rulers of apartheid South Africa and military Chile was mere hypocrisy. But there was no trickery in the disgust felt by most people at a system which built magnificent palaces for its rulers, alongside barbaric orphanages for its unwanted children. Most devastated were the long-standing supporters of the Communist Party. These people had spent their lives supporting the poor against the rich, the weak against the strong. They sincerely believed the most effective way of achieving a fairer, more equal world, was to promote the joys of 'the socialist countries'. Now it was apparent that in doing so, they'd been backing the rich against the poor, the cruelly strong against the desperately weak.

Year after year they had yelled in Wimpy Bars and written in the *Morning Star* that people in the socialist countries were immeasurably more contented than people in the West. But as their model states collapsed, the inhabitants were overjoyed at their passing. The followers of the tyrants weren't the same as the tyrants themselves. Ceauşescu lived in a palace. Most Communist Party members in the West were poor working people whose inspiration came from fighting for a cause. How must it feel for it be revealed that a lifetime's commitment has been so flawed? I wasn't better than them, just luckier, to be angry and eighteen at a time when it was much easier to see that Russia wasn't socialist, it was shit.

Around that time a local historian told me he'd been searching through archive material on the Croydon Communist Party in the 1940s. At one time they had fifteen factory branches in the area. They'd been formed by working-class people dedicated to opposing fascism, supporting unemployed marches and backing the Spanish republicans against Franco. The secretary for this activity had been a fiery young woman called Queenie Knight. She had spoken to mass meetings of engineers and tirelessly knocked on doors to convince wavering members of their value. She had organized demonstrations and fundraising events, sat up all night printing leaflets, and hoped and believed and felt as I had at twenty, but with greater effect. All I had over her was hindsight.

My friend Dave Davies, who joined the Communist Party as a naval electrician in 1942, came to terms with the deceptions of Stalinism after the demise of the East European regimes. But he stays in touch with his old comrades. 'One week,' he says, 'they sink into their beer and say "Where did we all go wrong?" The next week, they say "mind you, there were a lot of progressive things about the socialist countries". So I say to them, "Listen. Stalinism is like smoking. It's no good trying to give it up one stage at a time, you've got to give it up all in one wallop and be done with it".'

Chapter 17

As dictatorships in Europe faced meltdown, the fallout sprinkled through Britain. The idea settled in the backs of millions of minds, so mildly that most weren't aware of its presence, that apparently unassailable leaders were due their comeuppance. Thatcher had been careful throughout her first two terms to take on one group at a time. Now she got cocky. The poll tax would make everyone pay the same local taxes. In the words of Nicholas Ridley, 'The Duke would pay the same as his gardener.'

One of the marvellous aspects of the campaign against the poll tax was here was a movement that couldn't be blamed on outside agitators. During the miners' strike, they could shout 'some of them weren't even miners'. And they could yell 'some of them weren't even printers' during Wapping. But *everyone* had to pay the poll tax. So they couldn't scream 'some of these demonstrators, well they're not even, you know, they're not er, thingy, well they're not even people. They're squirrels and canoes and bits of string'.

I started doing a joke in my act, which got such an enthusiastic response it made me feel slightly uneasy. It went, 'Margaret Thatcher said many people would be better off under the poll tax. And to be fair, in my case, it is true. Because I always used to pay the rates but I'm never paying the bloody poll tax.'

Were audiences at places like the Comedy Store and Jongleurs Comedy Club really cheering the prospect of breaking the law to defeat Thatcher? Or was there an unintended pun in there somewhere I hadn't spotted? Political popularity was a disturbing feeling, and some decided that being disliked was a virtue. At a meeting that Jeremy Hardy and I spoke at, on comedy and the left, someone said it was unprincipled to be a popular comedian, because 'popularity is always at the expense of politics'. Jeremy replied, in that case, Lenin must have turned to Trotsky during the Russian revolution and said, 'Shit, Leon, this is disastrous, they like us.'

Much of the left had become used to relating to a small minority of dissidents, becoming like computer experts or jazz aficionados, unable to connect with anyone outside their own circle. If a bus driver asked them what was the point of being a socialist, they'd say something like 'to establish a hegemony of ideas amongst the working class'. So they were puzzled at how left-wing comedians managed to speak to rooms full of strangers. And some of them thought a gig was the same as a speech. After a show in Sheffield to around 400 people, I was approached by a student who was furious because I hadn't mentioned Nicaragua. I often wondered whether right-wing comedians received similar treatment, whether Jimmy Tarbuck was harangued by Young Conservatives after his gigs for not mentioning the benefits of privatizing British Gas. Local activists would approach me ten minutes before the start and ask if I could do something in the act about the campaign against repression in Iraq.

Sometimes the most embarrassing people were those who sought to defend me. I spoke in my act about subjects like the tedium of work, the characters on my estate and the frustrations of being a kid. So some socialist fans would congratulate me for 'drawing the audience in and making them laugh at capitalism', as if it was part of a grand strategy, and when I'd got a laugh from an impersonation of my great aunt, I was half-way to converting them to a Marxist theory of the state.

One night, when I commented to an SWP member in the audience that the act which followed me had gone down badly, she looked at me with horror. 'You shouldn't say that. He's one of the most active people in the local Labour Party, and very good on South Africa,' she said. Another common comment was that the rarefied atmosphere of the showbiz milieu could lead to me becoming estranged from the labour movement, so it was essential I combined my comedy lifestyle with 'day-to-day political activity'. I wondered if they wanted me to do some flyposting during the interval.

The tensions grew when I reached the point that comes to many comedians, when you become accomplished enough to do consistently well but are unknown enough to be worth discovering. Suddenly I was on a settee, doing chunks of my act on the *Des O'Connor Show*, with Des wiping a fictitious tear from his cheek in response. What would that bloke from Sheffield think about that? A golden opportunity to talk about Nicaragua on peak-time ITV and I blew it again. Backstage on the *Des O'Connor Show*, I wandered into a room and bumped into a co-guest, Donny Osmond. This was the moment when I knew I was no longer eighteen. At that age, I'd have imagined that in the unlikely scenario of finding myself alone in a room with Donny Osmond, I'd have accused him of being a sickly Mormon hypocritical anti-gay putrid symbol of the cesspit that is clean-cut America, who should have been locked up for 'Puppy Love'. Instead I said 'good luck with the Christmas single Donny' and shook his hand. I got on well with Des. I wonder what he'd have thought if I'd broken a pause in the conversation by telling him I was in favour of the state being seized by a democratic collective of workers' councils. Even stranger, it was expected of SWP members that they should try and sell papers to their workmates. But that becomes a bit tricky when your workmates are Des O'Connor and Donny Osmond.

Jokes like the one about the poll tax did seem to earn a laugh of defiance, and the irreverent spirit wasn't confined to that issue. The previous year, a movement had grown in response to the decay of the Health Service, culminating in protests in most towns and a huge march in London. I got a local seamstress to embroider the words 'COMEDIANS DEFEND THE NHS' on a banner. Though there wasn't the time to add a scene of hungry comedians walking towards a grimy microphone and a portrait of a militant comedian from the general strike. Around forty comedians marched behind it on a day that was joyous and optimistic because, unlike the marches of 1981, this felt as if it represented millions more who weren't there.

One of the moments which revealed a gradual change of mood took place following a postmen's strike. The local Post Office had employed a new manager, fresh from a business management course, who threatened the strike leaders with disciplinary action. I and a few others distributed a leaflet proposing that if this was carried out, the staff should stage an immediate walkout. The new manager was so outraged he wrote his own leaflet in reply. Then to make sure everyone understood what he was complaining about, he reprinted the original leaflet and handed it to every postman on every shift. The workforce thought this was hysterical, as it made him probably the only manager in the history of industrial relations, to ensure the thorough distribution of a leaflet calling for his own workforce to go on strike.

Something was stirring. Suddenly, you didn't get lectures on how Thatcher had made it possible for ordinary people to cash in on the property boom, because interest rates were rocketing and the dreams of ordinary people who'd bought houses were being shattered. Many people who had made a few quid out of shares, who Thatcher and Kinnock believed to be irretrievably converted to state-organized selfishness, were facing in horror the bill for their ride with the Tories. The Health Service was crumbling. Their parents' house was on offer to a shark from the city. And round the corner was the poll tax. These people weren't screaming for Thatcher's head, but they were no longer jumping to defend her. So millions who hadn't voted for her were regaining the confidence to take her on.

For a while, those who had never liked her would greet each other with a perky 'hiya', in the way that strangers say 'good morning' on the first sunny day of spring. We were creeping out of our ghetto. Thousands punched the air to Carter the Unstoppable Sex Machine's 'Sheriff Fat Man'. Elvis Costello released *Spike*, a haunting soliloquy of bile against Thatcher, including the chilling 'Tramp the Dirt Down'. 'When England was the whore of the world, Margaret was her Madam . . .' and ending 'When they finally put you in the ground/I'll stand on your grave and tramp the dirt down.' Rik Mayall was Thatcherite MP Alan B'stad. Or there was the more sophisticated version at the cinema, *The Cook, the Thief, His Wife and Her Lover*. Suddenly greed wasn't good.

Two events turned the tide further. After a battle with Thatcher, Nigel Lawson resigned as Chancellor. Then the ambulance dispute began. Collections for the ambulance drivers took place in almost every shopping centre and were ridiculously easy. In some ways they were *too* easy, like the puzzle corner in a local paper, and would have been more fun if they'd offered at least some challenge. Everyone supported the ambulance drivers, especially after Kenneth Clarke called them 'glorified taxi drivers'. My mum told me she always put money in their buckets. Radicalism was deprived of its shock value. Imagine being seventeen, shouting 'I support the ambulance drivers', and finding your mum saying 'so do I dear, I gave them all my change outside KwikSave'. Where would be the fun in sneaking ambulance drivers into your mum's house to sleep on the settee, only for her to find them, tell them they were marvellous and fetch an extra blanket?

The TUC called 'fifteen minutes of action' to support the ambulance crews during a lunchtime in January 1990. Fifteen minutes. Even then you couldn't be certain they wouldn't panic, and call it off after eleven minutes. We arranged a meeting with the union steward from the ambulance depot and called for a demonstration in the local park. From then until the fifteen minutes, I felt a breathless hole in my guts every time I thought about it. How many would be respectable? Fifty? Forty? What if there were seven of us and the local paper? This is the gut-wrenching procedure of organizing a public event. You announce it, imagining the hundreds of people bound to support it. Then two weeks away, only eleven are definitely coming. With one week to go, the figure has dropped to five. On the morning of the event, you admit to yourself that even when you were predicting hundreds, you'd have settled for thirty. On your way, you stop to give someone a lift, but they're not coming. If the reason is they have to work, you want to beg them to bring their work with them, even if it involves driving a bus. If they tell you they're exhausted, you feel like suggesting they bring a mattress and sleep through the meeting. As long as they're there it counts. Then you get there. There are two others, setting out chairs, then usually a moment of deflation, when someone comes in, almost sits down and says something like 'Is this the right room for the Turkish dancing class?'. So you wait by the door, muttering 'Where the bloody hell's Kevin?'. All these emotions are heightened many times over by calling a demonstration.

By the time I set off for the park, I was simply hoping to beat the ten on that march for jobs. But there was an unexpected twist. At one edge of the park was a registry office, which often led to wedding crowds posing for photographs on the spot where the demonstration was due. And on this day at this time was the biggest wedding crowd I'd ever seen there. I galloped through the park in the hope of persuading the crowd to leave, as if this couple would be prepared to tell their children in future years that they hadn't got any wedding photos because twelve people wanted to make full use of the TUC's fifteen minutes of action. Then I realized this crowd had placards. The scenario which hadn't occurred to me was that the crowd of several hundred were here for the demonstration. A student brought everyone from his course. Hundreds of council workers came from the town hall. The union official from the Post Office led around 500 postal workers across the road into the park. Eventually the crowd was estimated by the local paper at 2000. It was almost as if it was a terrible mistake. They listened to speeches, cheered the union steward from the ambulance depot, and after fifteen minutes went back to work. The three of us who had done most to organize it were stunned. We went to the pub and contemplated what you're supposed to do when 2000 people turn up. And we must have looked so perplexed that if anyone who wasn't on the demonstration had seen us they'd have thought 'oh dear, they must have got less than ten'.

After six months the dispute ground to a halt, but the mood amongst the crews and their supporters was nearer to the postmen than to the choking miners of a few years earlier. Soon after it ended, almost every town in Britain had an angry protest against the poll tax, including places like Weymouth and Bracknell. Every newspaper was discussing the possibility of Thatcher being dumped, and Michael Heseltine was assuring us on an hourly basis that he couldn't foresee any circumstances in which he would stand against her.

The sense of anticipation transformed the average socialist weekly meeting. A group of builders arrived, covered in plaster, who we assumed were looking for another event, probably one which involved a game of cards. They all shared the classical builders' ability to slip 'fuck', or a derivation of fuck, between any two words. The speaker began his talk, on crime, saying that attitudes depended on whether the criminal is a car thief or insider dealer in the City. A cry went up of 'he's fucking right'. From then on, one or more of them repeated this phrase after each sentence, so that if a sentence passed by without it, the poor speaker must have felt quite rejected, and within his rights to say 'What's the matter, was that fucking wrong?'. Fresh from our success with the fifteen minutes of action, we called a march against the poll tax. The following week, I started the meeting with a patronizing plea to be as imaginative as possible in getting support for the demonstration. One of the builders shouted, 'He's fucking right. I fucking tell you what the fuck I fucking done. My fucking mate hires out these fucking aero-fucking-planes, for fucking birthdays and that, where they fucking hang all fucking letters say "happy fucking birthday". So I've fucking persuaded him to fucking fly all over fucking Croydon during the fucking march, with a load of fucking letters saying "No Poll Tax". That should fuck the fuckers.' My glee was tainted by the worry that the whole of Croydon would look up to see a plane trailing a huge message: 'No Fucking Poll Tax'.

The changing atmosphere seemed to upset many long-standing campaigners. There's a rhythm to being miserable that is quite satisfying, and it can be disturbing to have that peaceful depression shattered by a load of cheerful bastards. Some of them had become so institutionalized into studying theory, you were wary of handing them a megaphone on a march against the poll tax in case they shouted 'the result of the expropriation of the proletariat was referred to by Marx as surplus value'.

To organize the campaign involved getting people who weren't used to such activities, going down streets giving out leaflets and knocking on doors, which always leads to magnificent chaos. The first law in this situation is that someone in every group starts moaning. 'Why are we going down this road first? Surely it makes more sense to go down the other side of that road and then back up this road. I mean, this way we walk down that side of the road and then we have to come back again, which is a waste of time.' And as they wander off with the leaflets, you can still hear them muttering 'it's bloody ridiculous'.

Or there's the over-organized ones, who come into their own during flyposting, having prepared each individual poster by rolling it up so it unfurls easily on to the wall. Then they get offended if it isn't put up perfectly straight, perpendicular to the pavement. So they stand there adjusting it and readjusting it, although the lookout is shouting 'Police!'.

One week prior to our march was the national demonstration, on the weekend the poll tax came into effect. The atmosphere leading up to it reminded me of being fifteen, when someone is having a party that everyone talks about for the week beforehand. I would ring people to see if they were going, and they would tell me they were bringing ten of their mates. On 31 March around 200,000 people assembled in Kennington Park. The normal procedure on marches was for a few groups bravely to try breathing life into the event by banging drums or dressing up as Douglas Hurd. But they always seemed like singers who plead with their audience 'come on, let's try it again, and this time really clap as loud as you can'. This time was different.

If you saw someone you knew, they didn't greet you with 'hello', but with 'isn't this fantaaaastic'. The same busking bands were playing, but instead of being seen as a nuisance, groups were dancing to them. Crowds of middle-aged women from towns such as Maidenhead clustered behind homemade banners. 'No poll tax' roared above the whirring of the helicopters. For ten years I'd shouted on demonstrations that various things should be scrapped, smashed or stuffed, without believing they would be. Today I was amongst a crowd shouting a demand we thought we would win. The Tories' mistake was to believe their own propaganda. The poll tax was so blatantly unjust, almost everyone opposed it, without stopping to assess whether they personally would save a few quid.

Even if someone would benefit personally, they knew the tax would bankrupt larger families. They knew it was wrong for the duke to pay no more than the gardener. The 1980s had been bleak, but they hadn't turned the entire country into savages fending for themselves.

It took several hours for this carnival to thread through South London towards Trafalgar Square. Then it got stuck in Whitehall. No one could go forwards. No one could go backwards. In the distance, by the Whitehall Theatre, someone was dragged across the road and hurled into a van, limbs lashing out in all directions like a cat being put in a box. A chant went up: 'Stasi Stasi' after the recently deposed East German police. Still no one could move. Pieces of balsawood from the placards started floating across to the increasingly edgy lines of police. Most people were still singing. They were still singing when a line of police horses appeared to our rear. There was a sense of 'oo what's happening' as if the animals were part of a display, kindly laid on to entertain us while we were stuck.

'Here we go,' I thought. But the contagious fear that usually spreads through the crowd on these occasions was missing. The horses started fidgeting. The police seemed to stare blankly, like sprinters in deep concentration in the moments before a major race. Then they charged. Everyone ran into the few gaps made available as barricades were flattened, and many screamed. But as well as screams of terror, there were screams of fun, like those you hear from children when an adult chases them round a garden pretending to be a dinosaur. After a few seconds, the running stopped. This ritual of the interrupted charge was repeated several times, and then a police van arrived, hurtling into the crowd. It was immediately surrounded by demonstrators who tried to rock it over.

Most people who were there that day claim to have seen the incident which started the riot. But I expect the truth is that scenes like this were repeated throughout the area. No one action sparked the battle. Two forces were closing in on each other, one brimming with complacent confidence, resting on years of dominance, the other bursting with renewed vigour and popularity. Thatcher, her minions, her press and her police were like a boxer who's become too used to winning and doesn't notice the hunger and speed of his next opponent, or the flab accumulating on his own stomach.

By a combination of pushing and fleeing, I made my way to the Strand. Ahead of me a building site was on fire and Trafalgar Square was packed with jubilant dancing demonstrators. Vans continued screeching into the crowd, but each time with the same result, first surrounded and then rocked. By my side, someone from the Revolutionary Communist Party was on the phone, saying 'there's nothing much going on here, just middle-class kids at play'.

In every direction lines of protestors were skipping around the immobilized traffic. From the side-roads that led to the Thames, from burger bars and coffee shops and from the middle of the square came spontaneous cries of 'No poll tax – No poll tax'. Segments of the march, including the homeless, had broken away to parade around the West End and riot. This might not have been a productive way to protest, but the people who did it were the most desperate victims of the decade of greed. They were on day release from hopelessness, and could no more be expected to behave than a sailor on shore leave could be expected to return early from the pub after a gentle half of bitter.

Marches weren't supposed to end like this. Normally, you filed into an orderly crowd and listened to the speeches – an actor, a maverick Liberal MP, Tony Benn and a clergyman – and clapped at each sentence that ended 'sweep that woman out of office'. Or you went to the pub. But today you watched the smoke drift over the spot by the Foreign Office, where I'd once stared in bewilderment as the police snapped those placards.

The press and politicians shook with predictable fury. But every other rule concerning the aftermath of a riot was broken. 'Here we go,' I thought again, as I stood in the newsagents the next morning behind a woman tutting as she surveyed the newspaper pictures. 'Well what does she expect,' she said. And that appeared to be the official statement from the pubs and launderettes of Britain. Thirty-first of March 1990 was the day that 'what does she expect' took over from the long-running 'isn't it terrible'.

Two days after the demonstration, I was performing at the London Astoria, in the heart of the area still littered with debris. The show was to be broadcast on BSB, the ill-fated satellite station. The host was Jools Holland and the recording started at six o'clock, so the live audience of around 1,000 was made up largely of office workers. Mark Thomas was on in the first half and walked to the microphone accompanied by a classical American showbiz blast from the house band. He started with, 'What's all this fuss about the poll tax riot? We pay the police's wages, we're entitled to kick them about a bit.' And the crowd cheered and clapped and roared, and if they'd had their hats, they'd have thrown them in the air. As the noise receded, he followed this up with, 'There's a difference at McDonald's. Yeah, no fucking windows.' And off went the crowd again. All it needed was for the drummer to follow it with a 'durum tss' on the snare and cymbal.

In opinion polls, the majority blamed the riot on the police and the government. Labour shot to a 20 per cent lead over the Tories. This time, the Tories and the police had lost the battle they started, not because of the prowess of anyone there on the day, but because the tide was with the protest. Croydon police, however, took a different view and banned our local march.

We met the chief inspector, who opened a folder marked 'Poll Tax' and told us he had heard, through a source he wasn't prepared to disclose, that anarchists were preparing 'to come to this march and burn down Croydon'. Did he mean the whole of Croydon, or was it a moderate anarchist who would be satisfied with just the shopping centre? From his folder he took out a poster advertising the march. An officer had scraped it from a wall because someone had scrawled along the top in biro 'bring a bottle'. 'Look at that,' barked the inspector, with a sense of drama that deserved a 'dun dun duuuun' you get in thrillers when a murder is revealed. Did he honestly think this undercover work had prised open an anarchist plot to throw bottles, using the secret code 'bring a bottle'? The other flaw in his logic was that if these anarchists were going to carry out the greatest act of arson since the bombing of Dresden, would they be deterred by the march being banned. As if they'd say, 'If we get done for burning down Croydon, we'll be in enough trouble as it is. So let's not make it worse by going on a march without police permission.'

The chief inspector said he was holding me personally responsible for telling everyone who was coming that they shouldn't attend, including, presumably, the thousands of anarchists. The next day he rang me back and said proudly, 'I think we can safely say no one will be coming to the march this Saturday. Because I am due to announce the ban on an interview this evening on Croydon Cable Television.' Despite this primetime broadcast and the front page of every local newspaper carrying the story of the ban, around 100 people turned up anyway, along with seven bus-loads of police. The chief inspector allowed us to hold a rally, thanked me for being co-operative and shook my hand. And in that moment I doubted whether I could ever lead a revolution, because for a moment I thought 'ah, he's not so bad after all'.

The impact of the protests was to make it seem legitimate not to pay the tax, giving non-payers the assurance they weren't alone. A few cases came to court, of which the most prominent locally was that of anti-poll-tax campaigner Billy. Trade unions sent delegations to the case and banners surrounded the court. Protestors stood on the steps with placards and a noisy group filed into the gallery to cheer Billy when his case came up. The local press and radio were there, sitting through a litany of cases involving pub fights and raided electric meters, until the magistrate said, 'Ah yes. Next we have the young man who hasn't paid his community charge.'

'Go on Billy,' everyone shouted, in the encouraging tone with which snooker fans shout 'Go on Jimmy' at Jimmy White. Everyone fidgeted nervously. The local paper's photographer jostled for position. A clerk of the court stretched up to the magistrate, who was leaning forward. Were they delaying the start deliberately for dramatic effect, as if we were waiting to see James Brown? The clerk wandered away, and the magistrate said, 'Well it seems we no longer require to hear this case as the outstanding debt was paid in full this morning.'

'My dad paid it for me,' said Billy, as he emerged outside to his less than hero's reception. 'Only I didn't know how to tell you.'

Nationally the poll tax campaign had shaken Thatcher's credibility to such an extent that even her colleagues were accepting she couldn't win another election. So when the issue of Europe popped up, her opponents inside the Conservative Party were ready to go for her throat. Geoffrey Howe, the deputy leader, resigned and made his famous speech revealing her anti-European stance at recent summits. Heseltine announced he was standing against her because these circumstances were 'unforeseeable', as if we'd entered a new ice age or war with Norway.

Could this be it? Could this be the end of her? On her tenth anniversary as Prime Minister her fans had chanted 'ten more years'. And who was to say they weren't right? But now she could be gone. On the day of the vote I looked at a clock every few minutes, to make sure seven hours hadn't passed by without me noticing and I'd missed the news. At six o'clock, with a crowd of anxious co-Thatcher-detesters, I was in front of the news unable to sit down and unable to stand up. Out came the figures. Having spent all week studying the permutations and probable outcomes, suddenly none of us could work out what it meant. For a moment no one knew whether she was Prime Minister or not. Then out she came through those doors in Paris to stride down those steps and take the stage declaring she had all but won. I might have hated your guts Maggie but you were wonderful at creating a sense of drama.

The next ballot would take place the following week. On the Thursday morning I went to a friend's house to borrow a book. And while I was there it happened. He was listening to a dance music station, the sort that wouldn't interrupt its club-mix hour if war was declared. But it did for this. 'It has just been announced that the Prime Minister Margaret Thatcher has resigned.' Wahoooooooooooooooo! Eighteen. I was eighteen when she got in. Eighteen and just started at the Post Office and living with my mum and dad and frightened of chatting up women and now I was thirty. All that time. All that time she'd strutted across my and millions of other lives, the symbol of every rotten selfish vindictive side of the human condition she could rake up and cultivate, like an evil scientist nurturing a test tube of greed and releasing it across the whole planet. And now she was gone. Maggie Maggie Maggie, out out out. It took eleven years but we did it. For a moment it all seemed to be over, how I imagine it felt on VE Day. There was no need to be a socialist any more. We could all go back to getting on with our lives. She was gone. And not just because of an internal coup. If it hadn't been for the campaign against the poll tax, would her credibility have slid to the point that made her vulnerable? She'd won a thousand battles, but each one had taken its toll. Now she would be replaced by another Tory. But that wasn't the point. Every time a bully gets toppled it sends a message to every other bully and their minions that you can't get away with everything. There are always more of us than there are of you. In any case, she was gone. How can you chant 'Maggie Maggie Maggie, out out out' for eleven years and not be delighted when Maggie is finally out? That would be the most extreme version of that trick spoilt kids play, when they moan and whinge for a chocolate ice cream, then when it comes, say they don't want it. Ha ha.

A few days later John Major was Prime Minister. His job, I had no doubt, was to tidy up after her to leave everything ready for a Labour government. Major was, he said, grateful for all the marvellous work she had done. Though privately, he admitted later, he thought that in her last years as Prime Minister she had been suffering from a split personality. That's really bad luck isn't it? To have two personalities and for them both to be rancid old bags.

Chapter 18

The danger in reaching thirty isn't in becoming more right-wing, but in becoming sensible. It creeps up on you, sensibleness. And it happens in a series of justifiable stages. It really *does* make sense to take advantage of the easy credit option and get a posh settee, rather than a cheap one that will need replacing in a few years. Then, as you don't want the thing scratched, it makes sense to tell everyone to take their shoes off if they go near it. Until if anyone walks past it with a glass of red wine, you shriek as if they were carrying a capsule of deadly anthrax. Though even if they *were* carrying anthrax, the sensible person would think, 'I know it can wipe out Guildford, but what sort of stain does it leave on leather?'

It really *does* make sense to keep the house organized. But with each step of planning, you move nearer to giving visitors guided tours of the house, which go, 'This cupboard is for chutneys, and this one for marmalade, jams and affiliated spreads. There's a jar here with "flour" written on the front for flour, so we don't mistake it for a bag of onions. And in this room all the furniture is in alphabetical order so we know where everything is.'

The menace of sensible is that it's incompatible with passion. I bet Che Guevara never had all his Christmas cards sent out by the middle of November. At thirty, you find friends heading in this direction and it's distressing. They're doing things like buying cans of beer and leaving them in the fridge for a week! Next they're saying 'we're hoping to go to the Lake District next summer' and you're remembering when you set fire to a litter bin in the high street together for no reason at all. Here is your mate who battled alongside you to scramble to the front of a Damned gig, saying 'I met this copper last night, he was a really nice bloke'.

Maybe this is one of the reasons why the friends you make in your mid-twenties seem to be the ones that stick with you for life. The friends you make earlier on have still got major personality changes to go through. But sensibleness is a bit like baldness; if there are no signs of it by the time you're twenty-eight, you're probably safe. This isn't to say you don't change. When I was eighteen, if I disagreed with someone, I would probably snarl 'that's bollocks that is mate'. But at thirty, having mellowed, I was more likely to say calmly 'that's bollocks, if you don't mind me saying'.

One of the difficulties is that at eighteen, the whole adult world can appear as the enemy. Conversely the adult world excuses teenage radicalism as youthful exuberance. I knew a teenage vegetarian civil servant who went home for Christmas dinner and, as the family was cooing at the turkey on the table, he picked it up and threw it out of the window. I'm sure everyone was distressed, but not as much as if the civil servant had been thirty. By thirty it's apparent that you have to get on with other adults, as you work alongside them, socialize with them and marry them. In my case I was also supposed to make them laugh. It's not that the teenage radical becomes a thirty-year-old conservative, but the active radicalism can give way to the safer practice of just thinking radical thoughts. The worry is not that if you went round with a collection sheet or petition, the others would think you were wrong. The worry is they would think you were weird.

A common trick is to pretend you've stuck up for your point of view, when in fact you haven't challenged the person you were talking to at all. After the rent strike I visited one of the other flats in my block, to find the tenants' dad was there. He'd been in the RAF at the time of the Suez crisis, and we got into a discussion about the affair. I said the outcome was a symbol of Britain's declining position in the world and he agreed. He said Nasser wasn't a Marxist as the British claimed, and I agreed with that. We talked about planes and America and Israel and canals, and we both agreed, for about an hour. A few days later my friend said that as soon as I'd left, his dad had said, 'Well that was a funny conversation. All the way through, he wanted to say "we should never have been there", and I wanted to say "we should have bombed the bastards".'

In some ways I missed the naked rage I'd felt at eighteen, but there are advantages to being a thirty-year-old agitator. One of the most alarming benefits was that people were more likely to take me seriously. Instead of dismissed as 'young man', adults would sometimes ask what I thought they should do. It was tempting to say, 'How the hell should I know? You're supposed to tell me not to be so ridiculous.'

The pressure to conform was also easing, as the flow of Conservative dominance waned. But in the summer of 1990, Saddam Hussein's army rolled into Kuwait and renamed it the 'nineteenth province of Iraq'. US President George Bush assembled an international coalition to drive him out, and Britain gave the most enthusiastic backing. Governments dusted off the old arguments about war; only the names were changed. Saddam was a tyrant. Which he was, but armed by the same governments now threatening him. Saddam gassed the Kurds. Which he did, but the man who vetoed the UN resolution condemning this was George Bush. Saddam was undemocratic. Which he was, but Kuwait was ruled by the Al-Sabbah family, who held all twenty-two of the main government posts. So *Election Night Special* in Kuwait was hardly worth staying up for. And the main ally of the US in the region was Saudi Arabia, ruled by King Fahd whose method of elections was one man, one vote – his.

Another trend I recognized from the days of the Falklands was for everyone to become military experts, this time with elaborate reasons for why the war either would or wouldn't take place. And everyone referred to Saddam's 'elite Republican Guard', as if 'elite' was part of the name, like 'Athletic' in Charlton Athletic. Just before Christmas, Bush set a deadline for Saddam to withdraw from Kuwait, his response being to promise the 'mother of all battles'. This was destined to enter popular vocabulary, especially in places like the playgrounds of Swanley – 'you looking for the mother of all smacks in the 'ead or what'.

As in the days before the Falklands War, the tension mounted, but more so. Back then no one expected the war to escalate beyond the two countries involved, but this could go anywhere. Serious programmes and articles predicted years of conflict and environmental armageddon. We got over 100 people to a local anti-war meeting, which wasn't bad, but probably some way short of what was required to stop armageddon. Nonetheless, this level of opposition was different from the Falklands, and 100,000 demonstrated against the war on the weekend before the deadline.

That week I visited the local mosque to ask permission from the imam to distribute leaflets at the Friday prayers. He listened intently while I put my case and invited me inside, as long as I removed my shoes and socks. 'Peace be with you,' he said, and he explained the format of prayers, pointed out the separate balcony where women pray, and showed me where he was hoping to get some plastering work done in the summer. Then I was taken to an elder, who sat serenely amidst his black robe and straggly beard, slowly nodding and muttering the odd word in Arabic, looking exactly as an elder is supposed to look. It would have been so disappointing if he'd been in a t-shirt, with a pot belly and watching *Brookside*. This was all making me feel extremely humble, especially when the imam turned to me and said 'the elder says you will remain in his prayers as a brother of peace'.

That Friday a group of us arrived at the mosque with our leaflets and petitions. The scene outside a London mosque in the moments before Friday prayers feels as if it should be the start of an epic movie. As they arrive in robes, veils, suits and smart casual-wear from Gap, you're aware that the presence of every one of them is the culmination of a fascinating story. Wars, economic crises, exchange rates, interest rates, wealthy uncles, appeals for doctors, and cyclones have driven this elderly man, that veiled woman and that teenager with an earring, from Kabul, Karachi or Istanbul to Thornton Heath on a Friday afternoon. Like watching employees arrive for work, the keen ones are early, but with a minute to go, a handful of youthful muslims are sprinting the last 100 yards, untangling Sony Walkmans from their ears, to scamper home just in time.

We waited with clipboards and petitions, until the first person emerged. I got into position to obstruct his passage in classic petitioner's fashion, but he appeared to be looking for us. Dozens more poured from the mosque doors, marching across to the three of us and signing their names. The leaflet, someone told us, had been translated and read out in the prayers, with a recommendation that everyone should add their names. Queues of muslims lined up to sign our flimsy petition opposing the probable war, until we'd used up every space, front and back. So we found some scraps of paper in various pockets and filled them up with names, until my last two signatures were written on the back of the shiny bit from the inside of a fag packet. The task was made harder, but more memorable, by the eagerness of so many to discuss the war. What did we think of Israel? Could the United Nations be trusted? Why weren't the Labour Party opposing it? How can Arab leaders be supporting America, instead of backing their Arab brothers? As the debates crackled with passion on the pavement, I wondered when the last time such a scene had taken place after a Church of England service at somewhere like 'St Georges on the Meadows'. Or when a vicar last translated an Arabic leaflet into English and read it out during the harvest festival.

Despite this, on 15 January 1991, the television screens exploded with excitement. Journalists' hotels shook to the rumbling of nearby explosions, trails of surface-to-air missiles flickered in arcs across the night sky, and it was all LIVE, through the night, as it happens, right here after the break. Expert after military expert peered at us from the screen explaining the dazzling technology of the weaponry being hoisted on Baghdad and Basra. The marvellous and astounding news was there were no reports of casualties at all. Diagrams, grainy film and more experts helped to explain the ingenuity of the precision bombing. Cruise missiles were hurtling down streets and turning corners, heading across squares and piling into the exact window necessary to inflict the maximum damage. It made me wonder why we hadn't been using the things for years as taxis. Saddam's palace was a victim, ho ho ho, and I thought they were going to tell us the precision bomb had flown across his mantelpiece and broken all his favourite ornaments. Every day we were treated to a film demonstration of such accuracy at work, fronted by Commander-in-Chief Stormin' Norman Schwarzkopf. He was the bear of a man who, if he hadn't led the military, would have to have been a wrestler. He announced the destruction of a city with a cuddly smile that you feared would get cuddlier if only he was permitted to detail the charred humanity resulting from each hit. As the war went on, it slipped out that only 70 per cent of these weapons hit their target. This figure was reduced to 60 per cent, and some years later they admitted it was 25 per cent. A more honest version of the daily press conference would have begun with a cube-faced general barking, 'We can confirm that our missions today were once again an outstanding example of precision bombing, in that all our weapons aimed at Iraq landed on Iraq. Just one went astray and hit Belgium.'

It felt as if we were at the start of the most dramatic global event of my lifetime. What if Israel couldn't be kept out of the war? Would America use nuclear weapons? And in front of us, even now, the glittering sky and spectacular flashes creating instant dramatic silhouettes of the Baghdad skyline, were providing this optical feast at the expense of unimaginable screams of pain and anguish. Who could tell what torture was being inflicted, how many desperate women were running hysterically down the streets in response to finding the scorched remains of their family? 'Now I'm joined by Paddy Ashdown,' said the man on the television.

There are many reasons for organizing anti-war movements at times like this, but as I got to bed, one reason struck me that I recalled from the Falklands War; the preservation of your own sanity. The following night the Iraqis fired a Scud at Israel, and the politicians and media were apoplectic. For all their military expertise, they seemed to be unaware of the likelihood in a war that at some point your opponent will fire back. Suddenly the Americans announced their surprise weapon the Patriot missile, capable of immobilizing the evil Scud in mid-air. The whole thing was being conducted by someone obsessed with comics. It looked as if they would announce that Saddam had said, 'Ha ha ha, you poor deluded fools, now I have my faithful Scuds, nothing can stop my deliciously evil plan to rule the earth.'

The propaganda became more and more ridiculous. One day the main item on every broadcast was about the discovery of an oil slick, which could only have been deliberately caused by Saddam out of pure evil. The more likely explanation, that an Iraqi oil tanker had been bombed, was not even suggested. No, the only plausible theory is that Saddam is so crazy, his military strategy is to pour oil in random places. The bloke was probably running up and down hillsides emptying tins of Castrol right that minute. The next day the coalition announced, and the media lapped it up, that out of care and concern for the environment, the Americans had sent down precision bombs that had somehow stopped the oil slick from spreading. It really wouldn't have surprised me if they'd announced that another bomb had scooped up the oil, poured it into a barrel, rolled it down the hill and poured exactly the right amount into an American general's Land-Rover.

Then three American airmen were taken hostage after being shot down. New levels of outrage were reached as the airmen appeared on Iraqi television, 'clearly scratched and bruised', proving they'd been beaten. Not once was it suggested there might be an alternative explanation for the scratches, that the airmen had been shot down from 30,000 feet. If someone told you they'd just been shot down from 30,000 feet, would you say to them, 'Oh have you? Here, where did you get those scratches and bruises? Have you been in some sort of fight?'

And each night Peter Snow clambered around in a sandpit, surrounded by toy helicopters like a spoilt child, adding to the impression that the whole episode was an elaborate computer game. Even when people were killed, they were collateral damage. Until with immaculate precision they sent a cruise missile through the roof of a bomb shelter. Suddenly there were the pictures of the human end to this digital extravaganza. Women in black were howling uncontrollably, their arms flailing above them, as nearby officials stepped carefully around the scattered corpses. Young men clamoured across each other to shout their story into any available camera. You could only guess what they were saying, but it was probably 'show this to the world. This is what the bombing has done'. I remembered my incredulity at those policemen snapping the placards outside David Owen's office, and could see the same desperate urge to tell everyone, multiplied more millions of times than could be measured. Five hundred people perished in that shelter, who in all probability despised Saddam, and unlike George Bush and his allies, always had done. Five hundred people who had no say in the status of Kuwait, not least because many of them were young children. And how did those responsible react?

At first they blamed Saddam for fooling the Americans into thinking the shelter was a military target, to create a propaganda coup. They soon dropped this and switched to simply blaming him for bringing this action on his own people. But whatever line they came out with, one thing was certain – they didn't care. They looked at this unimaginable suffering and misery, and their only thought was how best to sustain the approval ratings of support for their action. Now I felt that rage of the eighteen-year-old again. Here was that old sensation, that burning in the stomach that seems to contract your whole body and tighten your face, and frighten yourself that you could batter those responsible in a fearful unrestrainable frenzy.

The seven weeks of the Gulf War was possibly the most political time I have ever known. The poll tax campaign was rebellious but this raised every issue about who does and who should control the world. We said they tip food in the sea, to keep the price up, without a thought for the starving whose lives could be saved. We said they spent more money each day on arms than would be needed to provide medicine throughout Africa for a year. But here was visible daily proof of what they were like.

   The neighbours wanted to talk about it. The bloke who served me in the building society talked to me about it and joined the anti-war campaign. I was a guest on *Kilroy* to argue about it with Rick Wakeman. He felt that entertainers shouldn't get involved in anti-war campaigns. I was so proud that I'd thought he was crap even when I was fourteen.

   A majority supported the war, but this disguised two facts. The one-third of society who opposed it were doing so despite round-the-clock propaganda, which forced them to question every aspect of the way the world was presented. And most of those who backed the war were keen to listen to and accept many anti-war arguments. There was a distinct and welcome lack of militaristic dustmen, excitable engineers and singing patriotic transsexuals. The most infuriating types, after the generals and politicians themselves, were the middle-class liberal bombers, with their pacifist reasons for supporting the slaughter. 'Oh I couldn't put my name to that,' said one prominent feminist when I asked her to support an anti-war event, 'as I have such trouble with the way muslims treat their women.' Whereas the West was treating muslim women with more respect, allowing them to be incinerated in any outfit they like.

After seven weeks of intense bombing, the elite Republican Guard were a pushover, decimated in under a week of land war. As a goodbye wave, the Americans carpet bombed the road to Basra, killing between 10,000 and 50,000 conscripted soldiers. I had organized a launch meeting for 'Comedians Against the War'. But the day before the meeting the war ended. I had to fight the temptation to think 'oh couldn't it have gone on for just another few days, I was reckoning on getting about a hundred people to that'.

In the north of Iraq thousands of Kurds were driven into the mountains by Saddam's army as he reasserted his control in that area. But whereas the bombing raids had taken place at the rate of one a minute, the flights to help the Kurds came at ten a week. The coalition couldn't be expected to target the food and blankets required to save these people, they claimed. But days earlier they'd been boasting they could send missiles through any window they liked. From the way they'd been bragging, you would have thought they could not only provide food, but send down plates, meat, two veg, a knife and fork in the correct setting and a slice of lemon on the side.

I was thirty, and the world hadn't shaped up in the way I'd hoped when I embarked on this project as a teenager. At that time, thirty was a misty distant star. I knew people got to thirty, but it couldn't happen to me. And if I ever did arrive at the end of that enormous expanse of time, surely we'd be well on the way to redesigning the world by then. In the sense that I'd hoped by now to be living in a world free of wars and famine, there was no doubt the political project I'd set myself had been a failure. By the time Trotsky and James Connolly were thirty, they'd led general strikes, been arrested, exiled, escaped and become feared by the rulers of empires. I'd sneaked a couple of steelworkers on to a settee. But whatever the account so far, I was relieved not to have taken the other route and become sensible.

Because the sensible disease can work in the same way with ideas as it does with lifestyles. It's not realistic to aim to overturn the basis on which the system works. It's sensible to be practical and aim simply to get a kinder government elected. But in order to get elected, you have to be sensible and check the opinion polls before making statements about gays or immigration. Once you are elected, you have to make a few cuts in services, to balance the budget. Otherwise the other lot will come back and they'll be worse. Eventually arms can be sold to dictators and crooked millionaires defended, reluctantly of course, because what else can you do but be sensible? So that bit by bit, people who were once driven by outrage against injustice, spend their whole lives justifying the injustices they're carrying out. From Neil Kinnock down, sensible politicians had watched the gasping, wailing women pounding the ground in despair alongside the ashes of their families in that bomb shelter, seen the grisly pictures of the roasted conscripts in their trucks on the Basra road, and thought, 'How should I react to this if I want to secure the floating voter?'. As you get to thirty, the main thing is to not be sensible.

Chapter 19

Many Labour supporters reacted to the Tory years by assuming the population had gone rotten. A common phrase was 'there's no point in trying to change things in my area, they're all Tories'. If only the other side had been as defeatist in Labour areas and said 'there's no point in trying to privatize the buses round here, they're all socialists'.

Despite parading as a victor after the war, Major couldn't get ahead in the polls in order to call an election. He had an advantage due to the peculiar British system that allows the government to call it whenever it likes. Which makes it like a football team that's allowed to decide when their matches end, so if they're behind after ninety minutes they can say 'we're carrying on, until we get in front'. Although Major had to announce it before the summer of 1992 so, I assumed, we'd be rid of him by then.

It wasn't just the polls that signalled the end of the Tory era. The poll tax was scrapped when Major announced it was 'impossible to collect' as 14 million people were not paying. Even then, some Labour supporters said it was always destined to fail, as it was ill thought out and 'upset the middle classes'. Although a year earlier the same people had said there was nothing anyone could do about the poll tax, as they're all Tories round here.

More impressively still, Nelson Mandela had been released. The apartheid regime's reasons were complex, but anyone who had participated in the protests, meetings and marches, boycotted South African grapes or Barclays bank, backed the ban on cricketers and singers, or supported the movement in South Africa itself, had contributed to apartheid's surrender. Their side had tanks and oil and diamond mines and Margaret Thatcher, and we had a few placards and a song by the Specials, but eventually we got our way.

There was a series of inspiring fundraising benefits for the Birmingham Six. Women like Breda Power, niece of Billy who was one of the six, were so poignant, not because they broke down in tears but because they didn't. At one point they had been expecting to lead the normal life of a working-class Irish family living in Britain. Then they were forced to become full-time activists, speaking in theatres to hundreds of people and debating on Channel 4 news with spokesmen from the Home Office. They were ordinary people, made extraordinary by events. Then suddenly the six were released. There was Paddy Hill, whose bemused features had stared at me from a thousand t-shirts, in the flesh venting seventeen years of anger into any available microphone outside the High Court. We had learned their names but it was hard to attach them to the real characters holding each other's arms aloft. That night I went to a party at the Irish Centre and there they were. There was Billy Power, and we had a brief conversation about the Gulf War. Not only was he out of jail, but he was lucid, intelligent and charming. 'This,' I slurred to the organizers of the campaign as I rocked in all directions with a bottle, 'is a feeling we shall have to get used to. We're going to start winning.'

The next major event was the failed attempted coup in Russia, which led to the collapse of the Soviet Union and the triumph of Boris Yeltsin. What brought home to me how fast the world was changing, was when just after that at Brixton underground station I realized the escalator was still broken. It had first gone out of action in September 1989. As I clambered up the stairs behind old women dragging their shopping trolleys, a thought occurred to me: it had taken longer to fix this escalator than it took to bring down the Berlin Wall, dump Thatcher, incinerate Iraq, release Nelson Mandela, free the Birmingham Six, finish Soviet communism and for David Icke to believe he was the turquoise son of God.

And now there was another world recession. The boom built on credit had gone bust, leaving millions in unsustainable debt. So here we were again. Thirty people applying for every bar job, mini-cab firms overflowing with desperate drivers, burger bars staffed by university graduates. But each recession, like each ice age, has its own special feature, leaving a distinctive trail of destruction. This time, among the usual casualties were middle managers, salesmen, accountants and bank clerks. My mum rang to tell me 'you know Michael the bank manager, he's been made redundant'.

And this time the victims of the slump weren't just losing their jobs but their houses as well. Repossessions ran at record levels and the phrase of the age was negative equity. With no job security, no one was buying property, so values plummeted below the price paid in the first place.

But at least we'd soon be rid of the Tories. I started counting the months. It was almost like waiting for an operation that would cure some dreadful affliction I'd had for thirteen years, although I didn't know the exact date of the surgery. February came, then March until there was all the excitement of the Prime Minister going to the Queen and it was set for 9 April. All the polls put Labour ahead. No Tory posters went up anywhere. The last four years had involved one crisis after another for the Tories. The Health Service, the ambulance dispute, the poll tax, ditching Thatcher, the miscarriages of justice. For long periods, they'd been 20 per cent behind in the polls. They'd lost unloseable by-elections, in places like mid-Stafford, where they were all Tories round there.

It didn't seem fair the Tories were even allowed to take part in the election after that. It was like a runner who'd come last in all of the heats still being allowed in the final. But the last four weeks couldn't wipe away the legacy of the previous five years. Which is why I didn't get as annoyed as I should have done about the Labour campaign. Their most baffling decision was not to mention the poll tax. It was like Kinnock's Westland speech all over again but lasting a month. All through the election, I wanted to scream, 'Bring out the poll tax, you idiots. Fourteen million people didn't pay it, even if you only get them, you've walked it.' It was like watching someone playing cards, when you know they've got ace, king and queen of the trump suit and instead they put down the four of diamonds. Perhaps they wanted to lose. Maybe, even if they were 30 per cent ahead with a day to go, Kinnock would say 'and one more thing, if we win I'm going to kick everyone in the crotch'.

And how could they let the Tories walk over them with this tax stuff? 'Labour's Double Whammy', said the posters. Why didn't Labour say, 'That's right, the top 1 per cent who pay 70 per cent less tax than they did before are getting a double whammy to repair the damage done to the Health Service.'? Instead they said nothing and Heseltine walked all over them. You could almost hear the Labour front bench, getting to the TV studios and whining, 'Oh dear, it's Heseltine. I don't want to go on against him, can't you do it, I'm feeling a bit queasy.' Labour said it was going to spend £600 million extra on education. Which, when you work it out, is roughly a curry each. But they couldn't defend it. There would be Heseltine, 'Where's it going to come from, this 600 million? Tax tax tax tax tax.' And the Labour spokesman would look apologetic, as if he was about to say, 'Oo I'm sorry Mr Heseltine, I hadn't thought of it like that, maybe we'll phase it in over a hundred years a farthing at a time.' And I'd be thinking how I would love to be on the programme. Because when Heseltine asked where the money was coming from, I'd say, 'From you, that's where. You're worth 60 million on your own, we only have to find nine of your mates and we've cracked it.'

There was a Labour broadcast called 'Jennifer's ear'. It was a moving story about a girl with 'glue ear' who hadn't been able to have the simple operation needed to restore her hearing. But the Tories attacked them for exploiting the girl's suffering and Labour went on the defensive again. Why didn't they say, 'Look, everyone knows someone who's had operations delayed and delayed like that. Except for you because you all use private hospitals.'? But they were desperate not to upset the middle ground they'd been chasing all these years. They believed, it seemed, they were all Tories round here, and daren't utter a word that might inspire the millions who could sweep them into office.

Despite all that, they were sure to win. They had to win. What did Major look like stood on his box in market places? Who would be fooled by the image on that broadcast of a simple boy returning to his humble roots? I performed at an election comedy night, in the Royal Court theatre in Sloane Square a few days before polling day, and performers and audience were buzzing with anticipation. A comedian I'd never met before, grabbed me by the shoulders. 'They're on the way out Mark, aren't they,' he said, wearing a beaming emotional smile as if he was greeting a long lost relative at an airport. 'They are,' I told him, and he laughed maniacally, like an evil emperor in a kid's cartoon, as if my reassurance was the confirmation he was looking for. Each morning my first thought was 'four days to go', 'three days to go' and so on, before scurrying through every newspaper for the latest opinion polls.

But a sober analysis would have conceded that Labour weren't ahead by much. And though there were no Tory posters, on the council estates there were no Labour ones either. And there was one nagging fact that wouldn't go away. Shortly before the election was announced, there had been a council by-election on my estate. The Tory vote fell from 1,100 to 900. But the Labour vote fell from 1,300 to 700. The drilling man's wife had voted for the Liberals and was going to do the same in the general election. She was baffled at how, after the abuse we'd taken from the Labour council, I could even consider voting Labour.

Over the final two days the press hurtled into a frenzy of vitriol about the destitution we'd be reduced to under Labour. They would ruin our schools, take all our money, give back the Falklands and put Tony Benn in charge of everything. It was like being in a family that hated the person you were preparing to marry, and in every room you entered there was someone screaming 'don't do it, you idiot, they will destroy you'. The *London Evening Standard* printed an eight-page election feature, packed with information on how miserable your life would become if Labour won. And instead of coming out fighting, Labour just sat back and trembled. Except for a rally in Sheffield, in which Kinnock, apparently overwhelmed, walked out in front of the crowd and screamed 'yes yes yes' as if he was auditioning for a porn film.

The rage from the press confirmed why it mattered so much that Labour won. They may have been sycophantic fools, led by a man who exuded a unique cocktail of arrogance and incompetence. Parliament may not have been the body that really decided who worked, who was sacked, who bought extra homes and who had none. But where Labour bowed before the millionaires, the Tories *were* the millionaires. The *Sun* was owned by Rupert Murdoch, so of course it would advise that if Kinnock got in, would the last one to leave turn out the lights.

Conversely, the more desperately someone wanted a fairer society, the more anxious they were that Labour should win. Despite Labour's best efforts to appear otherwise, in most minds

Labour stood for reversing the growing inequality, and the Tories stood for extending it. Which is why many of the people who had said the election would be of no interest became the most enthusiastic about the great day coming. How could anyone who had shouted 'Tories out' over the last thirteen years, even if it was at the telly, not be planning every second of the joyous night which would put the Tories out. One poll even put Labour 8 per cent ahead, though most had them between 2 and 4 per cent in front. On the day before the election, I met a comedy colleague known for his cynicism. He was awash with enthusiasm for the election, wearing a heartening glow that made him almost unrecognizable, as if he'd grown a beard. As I was leaving, he said cheerfully, 'I met the election agent for Battersea today, and he's fairly confident he'll retain his seat.'

What did that mean? That played on my mind all evening. They had to win dozens of Tory seats, so there shouldn't be the slightest doubt about keeping those they already held. It occurred to me that my assumption Labour would win was devoid of all science. I had nothing to support my view that Labour would win except 'of course Labour will win. After all that's happened, they must do'. But why must they? That night in Croydon Labour Club, a Labour canvasser told me he'd been getting a frosty reception all day from people he expected to be solid Labour voters. A chill ran through me. I felt like a TV detective who suddenly realizes the guy he's convicted is innocent. As I left the Labour Club that night, the barmaid said, 'See you tomorrow then Mark, I've ordered a whole crate of champagne.'

The day arrived, 9 April 1992. The Tories had suffered one chaotic trauma after another. They'd been in for 13 years, just like in 1964 when they were beaten. And it was a glorious sparky spring day. But when I studied the facts instead of the omens I went cold. Here was the day I'd been longing for, counting the days towards, and I was hating it. I felt I must know how a woman feels who's spent her whole life looking forward to her wedding day, then on the day realizes she doesn't like the bloke she's about to marry. I kept telling myself I was paranoid and that, oh I'm sure it will be all right.

At the Labour Club, the *Daily Mirror* election chart was on the wall. A scrum of people crowded around it, studying the details with great care and a pencil behind the ear, making the place seem like a late-night bookies. The bar was frenetic, the mood optimistic and only slightly uneasy, as if we were about to watch a horserace involving twelve dud horses and our champion sprinter. Almost unnoticed, the exit poll results were announced: the Tories ahead by 4 per cent. More people flowed in from the street. 'Wooo hooo' shouted a crowd arriving with plates of sandwiches. There were shouts to those squashed at the bar, waving fivers and tenners above their heads, to 'make that *five* pints please'. Each new contingent was cheerfully welcomed as they arrived. But a growing concern was spreading outwards from those paying close attention to the BBC. 'How are you doing Mark, I haven't seen you for ages,' said a civil servant I hadn't seen for seven years. 'I've got two kids now,' he told me. 'Labour are going to lose,' I said.

Rapidly the anxiety spread around the room. Over a five-minute period, the banter withered. The exuberant cackle, punctuated by bursts of laughter from odd corners, and strangely identifiable shrieks that can be attributed to someone you know amidst the burble of 200 people, gently subsided. Now, every action was dominated by confusion. Instead of forthright demands for 'four bitters and two lagers please, Wendy love', was 'oh, er, two of those and, I don't know, a bitter I think'. The cackle became a rumble of murmurs. Every couple of minutes, the group nearest the television screen waved their arms and emitted an angry 'shhhh'. The experts were predicting a hung parliament. Labour leaders were calling it a massive rejection of the government. What did it all mean? Occasionally the door would swing open and a bunch of new-comers bound in, joyfully taking off their coats and each insisting they bought the first round, before picking up on the sense that something was going horribly wrong.

Then the first results came in. There was more confusion. Would Major have to resign? Would he form a coalition? Everyone had their theory – until Basildon. Labour had to win Basildon and lost. There was no one moment when everyone gasped. Everyone had their own personal instant when they said to themselves 'we've lost again'. As more people went through this barrier, the room descended from confusion to despair. The chatter was subdued, the occasional ironic laugh burst through the gloom and made everyone gloomier. Then the crying started. A woman who appeared to be the same age as me sat on a ledge and unashamedly sobbed into the curtains. Someone dropped and smashed a glass. The woman next to him snarled that this was typical of him, the idiot. 'All right, it was a fucking accident,' he snapped back. If it hadn't been for Basildon, that smashed glass would have been greeted with a chorus of 'wahoooo' while the culprit went to the bar to fetch a dustpan and brush and replace the drink.

The Socialist Worker contingent gathered together and devised a strategy for the rest of the night. We should emphasise to everyone else, we decided, that the tide which had swept the Tories into their crises of recent years wouldn't be reversed by this one night. Formally, it was faultless. Realistically, it was bollocks. We might as well have wandered around a crowd at an airport, which had just been informed the plane with their families on board had careered into a mountain, and told them to pick themselves up as they were bound to get a new family after a while. The room thinned out steadily. I asked the civil servant what his kids were called. Ivor Crewe was still rolling out the details, and as each result was declared a handful of obsessives studied the beer-stained *Daily Mirror* chart, as if there was a chance we might discover that everyone had added it up wrong and Labour had won after all.

Then, suddenly, a local twist. Flashed on the screen, unnoticed while John Prescott huffed and Norman Fowler beamed – 'Croydon North – Labour gain'. In an instant the room was transformed from collective despondency to unrestrained ecstasy. People were jumping, literally jumping with both feet as if they were circuit training. A man I'd never met before jumped five or six times next to me until, out of breath, he grabbed me like a wrestler. There was a tear on his cheek. 'Every moment of the last four weeks I've been working for this,' he blustered. Then he hugged me so tight that I coughed. Why had this man worked so hard? Not for himself, not for any gain in his own life, not for money or status or ego, but because he wanted a more equal, more just world. Whether Kinnock would have brought us one, we will never know.

But for a moment his efforts were rewarded. At least Labour gained Croydon North.

As everyone remembered the big picture the room thinned out further, leaving around sixty of us poring masochistically over the rotten bones of the night, carrying on drinking with no chance of getting drunk. Without any doubt it was one of the most awful experiences of my life. It was obvious the same scene was being acted out all over Britain. The most active, selfless campaigners, who had faced the wrath and scorn of their contemporaries through the Thatcher years, were once more utterly, cruelly rejected. Never has so much champagne remained as woefully unopened as that night.

But one factor was overlooked, and has remained overlooked ever since. The only places in which Labour increased their vote by an amount which, if it had been reflected everywhere, would have won them the election, was where the candidates were known as left-wing. The swing to Labour in Jeremy Corbyn's constituency was double the average. The same was true of Tony Benn and Bernie Grant. In Coventry, Dave Nellist stood as a Militant candidate against Labour and got almost as many votes as the winner. This wasn't necessarily because they were left-wing. But it was because they offered a distinct alternative to voters, could raise the memories of the ambulance dispute and poll tax, and motivate their followers to campaign.

But defeat never takes people to the left. The dominant conclusion is always that we were asking too much. All the statistics, all the evidence, all the subsequent reports that showed the main reason why people didn't vote Labour was they didn't believe the promises, were all ignored for the convenient theory that 'we were still too left-wing'.

As I was driven home that night, I was overwhelmed by another thought. Did the side I supported always have to lose? Couldn't I just once know what it was like to celebrate a victory? Never mind the politics, this just wasn't fair.

What did happen to all those people who supported the marches for the Health Service, the four and a half million who signed the ambulance workers' petition and millions who backed the poll tax protests? You didn't find anyone saying that, on reflection, the poll tax was a good idea and the ambulance crews *were* glorified taxi drivers. Elections measure votes cast but not the manner in which they're cast. At the last three elections, a layer of the population had marched into the polling booth and marked a sturdy X by the Tory name. This time, they had sauntered in, sighed and thought 'oh well, Tory I suppose'.

Which is why no one put up posters, or wore badges, or crowed in workplaces or pubs that they were voting for the Tories. Of those who admitted to it, most lied about the reasons, like sportsmen who went to apartheid South Africa declaring 'we'll be building bridges through sport' and never 'wahey, with all this cash I can buy a stinking great boat'. Similarly Tory voters mumbled about the Tories being best for economic growth and so on, but never 'I reckon I'll save two quid a week in tax which will pay for a new lawnmower, so bollocks to the Health Service because I'm not ill'. This explained the discrepancy between the polls and the result. A percentage of Tory voters were ashamed of what they were doing and daren't admit it, not even to the pollster, nor probably to themselves.

This made the Tory victory extremely fragile. The *Sun* said that John Major was master of all he surveyed. The *Financial Times*, asked 'How does it feel to be waking up in a one-party state?' But they were wrong. I'd been hopelessly pathetically wrong in my instincts about the election result but I was certain I hadn't been wrong about the tide turning against the values of the free market. For the whole weekend, amidst unmitigated gloom I told people to perk up, that it wasn't the end, that the Tories would soon be back in trouble. I must have appeared like an irritating court jester, dancing and jangling across a sea of corpses on a medieval battlefield.

On the Sunday night, I went to see my friend who lived upstairs, who hadn't been out of the house all weekend, unable to face the newly re-elected Tory world. I gave him my prognosis and wondered whether I'd offered him some solace. It wasn't as bad as all that, it really wasn't. I got downstairs, slumped on to my bed and wept.

Four days after the election, I saw the cynical comedian. 'Have you heard the good news?' he said, 'Labour are 3 per cent ahead in the polls.'

Chapter 20

It was a miserable few months. Jimmy White played Stephen Hendry in the Embassy World Snooker final. All decent people wanted Jimmy to win. He was a lad, one of us, and took outrageous gambles. Hendry was the nineties Tory, not an expression out of place, sensible and, like Major, had recently taken over from the other Tory who had dominated the eighties, Steve Davis. Jimmy went 14–8 ahead, needing four more frames to win. Surely he couldn't lose from here. Then Hendry won the next seven to go 15–14 ahead, and it was uncannily reminiscent of election night, right down to it being Jimmy's fourth successive defeat in the final. As another moment of triumph unbelievably slid away, I rang the cynical comedian, who I knew would be transfixed in the same despair. Hendry sank a black to ensure another frame, and we agreed 'that black was Basildon'. When Hendry won, I had to go out for a long walk alone. I was accustomed to the ruling class getting almost everything their own way, but surely they could let us win the fucking snooker.

Most Labour supporters blamed the Tory victory on 'people', for being stupid, or too well off, or Southern. Over the next year, whenever I went to a Northern town for a gig, someone would tell me it was the fault of us posh bastards in the South, for all being middle class down there. I usually replied that if there were no working-class people in the South, who did we get to fix the drains? If they were overflowing, did we say 'my goodness, what a pong. I'd better ring a Northerner'.

A more sophisticated argument was that despite the compromises, Labour were still rooted in the traditions of a disappearing working class. Old Labour values could appeal to blokes who poured out of factory gates but not to the aspiring business sharks we'd all become. The modern young person, said Peter Mandelson, was more ambitious than their grandparents. As if our grandparents endured the slump, the means test and whooping cough because they were happy like that, and never set their sights on a cappuccino machine.

From a Marxist point of view, class originated in neolithic times, when one group was first able to seize the surplus that had hitherto not existed. Had it really travelled through Ancient Greece, the Byzantine Empire, the middle ages, the industrial revolution, global industrialization, but been wiped out on 9 April 1992? In Croydon Labour Club, the pictures of Kinnock were removed and replaced with a huge photo of the safe pension-plan salesman features of new leader John Smith. The same week, all the pictures of local May Day marches and delegations to the miners' strike were taken from the walls.

Then the army of academics pushing this theory must have heard an irritating buzz, like that of the distant but audible fly that prevents you from getting to sleep. It started on a Wednesday: Black Wednesday. Usually, days that become known in history as 'black' involve pillage, siege and massacre. Which may confuse the historians of the future, who trawl through the accounts of Black Wednesday searching for a slaughter, or at least a military coup, finding instead the pound crashing out of the European exchange rate mechanism. Chancellor Norman Lamont threw £10 billion at the money markets and threatened to double interest rates to rescue it, eventually giving up in humiliation.

A few weeks later Michael Heseltine announced the closure of almost the entire British mining industry, proving Scargill's predictions at the time of the strike to be an *under*estimate. The next day a national tide of outrage grew, making it almost impossible to sound like an extremist. A Socialist Worker member contacted me, and suggested we visited local workplaces, putting the case for a general strike. General strike? You can't suggest a general strike. Wouldn't we sound like these groups who call for a general strike over everything? If one of them had been involved in our protest over the burglaries, they'd have demanded the TUC called a general strike for stronger doors. Their strategy seemed the same as that of a child who goes on and on and on that she wants a lollipop, hoping the TUC eventually said 'all right, you can have a bloody general strike, as long as you promise to keep quiet'.

We printed a demand at the top for a general strike and to start with took it to a local bus garage. In the canteen, I approached a group of drivers, but two sentences through my pitch, one of them shouted, 'Haven't I seen you on the telly?'

'You might have done,' I said.

'I knew I'd seen him somewhere. You were on that thing on BBC1 a few months back. Or was it that one with wotsisname?'

'No, it was the one on BBC,' I said. 'Anyway, we can't let Heseltine get away with . . .'

'No it wasn't. It was whaddyacallit, *Saturday Night Live*. With that Stavros. That's where I've seen yer.'

Then another one started. 'Were you on with Stavros? Do you know him? What's he like?'

Then one of the drivers took the sheet and walked off with it. So I'd lost my copy of the letter, and if I couldn't convince a bus driver that I hadn't been on *Saturday Night Live*, persuading him to demand a general strike was a little ambitious. But a few moments later, the driver who'd taken the letter returned, having collected the signatures of all eighteen of the drivers who were in. 'I'll sign it,' said the bloke who'd seen me on the telly and so did the others.

And so did almost everyone else. On the Saturday, I helped with a stall in the shopping centre, surrounded by posters demanding 'General Strike Now', while a constant stream of shoppers came past to give their names and go on the following week's demonstration. The *Sun* had a front page that was completely blank, except for a heading 'This is what Michael Heseltine knows about industry'. *Socialist Worker*, with its headline 'General Strike Now', achieved its record ever sale.

The first demonstration, on the Wednesday, drew around 150,000, but it had a different feel to anything I'd seen for at least ten years. Each contingent was packed with delegations from the relevant workforce, behind the appropriate union banners. This, as the books and theses pronouncing the death of the working class were being bound and printed, was the organized working class on display.

And just to complete the 1970s feel, my mum was coming to

stay. She hadn't been since I first left home and now she was coming on the week that everyone agreed there should be a general strike. She wouldn't understand. Even if there was an actual general strike, she would say 'well I'm sure there'll be another one soon dear'. So the outcome was I was a complete bastard. I took her out for a meal, bolted the lot down in one gulp and dragged her back home because I'd arranged to meet a local train drivers' rep. The next evening, six people arrived for a meeting in the living room, which took place around my mum who was trying to watch *Emmerdale Farm*. On Sunday she stayed at home while I went to the second demonstration, which was bigger than the first and took place through swirling, torrential, unceasing rain. The adversity seemed to make everyone even more invigorated. But what next?

The local trade union movement called a meeting, to which Dennis Skinner was invited, to discuss the campaign to save the pits. Around 200 people were there, of which thirty were supporters of the general strike letter and we were confident the meeting would vote to support this. Dennis Skinner finished with the line 'the chance to win only comes along once or twice in a lifetime. One of those chances is now'.

The last official speaker finished. Then the secretary got up and announced the meeting closed, with no discussion permitted. Stewards from either side began shuffling people out of their seats. They would rather wreck the whole thing than discuss a proposal from Trotskyists. A teacher stood on a chair and appealed for people to stay. Now there was utter confusion. As the teacher climbed down, a trade union official, covered in official badges worn like medals on a Chelsea Pensioner, pushed her so she almost fell over. Then Ted the gas man bound in two leaps across several rows of seats and grabbed him. This was one of those moments, like the instant before you drive into the back of another car, in which time stopped. During the second in which he had this official by the throat, a full debate went back and forth in my head. If Ted thumped this bloke, we would lose all sympathy and probably be barred from the local movement forever. 'Leave him,' I said, as if I was separating a scrap outside a nightclub, and I should have added 'he's not worth it'.

By now dozens of people were screaming at each other, while

everyone else stared in amazement. They'd only come to support the miners and the room looked like a bar fight in a Western. It must have seemed as strange as going to a whist drive that ended up with the pensioners all nutting each other. 'Did you have a nice time?' asked my mum when I got indoors.

The official labour movement had travelled so far down the road of timidity that it sat and watched this chance to win evaporate. But the Tories, six months after John Major was master of the one-party state he surveyed, were 24 per cent behind in the polls and stayed there. In by-elections they lost seats like Newbury and Christchurch, their sixth safest in the country. The trend of growing contempt for Tory values, having been violently interrupted at the election, resumed. When I took two women from the Timex strike in Dundee to the Post Office union, the official summarized the Tories' dilemma. He said that in 1984, when people donated to miners' collections, it was as if they were supporting victims of a disaster in another country. But now, anyone on strike appeared as spokespeople for the same issues they were confronting themselves.

It was as if there was a collective 'sorry' from millions who'd voted Tory. And as the months went by, John Major and his government lurched between appearing vengeful and pathetic. He was despised when he broke his promise and put VAT on fuel and derided as an idiot for the Citizen's Charter. 'Back to Basics', the code on family life, reached its nadir when Tory MP Stephen Milligan was found dangling from a flex wearing suspenders with an orange in his mouth. The next day I was at a comedy club in Middlesborough, in which there was a competition for the best Stephen Milligan joke. Second place went to 'The man from Del Monte says "yes YES *YES*!"' But the winner, awarded to the joke that received the biggest cheer, was 'Ha ha, dead Tory.'

The divisions splintering the Conservatives made sense, if they were seen in the context of the low regard in which they were held. Neither side could restore Tory popularity, so they behaved like friends lost in the woods, bickering, blaming and plotting. The one point saving Major was the depth of his party's crisis. There was no point in his colleagues getting rid of him, as no one could save them and anyone new might bring the whole thing crashing down.

*

The creed of individualism, of nothing having a right to exist unless it made a profit, had attracted sufficient followers for Thatcher and Reagan to dominate the eighties. But too many of its adherents were on the wrong end of downsizing and repossessions, or knew others who were, for this to continue. As it became harder to sell naked greed, the selfish eighties gave way to the corporate-caring nineties. Products were marketed as environmentally friendly or kind to third world nations. The drug of the age was the be-nice-to-everyone potion ecstasy. Jerry Maguire yelled 'show me the money' but found happiness when he rediscovered love and friendship, and as a bonus made more money than ever.

Two of the most popular television programmes were *The Simpsons* and *The X-Files*, both based on a cynicism about authority and government that would never have been so successful in the Reagan/Thatcher years. Grunge, led by Nirvana, became the first angry trend in white music for ten years to achieve mass popularity. And when I first played 'Killing in the Name Of' by Rage Against the Machine, which ends with a booming 'fuck you, I won't do what you tell me', I was back in my bedroom with the Clash.

The royal family hurtled into crisis when Charles and Di parted amidst soap-opera acrimony, and I knew the police were in trouble when my mum talked about the way the West Midlands force kept 'fitting people up'.

I was more optimistic than at any time since those early days of activism in 1978. But back then I was prey to naive enthusiasm, whereas this time it was due to vast experience and thorough analysis. There was sure to be an explosion in society of general strike-size proportions, because for John Major to blunder from one crisis to another, just surviving for four whole years up to the next election, well, that just wasn't possible.

There *were* bursts of activity, most notably in response to a revival of the far right, sparked by the growth of Jean-Marie Le Pen's FN in France. An Afghan in his twenties, Ruhullah Aramesh, whose family had fled the war in their country to find refuge in Thornton Heath, was chased by a group with pipes from a building site and battered to death.

We wrote a letter deploring the murder and knocked on every

door in the area seeking signatures to add to it, which almost everybody agreed to do. If we could turn this feeling into a march of several hundred local people, it would help to marginalize local fascists, so we met Ruhullah's family to seek their approval. Three of us sat in their small tear-stained flat, above a shop, with the murdered boy's mother and uncle. How can you know what to say in those circumstances? How should you sit? I chose a nervous perch on the edge of the settee, aware that a relaxed slump with crossed legs would be disrespectful. At what point, and in which tone, do you say 'anyway, with regards to the march'? How could these people know what stance to take, as the murdered boy's photo smiled proudly above the rickety sideboard provided by the landlord, and the uncle translated to his weeping sister our argument that it was vital to isolate the fascists? How lost can they have felt, in this baffling environment, while the shop below continued business as usual?

The murderers were convicted, and around 600 came on the march, the impact of which no one can tell. But a clue was apparent when I stayed with a friend in Edinburgh. He had helped to arrange a demonstration on the Muirhouse Estate, marching to the house of a fascist who'd been attacking a family from Botswana. About fifty adults from the area, each brought an average of three kids, one dog and a pushchair. The demonstration squeezed on to a patch of grass outside the fascists' house, where five lads yelled at us from a balcony, but not in equal measures. One was going for it, 'Away ye wee fucken' communist shites.' Two were swigging from a bottle of lager. And the other two occasionally made a wanker sign. But as their neighbours took turns to publicly denounce them through a megaphone, the racists started arguing amongst themselves. 'Fuck this, you said there'd only be a few of them.'

'Fuck you, they're just shits.'

'Fuck you telling me to fuck me.'

And two of them left. Then another two, announcing it was never their idea in the first place. Then a woman stomped through the crowd, with the stride of a wife marching towards a pub where she knows her husband is with another woman. She took the megaphone and, pointing it at the last fascist, announced she was his mother and couldn't imagine how he'd ended up like that.

Finally, as if it was a play with an implausibly overoptimistic ending, the lad came down himself, wearing only a pair of Union Jack shorts, his sunburned stomach flopping unashamedly down to the middle of the St Andrews cross. 'What the fuck am I supposed to do?' he shouted. 'I haven't got a job, I've got fuck-all. Fuck-all. I've got nothing. Tell me. Go on, tell me. What the fuck am I supposed to do?'

And I have no doubt he genuinely wanted an answer.

As the government unravelled stitch by stitch, John Smith appeared as a leader-in-waiting, as if he'd already been elected but due to a constitutional anomaly wasn't allowed to take over for another three years. Until I turned on the radio one morning to discover he was dead. I felt honour-bound to watch the meaningless train of experts and statesmen hastily whisked into a studio to agree that this was a time for mourning and not for discussing a replacement. But there was one dissenter – Denis Healey. There was one obvious choice, he said, and that was Tony Blair. I stood up, walked across the room and back, and sat down again. Healey had astonished me in two ways. First, I'd believed these characters when they said it was too early to talk about the future. But while the pot was still warm from the tea made to console Mrs Smith when they told her the news, someone was fixing a flying start for the succession.

And second – Tony Blair? I expected Healey to suggest someone right wing, but Blair wasn't even Labour. He was the smarmy one that hung out with the gang but didn't fit in. He was embarrassed by unions, even right-wing ones. He wasn't one of us, he was a la-di-da type. The press, especially the newspapers most hostile to Labour, became instant enthusiasts for his campaign. This became his main selling point, making the Labour Party the only organization in the world that allows its leader to be picked by its enemies, as if Manchester United allowed their team to be selected by Arsenal.

Blair was the human conclusion of the theory that class society was over. Subconsciously, his campaign slogan was 'let's face it, redressing inequality is a lost cause'. Ironically, my circumstances made me a model of the type who should have been attracted to him. In July 1992, I left my council flat for a mortgage and a garden. I had a last cup of tea with the drilling man, shook the coughing man's hand, and we all wished each other well. Though if it hadn't been for the rent strike, the removal van might have come and gone without them noticing. And instead of being angry at having no money, I was embarrassed, because the only reason I could leave this decaying estate and they couldn't, was that I had more than them.

For a few weeks I pined for the council estate spirit. Until my new neighbour, an accountant, called out to me, as I was getting in my car. 'I've been listening to the radio,' he said, 'and someone was saying it doesn't matter that England are playing Germany at football on Hitler's birthday. But I think you shouldn't give any encouragement to racists at all. Anyway, I won't keep you. Bye.' It was his way of saying, 'I know I'm an accountant, but you can trust me.' I was at the stage in life where you realize accountants can be pleasant people.

Instead of a squat and a few gigs in pub rooms, I had a mortgage and a radio series. Then I took a new girlfriend to a dinner put on by the entertainers' cricket team I played for. An actor at our table heard us talking about an anti-Nazi demonstration that had taken place a few days earlier in Welling, which had ended in a brawl. He leaned across and said, 'Oh you're not telling me you blame the police for taking the odd swipe at these loonies are you?' I showed my age by ignoring him and going to the bar. But when I came back, Bindy had her arm round his neck in a Nelson headlock, and in that unsensible moment our path to domestic sensibleness was assured.

If it was wrong to write off accountants, how absurd to categorize all office workers as middle class. Especially at the time when a new phrase was introduced into the vocabulary of office life – 'line managers'. Usually these were 25-year-old graduates from a business studies course. An electrician I knew had been transferred to an office job under a line manager who would walk round the office, see whose switchboard was flashing and stand over them shouting 'Calls'. Lecturers, like many professionals, were placed on short-term contracts. Salesmen, BBC producers and legal advisers started talking in the 'my fucking boss' language associated with postmen and train drivers.

The fastest growing areas of trade unionism were in banking and insurance. Computer programmers were well paid but clearly didn't think of themselves as management, as many of them installed viruses into the system, in a modern version of a labourer nicking a pile of tools as a swipe of revenge. Shipyards and mines may have been in decline but vast shopping centres were appearing in every available space. And supermarkets now employed as many people as the average factory, in jobs just as tedious. Though at least on an assembly line you're not expected to smile as you tighten each rivet.

The most impressive trade unionists I met at this time were usually in the fire service. In a campaign against the closure of a local station, I realized they're the masters at giving out leaflets or collecting money. Because everyone loves a firefighter in uniform and the firefighters know it. They give stickers to kids, who run round in circles showing everyone. Old people tell them they're marvellous, and half the women say 'you can save me any day'. And with no effort every leaflet is gone, every space on the petition is filled and the collecting bucket is full.

They also seem to be the best-read workforce in the country, with piles of books on subjects like the French revolution, which they read in the periods waiting for a call. While talking to a huge fireman, who looked like a cartoon drawing of a macho slob on a feminist Christmas card, I asked how long he'd been a fireman. His reply was, 'Oy, it's not fireman, it's *firefighter*. Now don't be sexist. All right.'

I did the gig at their annual union conference and got to know several firefighters from around the country, including Jimmy Fitzpatrick. It's often said you shouldn't meet your teenage heroes, though usually that refers to people like Robert de Niro and Ian Botham rather than an executive member from the FBU. But the same principle must apply. He did what so many trade union officials did when they met me after a union conference gig, which was to tell me jokes and try to impress me with stories of how militant they were. For some reason the greatest enthusiasts for this behaviour were always from Glasgow. And it's very difficult to know how to respond, when a slightly drunk nationally known union official, in a suit and loosened red tie slipping round his neck, burbles how he went into the Strathclyde region and brought out the whole area on strike just like that because there was no soap in the toilets. Especially when it follows without a pause from a story about two nuns and a cucumber, so if you weren't paying attention you could make the mistake of thinking they were part of the same anecdote.

I'd learned to be wary of trade union officials bragging about their militant nature, as it usually came just before a sell-out. For example, 'My proudest moment was punching Ted Heath in the mouth for the 1973 pay freeze. And that's why I'm telling you, the best way of beating this vicious management is to end this strike, accept the pay cut and not give them the chance to smash this union.'

It was one thing to say that unions were severely weaker than twenty years earlier, but another to claim the working class had disappeared altogether. And the aspect of the theory I found most infuriating was that the people most adamant that the working class was vanishing were the most unrepresentative esoteric middle-class media buffoons in the country. Late-night programmes on BBC2 were crammed with professors and broadsheet journalists pontificating on how obvious it was that Old Labour values were irrelevant these days, when it was their own business-lunch 'trouble with the builders/cleaner/nanny' lifestyle that bore no relation to the way most people lived.

They made me angrier than the Tories, these Bea Campbell, Suzanne Moore, Michael Ignatieff types. There was an army of them who had been liberals but wanted to justify their positions while maintaining they were still loyal to their old principles. So they adopted the fashionable theory that modern progressives needn't, indeed shouldn't, trouble themselves with the passé working class. Many of them were connected to the magazine *Marxism Today*, a self-parody which advocated champagne socialism as a serious strategy. These people were fêted by the media, yet their theories were invariably proved to be rubbish. They'd started out believing Eastern Europe was fair and progressive. Then they'd been devotees of Gorbachev, who would save the continent. Then they insisted Labour could never win another election without merging with the Liberals. Never were they anything other than spectacularly wrong. If someone from *Marxism Today* told you they were expecting you to have a wonderful day, you'd shit your pants.

As if to take the piss, aspects of traditional working-class behaviour became chic. Brasseries appeared in inner-city precincts, serving sausage, mash and beans for twelve quid. Broadsheet critics effused over the hidden genius of *Carry On* films and 1970s ITV sit-coms. The most popular names for boys born into middle-class families were Fred, Harry and Jack. Football became a compulsory middle-class topic. If anyone had thought of it, I'm sure they could have marketed rickets.

Theme bars sprang up in town centres, often with huge black and white grainy photos on the wall of dockers or gangs at work in a shipyard. I wondered whether there would be a chain called 'Scargills', where the bottles of lager had a lump of coal in the top and you were taken in by bus while actors yelled abuse and slung rocks at the windows. The word 'post-modern' crept into common language, as a vague way of describing this trend. The most lasting branch of this fashion was the invention of the new lad. Not like the old lad, coarse and leering over pin-ups in a mechanic's office, the new lad had tasteful photos from *Loaded* magazine on the wall by his Apple Mac.

The Major years stumbled on and interminably on. It's usually easier to remember each year of your twenties because you were probably living and working in different places and going out with different people, than later, more stable times. In a similar way the years of the second Major government blur into each other. There were no obvious markers, no big strikes, no huge campaigns, just a lame government tottering from one fiasco to another.

Jonathan Aitken, David Mellor, Major calling his colleagues 'bastards', John Redwood standing against him, beef, cash for questions, innumerable close votes in the Commons, and countless by-elections. They were perpetually 20 per cent behind in the polls, like a losing player hanging on pointlessly at the end of a game of Monopoly. Where fifteen years earlier, I'd winced in frustration while that woman behind me justified the pay rises of managing directors, the whole country frothed in outrage at the earnings of characters like Cedric Brown, head of British Gas. Privatized industries, once the backbone of Thatcher's popularity, were almost universally despised. Yorkshire Water even managed to run out of water and still charge people. Which was as ludicrous as someone going into a shop for a pint of milk, handing over the money, and the shopkeeper refusing to hand over the milk, saying 'sorry mate, it's leaked out of the carton'.

Events such as the Scott Inquiry, which damned ministers as liars, cheats and dealers in arms with Saddam Hussein, passed by without much comment, as it was like revealing that a well-known burglar in the area had stolen something.

In contrast to my early campaigning days, anyone expressing opposition to the government, such as animal rights protestors or Swampy, were popular. Tony Benn was adored almost wherever he went. But it was a long time since campaigns and strikes had proved to be the way to win. The 1992 election result proved to many people that even the mildest attempts to redistribute wealth could never win elections. The irony of the mass rejection of the Conservatives, was that the man in the perfect position to soak it up was the man who accepted most of what they'd done, Tony Blair. His selling point was that after so many defeats, he was offering so little, it might just be possible. To put it another way, the root of his success was pessimism.

It was as if his crusading message was, 'We live in a Britain that is crumbling. And that is why I promise a Labour government will change absolutely nothing. Now I know there are some in our party who cling to the old-fashioned idea that we should still promise to do a little bit about something. But unless we abandon this out-dated rhetoric, we will lose the election and never be given the chance to do nothing. So we will do nothing about poverty, nothing about privatization and shall not rest until we have achieved absolutely nothing. With 1,000 days to prepare for 1,000 years, that is the exciting message of New Labour, which I pledge to the British people.'

Chapter 21

There was one reason to be pleased about the advent of Tony Blair; it inspired a letter into *Socialist Worker* that I shall quote in full. 'Tony Blair? I'd rather have Lionel Blair. At least he'd dance round the Tories.'

The thought that someone had taken the trouble to write that down and send it off kept me inspired for weeks. I thought of sending in some of my own. 'Robin Cook? I'd rather have Thomas Cook. At least he'd send the Tories on holiday.' Or 'Margaret Beckett? I'd rather have Samuel Beckett. At least he'd leave long pauses between the words in his questions to the Tories.'

That aside, Blair was allowed to get away with almost whatever he wanted within the Labour Party, which became New Labour. He abolished the socialist Clause 4 of the constitution, which he claimed was 'out-of-date', having been written in 1918. This from a committed churchgoer, who presumably thought the New Testament was knocked up by Peter Mandelson in 1988. Though even the Bible must have been read by Blair selectively. Perhaps he had a version that told of Jesus in the temple, saying unto the widow, 'How can we expect the moneylenders to provide jobs when you're demanding an unrealistic minimum mite policy?' It must also have included a footnote, that rich men had no worries about entering the kingdom of Heaven, as Jesus made no stipulations about the size of the needle or the camel.

Marxism, he declared with glee, was a theory that could tell us nothing about the modern world, having been written in the 19th century. Which made me wonder whether the Blair household merrily slung their wineglasses around the room, confident they wouldn't fall and smash, because that old-fashioned gravity nonsense was written hundreds of years ago.

Blair could combine his conservatism, in a way the Tories never could, with a façade of modernity. He even spoke at music awards, saying, 'Great bands in the past have put music where it belongs: at the top, bands like the Clash.' Aaaagh. The Clash. He'd never stood in a record shop, hovering over the cover and feeling he'd done something deliciously evil as he handed over the money. What would he do if his defence spokesman said 'I hate the army and I hate the RAF'? What would he think if Robin Cook said 'I'm so bored with the USA'? Or Gordon Brown said 'I don't want to hear about where the rich are going'? When did Blair ever punch the air to 'Career opportunities, not one will ever knock, the only job they offer you's to keep you out the dock'?

Blair did all he could to liken himself to Bill Clinton. But when Clinton said he smoked dope and didn't inhale, the whole world thought 'baaa, you liar'. If Blair had said that, everyone would have thought 'you've never smoked dope in your life, you lying bastard'. But so many people had suffered the pain of so much Tory rejoicing, they wanted only to put their head down and hope, and wait, for Labour.

Blair said he admired Thatcher and was willing to sever Labour's link with the unions. These attitudes didn't make him popular, but to criticize him openly wasn't popular either. Any doubts had to be pushed aside because, please, please, this time Labour, even New Labour, had to win. This contradiction created a catchphrase of the age, 'he's just doing it until he gets elected'.

Socialists were in a curious position, in which millions of people agreed with much of what we said, but hardly anyone was willing to act upon it. It's a myth that most activists who drop out of campaigning become stockbrokers or columnists in the *Spectator*. Most get worn down by the nagging doubt that nothing you're doing is making any difference. History is full of heroes who have smuggled messages from South American jails, saying things like 'they can imprison my body but can never jail the spirit of a people that desires liberty'. But try standing in a shopping centre for an hour and a half selling papers, in which time your only conversation is with a woman who wants to know the way to Debenhams. It wasn't that the causes had gone away. It was more that the most plausible means of aiding those causes was to wait, and hope. Thatcherism was discredited, but the fall of communism in Eastern Europe and the Soviet Union, combined with election defeats and battered unions, had discredited socialism.

I underwent another experience which is reckoned to be a mellowing process; becoming a parent. Driving back from the hospital, leaving the three-hour-old wriggling product of the night's work with his mother, I had two thoughts. The first was directed at everyone else, as they walked home, filled up with petrol, or waited for a night bus to take them to the morning shift, which was, 'Don't just carry on as normal! Don't you know what's happened? Take the day off and line the streets or bow or let off fireworks but don't just cross the road like that as if this is like every other day.' The other was more political, that having witnessed the events of the previous twenty-four hours, I'd changed my mind: the feminists were right; women should rule, men are useless.

As if to confirm my fatherly mortgage-paying status, I was finding myself on the sort of radio programme where I'd be asked about the prospects for New Labour, and instead of the political bits taken out leaving only the jokes, the jokes were taken out leaving only the political bits. I did a radio series with Francis Wheen, whose knowledge of every political figure in the country is astounding. Suddenly I was embarrassed at how little I knew about the week's news, having been used to environments where people are impressed if you know the name of the Foreign Secretary. One night we were talking about the Labour Party, and Francis said, 'Do you know John?' 'John who?' I said. 'John Prescott.'

I just stared at him. Of course I didn't know John Prescott. What a daft question. John Prescott isn't someone you know. And it dawned on me I was moving in circles in which it was not unusual to know John Prescott. There's something seductive about this. It's fascinating to be surrounded by people interested in political ideas, even if they differ from your own. And there's all the inside knowledge. I sort of knew Prescott didn't like Blair, but I never realized he'd called him *that*.

Then I was asked to write a column for the *Guardian*, setting out the jokes I thought Blair should make in his conference speech. The next morning, as the piece appeared, I received a message that I should get in touch with Robin Cook. This was a joke, surely. I rang the number, while rocking the baby with the other arm, spoke to a secretary, and a man who sounded remarkably like Robin Cook said, 'Ah Mark, Robin Cook here.'

He wanted me to write his conference jokes. I declined the offer but we talked about the conference, and he said he was a fan of my radio series, particularly the one he'd heard that was a thirty-minute tirade about Tony Blair. But mostly I just wanted to shout, 'Fucking Ada, it's Robin Cook on the phone. Oy Robin, hang on a minute, I'm going to get the neighbours, they'll never believe this.' Now I was in the circles where I *did* know Robin Cook. And that night in the bath, I thought and thought to try and come up with the perfect joke, which I could have rung through and which may have become the first item on the nine o'clock news. And I realized how easy it can be, to think that mixing in those circles makes so much more impact than getting frozen in a shopping centre with a batch of unread leaflets.

Strikes were at their lowest level for 100 years. Those that took place were usually a result of an entire workforce being sacked and went on interminably, so that when they finally ended, it was like hearing that an ancient celebrity had died. A part of you thought 'that's a shame', but you also thought 'to be truthful I had no idea it was still going anyway'. The classic dispute of the times was fought by the Liverpool dockers. Four hundred of them, mostly from families that formed a community spanning most of the century, were sacked when they refused to cross a picket line. Their union leader Bill Morris went to Liverpool and cried, saying we all had to be proud when we told our grandchildren what we'd done for the Liverpool dockers.

Rob Newman, Jeremy Hardy and I sent out a letter to other comics appealing for money, and handed over the cheque at a gig I was doing at the TUC headquarters. The gig itself was fine, except for one table of top-grade civil servants that got drunk and heckled. At the end of the show a docker made a speech that went, 'I'd like to thank the comedians for raising this money, and all of yous, for supporting us like, in our struggle.' Then he walked across to the hecklers, leaned across them and said, 'Except for yous bastards. What the fock have yous lot ever done to support anyone but yer friggin' selves ay?' And for tension it was unbeatable, as he glared and they sweated. This wasn't a wild angry outburst from an unruly teenager. This was the considered response of a proud man, who demanded the same respect from those whose eyes he peered into, as they expected from him by right. Eventually, as their fidgets were followed by 200 sets of transfixed eyes, he'd won it, and turned away.

One irony of being a long-time activist is that at times when issues explode the routine you're accustomed to falls behind that of the newcomer. I was satisfied with the collection, but others organized a comedians' meeting and invited the dockers to speak. Activity burst from every corner of the room. Collections were organized for every London comedy gig over the next week. Then came the question of the benefit. A wearisome tradition had emerged by then, that no campaign could exist without a comedy benefit. Some socialists probably think the first stage of the Russian revolution was Lenin booking a comedy night at the Hackney Empire. So it was suggested we booked the Palladium. Lee Hurst marched into the offices of Mark Borkowski, a leading PR company used to dealing with people like Tom Jones and Dame Edna Everidge. They agreed to publicize the Palladium gig and the strike, and within days comedians were on every available news programme, culminating in Rob Newman on 'Richard and Judy' talking about the decline of the dock labour scheme. Stylish young clerks from the office, whose normal day's work might be lunch with Martin Amis, or accompanying Diana Ross to a TV studio, were ringing to tell me it was really important, right, that I went on *World at One*, because we really have to get the message across, right, about, like, what's happening to these dockers, man. The naïve frustration of virgin activists was sparkling. One comic was furious. 'I had a disappointing week. I rang forty people to see if they'd help with the collections, and thirty-three said they would, but seven of the bastards weren't prepared to do it.'

Ken Loach addressed our press conference and Channel 4 broadcast a film about the Palladium night. Then I was invited to speak at the weekly strike meeting on a Friday morning in Liverpool. I got myself in a frame of mind suitable for speaking to around forty strikers. But when I walked into the room I felt a sudden blast, similar to the sensation you get when you step off a plane and realize you've landed somewhere intensely hot. Not only was the room packed with over 500 people but it was buzzing with activity like an Arab market place. Groups of dockers were frenetically waving their arms, possibly discussing tactics for the picket line, or maybe horseracing tips, but whichever it looked impressive. I looked at my scribbled notes and panicked. Even worse, the meeting started on time. Didn't they know the rules? At the time it's due to start, there should be no one in the room except a caretaker putting out chairs and one fraught committee member screaming, 'Where the bloody hell is everybody?'

There was another guest speaker, from Sweden, and then me. One of the problems of public speaking when you're used to doing stand-up comedy is that two minutes without a big laugh seems cataclysmic. Even if I'm talking about a mudslide in Bangladesh, after one minute and fifty seconds it feels as if an enormous neon sign is flashing 'get a laugh – NOW'. And what if I got less laughs than the Swede? That would be disastrous.

While I was speaking, I was as fascinated by the audience as I hoped they were interested in what I was saying. In recent months, these people had travelled around the world, turning back ships in places like New York and Melbourne. They'd been on strike for over a year. They sat before me, proud, raucous, and barely visible through a solid cloud of smoke.

Better still was the following hours in the pub. Two dockers had spoken the previous evening, at a gay club in London, where one had been hugged by a lesbian and was still covered in sequins. Just as every class at school has one mad kid, who releases the frogs from the science block or climbs naked on to the roof of the gym, every strike has its slightly worrying loose cannon. With a mixture of coercion and charm, he persuaded everyone in the pub, including bemused pensioners and the bar staff, to wear headbands with 'victory to the dockers' on them in Japanese. Then we all had to have our pictures taken with a camera he borrowed off a passing tourist.

At ten-minute intervals, a frail and twitching character would sidle up to us, carrying a tray of lighters or something equally worthless, and plead with us to buy something from him for a pound. There, side by side, were the two faces of unemployment.

The opposition, defiant, inventive, and occasionally disturbing, and the result of that opposition being defeated, gaunt, tragic and a shameful waste of humanity. It was also four days into an election campaign, being fought between two parties who agreed that class society was a thing of the past.

This time I was certain, not pretending to be certain, but utterly unshakeably certain that Labour would win by a landslide. The layer that swung elections were not only furious with the Tories, they had been for four years. And they weren't just saying 'I think I'll vote Labour', they were saying 'thank God we'll soon be rid of these miserable creeps'. The Tories' plight reminded me of a comedian having a particularly bad gig. There comes a point when the audience has decided collectively they don't like you, from where your position is irredeemable. You could say the wittiest thing in history and everyone would look at you with contempt and think 'what's he on about?'. But someone in the audience saying 'you're a wanker mate' will get a huge laugh. Such was the hole they were in.

The most obvious reason for expecting a Labour landslide was that every opinion poll for four years had predicted one. But few pundits believed it. Every journalist I met in the months before the election assured me 'it will be much closer than the polls suggest'. The reason was usually 'because they will'. Sherie Dodds, a political writer on the *Daily Mirror*, said 'I think Labour's lead will fall by half'. Why half? Why not a fifth or five-eighths? A features editor on the *London Evening Standard* insisted to me that 'everyone in the know says it's impossible for Labour to get a majority higher than four'. I made a point of publicly predicting a huge Labour win wherever possible, partly to make a political point but mostly because I knew this was a chance to be a smug bastard.

With one week to go the complacency was shattered. A poll put Labour only five points ahead. That morning I arrived at our childminder's, who, up until then, had barely mentioned the election. As she came to the door she grabbed my shoulders, and said desperately, 'They can't lose can they?'

'Of course not, the poll is wrong,' I said, as if I had inside information it was a misprint. The confidence wasn't entirely fake, but a million hearts fluttered that day.

And it did prove to be only a frightener. On 1 May I woke at five o'clock, with the instant alertness with which a six-year-old wakes up on the morning they're going on holiday. I stacked a selection of records from 1979 and played them one by one, starting with 'Babylon's Burning' by the Ruts. To add to the symbolism, it was a gloriously sunny morning as we wheeled the pushchair to the local church to vote. Those I couldn't understand were the people who said they couldn't vote Labour because 'this time they'd gone too far'? Further than Attlee, who secretly ordered nuclear weapons? Further than Wilson, who backed the Vietnam War? What these people were saying was 'napalming a village I could tolerate, but privatizing air traffic control is overstepping the mark'.

Weighing up the party's policies was nothing to do with it. Real power in society lay with unelected businessmen, who would continue whatever the result. Labour, in most people's eyes, despite the efforts of the leaders, still represented caring instead of kicking your way to the front, sharing instead of hoarding, us instead of them. This would be a magnificent day for all those who wanted change from the eighteen Tory years of celebrated greed, not because Labour would deliver it, but because millions would feel more confident about demanding it.

'Labour landslide predicted,' said Dimbleby, in response to the exit poll. And the room in Croydon Labour Club, the same room that had witnessed such carnage five years earlier, hosted a practice roar of delight for the hundreds to come as the night wore on. An old engineer leaned behind me, to reach the switch for the light that hung over the huge photo of John Smith, which had never been replaced by one of Blair. Very quietly, as he pulled the cord, he said to himself, 'Here you are John, I want you to see this.'

I did an interview by mobile phone with Greater London Radio, and they said they would ring me for an update every hour. And from then it's all a blur. A cycle was set in place that went: 1) gradual building of 'shhhhh' from heaving sweaty room; 2) lip-biting silence as result was announced; 3) unrestrained rejoicing, hundreds of limbs cavorting in all directions, whooping, screaming and hugging; 4) exclamations and shrieks of 'I don't believe it' while dozens continued waving and bouncing on the spot as they

squashed to the bar for a huge round of drinks; 5) those monitoring
the TV standing on a chair and starting the 'shhh' in preparation
for another glorious Tory calamity.

The only thing wrong with that wonderful night was it happened
too quickly. It was like having your favourite twenty meals served up
in one night, at ten-minute intervals. There was hardly time to
savour Mellor when up popped William Waldegrave or Neil
Hamilton. I felt like shouting, 'No, not yet, we're still enjoying the
last one, let it linger. Can't we stretch these results over a week?' So
it was just one elongated bout of cheering, drinking, screaming,
delighting in the collective joy of the confirmation that millions had
finally, officially rejected the menace that had hung over us for so
long. It was such a hazy few hours that by the next day I could
hardly pinpoint in my memory a single incident. Just as if you tried
to remember the greatest night of sex you ever had, you'd be unlikely
to recall specific moments, just a fuzzy continuous night of joy.

Though there was one exception. The new MP for Croydon
Central, number ninety on the target list of seats, arrived to make
a speech to the ecstatic crowd. But two or three sentences in, up
popped some words on the screen that took the delirium to a new
level. No speech in history could have survived such a cannonball.
'Portillo may have lost Enfield'. Everyone yelped, not a screaming
yelp of victory, but those stifled disbelieving yelps like the one a
beauty queen emits when she's declared Miss World. And then it
happened. Every last granule of vocal energy from the tortured
throats of this jubilant mass were summonsed for our contribution
to the spiritual roaring taking place throughout the land. It was the
defining moment of a generation, like VE Day or the moon landing.
Portillo had lost.

I went home, dozed drunkenly on the settee, and as I opened my
eyes, David Evans, Tory oaf of St Albans, was losing his seat. By six
o'clock the phone was ringing every few minutes, to reveal
exhausted croaking voices garbling messages of untrammelled
delight. Just one worry nagged away, did I do another interview on
the radio? If so, the chances are it was a heap of jumbled drunken
swearing that probably got the station shut down. As it turned out,
when they'd contacted me, I was uttering such gibberish that they
didn't put me on the air. Though I definitely remember doing the

interview, so I must have been shouting into a mobile phone with no one at the other end.

Throughout the next day strangers smiled at each other as if it were a magical fairyland. Not everyone of course. Lurking amongst us somewhere were the 32 per cent that had voted Tory, who I hoped were suffering like we'd suffered so often. It was a day for suddenly breaking into a manic smile at inopportune moments, as if the country was full of dopeheads. Only for an hour did this sensation stop, when I went to a Channel 4 party that was packed with journalists and television executives. They were also delighted, but because they thought New Labour would be marvellous. 'Oh, and the number of women that have got in is so exciting,' someone enthused to me. This was an entirely different atmosphere to that in the club, on the train, in the street, where the celebratory mood wasn't because we loved Jack Straw or Harriet Harman. Every subsequent survey revealed that the poorer people were, the greater the swing to Labour had been. In Middle England, those who'd been shafted turned to Labour, but the wealthy who'd been courted with such passion by Blair for the most part stayed loyal to the Tories. Much of the victory had been gained in spite of the compromises, rather than because of them. However much he'd tried to dampen the expectations, a lot of people were thinking 'he's just doing it to get elected'.

On *Loose Ends* that Saturday, I started by saying, 'In my life I've seen the Jam live. I've seen the view from the top of the Empire State Building. I've even seen a new born baby. But I've never, ever, seen anything as magnificent as Portillo's face at four o'clock on Friday morning.'

Now the same media that had told us John Major was master of all he surveyed, then insisted the polls must close, were adamant that Blair had won by transforming Labour into New Labour.

A theory developed that the election result was a consequence of people having just got bored with the same government. But why would people have got bored after eighteen years but not thirteen? At what point do people get bored? Thirteen years and six months presumably.

So the first stirrings of unease with the new government passed them by. There was astonishment when Blair invited Thatcher to

Downing Street. Students were stunned when tuition fees were introduced. Especially by a government that announced its three priorities as 'education, education and education'. At least the last lot hadn't said 'this government has three priorities: mining, mining and mining'.

From those who thought he was just doing it to get elected, a bewilderment began to grow, as businessmen seemed able to elicit any favours they liked. The issue on which I found them particularly galling involved the Onibiyo family. Abdul and Ade, father and son, had been deported by the Tory Home Office after living in South London for twenty years. Abdul had been a critic of the military regime in Nigeria and following deportation was promptly placed in jail and tortured, as his supporters had predicted. I had two friends who fought a tenacious campaign for their return, and Jack Straw assured them that once Labour was elected, the family would be reunited. But after the election, he began proceedings to deport the rest of the family as well. None of us realized, when Straw said he would reunite the family, that he meant all together in a military jail in Lagos.

Eventually an independent judge overruled the government and sanctioned their return. At a benefit to cover the costs of the campaign, the family attended, leaving 1,500 people emotionally celebrating their homecoming. Abdul gazed around quizzically and asked, 'Why are they standing? Surely not for us.'

Nothing summed up the advent of New Labour more than the days following Diana's crash. Thousands queued to sign books of condolences and crowds flocked to her palace to weep and lay down flowers. But the royal family hardly seemed to care at all. Then up popped Blair to excuse the Queen, saying the reason she hadn't made a statement was because she'd been involved in 'complex funeral arrangements'. As if she would have loved to have said something but was too busy making fish paste sandwiches.

The most unlikely people confessed to sobbing in the street and laying flowers by any convenient memorial. At the time, my girlfriend was a union rep in the civil service and arrived at work one day to find twenty-six of her members insisting that the union demanded management flew a flag at half-mast from the roof. A pizza was named after Diana, a tomato seed was named after her, papers were full of memorial mugs, plates and beautifully crafted Diana-related tat, and Richard and Judy broke down on air.

Shortly after, I was on a television panel game and mentioned the silly rhyme we were taught at school to memorize the wives of Henry the Eighth, which went 'divorced, beheaded, died – divorced, beheaded survived'. I said the teachers of the future would have an easier rhyme to help remember the current royal family – 'divorced divorced divorced – divorced divorced crashed'. There was a collective yelp, and I wasn't asked back.

A ludicrous trend developed in liberal circles that argued Diana was a radical anti-establishment icon, in some cases a republican. This although her ambition was for her son to be king which, I would suggest, placed her on the moderate wing of the republican movement. But there was an anti-establishment element in the response to her death. There was a sense that the people cared but the establishment didn't, because she was an outcast from the family she called 'the firm'. Because she was associated with campaigns concerning Aids and in opposition to landmines, to some people she represented a compassion society couldn't deliver. And Blair could move adeptly into place as griever-in-chief and mediator between the crusty aristocratic establishment and its glamorous pseudo-radical modern wing.

Throughout this time it seemed there were fewer people calling themselves socialists than at any time for 100 years, but more people agreeing with socialist ideas than at any time for fifty years. Taking on the establishment was applauded, but few people thought it could succeed, so it felt as if many people wanted someone else to rebel on their behalf. Part of the Diana phenomenon was a curious manifestation of this mood. Though anyone who bought those tomato seeds was just mad.

One measure of the weakness of unions was that such strikes as existed were interminable, hardly seeming worthy of mention until they entered their second year. The Magnet strike went way past this marker, led by a steely articulate woman from Darlington called Shirley Winter. So many times I saw her speak, to crowds of a few dozen or thousands, each time striding to the microphone with a sense of purpose no politician could approach. She never used notes, never stumbled across a single word, was always concise, clear, bursting with spirit, and always got a standing ovation, this fitter's wife who had never spoken in public before her husband and all his colleagues were sacked.

On a protest outside a meeting of Magnet shareholders, I found myself standing next to.Arthur Scargill. Fifteen years after the time he was the daily front-page story, he was still protesting, having been marginalized, slandered and abused as much by the labour movement as by Thatcher. He reminded me of bands that have one huge album but still gig as joyfully 15 years later when hardly anyone can remember them. I said it was an honour to meet him. And he replied by shouting, about two inches from my face, about his steadfast defence of miners' pensions. Strangest of all was his habit of referring to himself in the third person. So I stood there, trying to nod in agreement, as Scargill yelled, 'What did Arthur Scargill do when the pension fund was threatened? I'll tell you what Arthur Scargill did. Arthur Scargill . . .' Afterwards Mark Thomas, who was standing nearby, suggested I should have said, 'This Arthur Scargill bloke sounds brilliant. I'm going to go and talk to him because you're a wanker mate.'

And the strike of Liverpool dockers wore on, despite the new government having a one-third shareholding in the company. Until one afternoon I received a call from a docker called Mickey Tighe. 'It's over Mark, they've called it off, we tried our best, I said at the meeting we had to carry on, we've let yous all down, I hope you don't think we've let yous down, they've called it off.' For several minutes he continued this coherent outpouring of emotional incoherence.

Bill Morris, the union leader, having won a standing ovation for his tearful 'grandchildren' number, had refused to campaign for a single moment of solidarity for the dockers, not even fifteen minutes. As the strike ended, he publicly attacked people like John Pilger and myself for giving the dockers 'false hope'. Morris could now look forward to sitting his grandchildren on his knee and saying proudly 'in two and a half years, I didn't once spread an ounce of false hope'.

That Friday I returned to Liverpool to speak to another packed, sweaty, smoky meeting. They were defeated but not broken, and perhaps slightly relieved, rather like a relative of someone who has finally died after a lingering illness. This time as I looked across them, I pondered their extraordinary journey together. How the photos of the most poignant, most violent or intimate moments would stay on their walls and never be removed in the hope of appealing to Middle England. But the scene also brought alive a great deal of history. When thousands of engineers poured out of Barcelona factories to fight Franco, these would have been exactly the sort that did it. When Trotsky wrote about legions of metalworkers forming themselves into instant battalions to defend their town against the White Army, this is what such a meeting must have looked like. Even in defeat, especially in defeat, they were an honour to have touched, and been touched by.

That's what was missing from the cosy political world of journalists and pundits whose life was centred almost exclusively around the professional political class. However fascinating, unless their outlook was connected to the turbulence, humour, joy and heartache of people like those before me, they would always remain sterile, with few people listening to them and fewer still taking any notice. I can understand how tempting it must seem to succumb to the lure of important people, beckoning you with the greatest bribe of all, the feeling that you mattered. But there is a price. Instead of the honour of embracing courageous opponents of military regimes, you face the shame of being part of the force that deports them. Instead of celebrating 500 opponents of injustice, you ignore them, lie to them and condemn them. And you never again sense or understand the pride, the intelligence, the commitment and the warmth that, even in defeat, was spinning round that room.

Chapter 22

Despite speaking at events such as the dockers' meetings, there were times when I must have seemed like a slightly cheeky member of the establishment, as if I was 'in', not least to myself. When I was eighteen, I didn't know a single person who listened to Radio 4. If I had met anyone who did, I'd have thought they had an unusual hobby and been slightly curious, as if I'd met a pot-holer or someone who bred snakes. At twenty-eight I thought the reason I was unable to get on Radio 4 was because it was run by Oxbridge graduates who, whenever they met me, displayed the expression you'd expect from someone in a room with a friendly pit-bull terrier. It was as if they were thinking, 'He seems all right at the moment. But at any minute he'll revert to type and go "oy cunt, do you wanna fat lip or what".'

Now I was on Radio 4, with an annual series, as a guest on panel games and chatting amiably with Ned Sherrin on *Loose Ends*.

At eighteen I just about knew there was such a thing as the *Guardian*. It was in the shops, along with *Amateur Boxer* and *National Geographic*, but I would never have considered buying it. It was like listening to opera or making your own salad dressing, it was something other people did, probably while they were watching BBC2. I'd have been fascinated to know there was a layer of society that raged with debate about the direction of this paper, or frothed with anger at the line of one of its columnists. It would have seemed as bizarre as listening to a row that was tearing apart the world of go-karting. Now I wrote for the thing.

I mentioned to our childminder that I wrote a column in the *Guardian*. She sounded impressed, so we chatted about the paper, and she said she got it free, every Wednesday. 'Here's the one from this week,' she said, and pointed at the current issue of the *Croydon*

Guardian, a freesheet local rag comprising of a front-page story about a fight outside a pub and nineteen pages of adverts for secondhand cars.

Sometimes after a radio show, I would go for a drink with people of the establishment like Ned Sherrin and Matthew Parris. The eighteen-year-old me would have been appalled. At that time I'd have thought the only reason for meeting such people would be to tip brown sauce over them as a statement against low pay.

The first few times I stayed in hotels that provided a hairdryer and mini-bar, I walked into the room and blustered 'bloody hell, look at this place', making sure I used every facility including the notepad at least once. But after a few years the novelty wore off and I'd be more likely to complain that I didn't think much of the place, because I couldn't get Sky Sports 2.

Almost invariably, I found the liberal Oxbridge wing of the establishment to be ruder and more exclusive than the conservative end. While I was at the *Guardian* I met the editor, Alan Rusbridger, only once. It was at a Christmas buffet and we were introduced, after which we stood opposite each other shuffling awkwardly as if we'd once been lovers. 'How are you, all right?' I asked. 'Hmm er yes fine,' he mumbled. Then he turned around and walked off. He didn't even say 'see ya' or 'bye' or even 'I'm off to find someone more interesting'. He just walked off, just like that. If someone with a South London accent had done that, I'd have automatically thought he was rude. But there's something about these people, that no matter how ill-mannered they are, you feel that it's your fault.

I had a similar experience every week when I rang the comment editor to discuss the subject for my column. He'd say 'Yes what are you going to do?' in a manner that was perfectly enunciated and yet so rapid it sounded like one word. And it exuded status. I'd feel instantly apologetic. Why had I been so foolish as to trouble this important man, who's so busy he has to rattle out his words at five times the normal pace? Then as I tried to explain my idea for the week, there would be these responses of 'hnn hnn', but even they would be said in the same tone. They must really work them at these posh schools. They even learn how to say 'hnn' in a superior intimidating way. There was something about that 'hnn' that said

'Do you think I care about your life, I once had lunch with Francois Mitterand?'.

Once I got a message to ring him at home, which I did, and his wife answered. And she was the same. I asked if David was there. 'No he's not,' she replied, the answer complete in around one fiftieth of a second, but with a definite upping of emphasis on the 'not'. And I started bumbling as if I was a servant who'd accidentally disturbed his master at a crucial point in a grouse-shoot. 'Right well er sorry for interrupting you sorry thank you,' I said. Until I put the phone down and recalled that the reason I'd rung was because I had a message to bloody well ring. I had the confidence to do forty minutes to 200 half-drunk Millwall fans at the Tunnel Club, but it all vanished in an instant once that liberal educated sneer went into action.

In the vacuum left by New Labour's abandonment of socialist principles, a simple thing like a newspaper column seemed able to make an impact. I heard from students who had photocopied a column I'd written opposing tuition fees and distributed them around colleges. A vicar wrote to tell me he'd handed out a piece I'd written on refugees to his congregation. A civil rights campaigner told me they'd visited Long Kesh prison and noticed a piece I'd written on Ireland was pinned to the prisoners' noticeboard. This was everything an egomaniac socialist comedian could ask for. Even more flattering, George Robertson, Peter Hain, supporters of the Countryside Alliance and various other targets took the trouble to write their objections to my jokes and send them in. This was fantastic. If I was pleased with a line I'd written, I'd smirk to myself that the minister this was aimed at would probably hear about it. What a great job, to slightly irritate leading figures in New Labour. Much more fulfilling than remembering tube maps.

Even better, I was invited on to *Any Questions* on Radio 4. The programme came live from Sandwich, twee lace-tablecloth Sandwich, in Kent. I was met at the station by Gerald Kaufman and Jonathan Dimbleby, and taken by leather-upholstered Jag the 100 yards to a hotel. As we entered, we were greeted by tables laden with immaculately prepared fish, salads, meats, trifles and cheeses, which would have taken us several days to get through and were clearly for show. Because anyone making a small dent in this buffet mountain would end up giving answers like, 'Leave it out Jonathan, I'm too stuffed. Never mind Sierra Leone, I could do with a good belch and forty winks.'

I nibbled a salmon and listened to Gerald Kaufman tell a story about going to Nicaragua with Harold. 'Who was Harold?' I asked. 'Harold Wilson,' he said. And I had to rapidly quell my normal instincts. Because normally if I heard someone say this, I'd reply, 'Oh right. You went to Nicaragua with Harold Wilson, did you? Well I went to Guatemala with Fidel Castro.'

So we chatted about films and Kent and the Tories and Harold, and he passed the pâté, and within minutes I felt myself drawn into the bonhomie of the situation. But none of it quelled the whirlpools of fear, swirling from gut to heart to brain, every time I contemplated how I would shortly be live on Radio 4 debating with famous politicians and Frederick Forsyth.

Jonathan Dimbleby opened the programme and took the first question, which was on the Macpherson report, compiled in response to police actions following the murder of Stephen Lawrence. Forsyth launched into bombastic tub-thumping praise of the police. But I could only think one thought; what the bloody hell was I doing here? Clearly there had been a dreadful mistake, and they'd mixed me up with Virginia Bottomley.

Forsyth finished, got a round of applause, and Dimbleby looked my way. 'Mark Steel,' he said. And it was such a battle, not to say, 'How the bloody hell should I know? I went to Swanley comprehensive and got kicked out and one night I smashed a load of windows in this poor bloke's greenhouse. You've got Gerald Kaufman here. He's been to Nicaragua with Harold Wilson, ask *him*.'

As the debate progressed, I had a piece of good fortune. Forsyth made the terrible mistake of being rude. He began one outburst against me with, 'I've *forgotten* more about history than you ever knew – boy.' As a result, his achievement was to drive this audience, dressed in Kent County Cricket Club ties or silk scarves and matching pearls, into opting to support the ranting Trotskyist.

Later, as I considered how it had gone, one thing troubled me. Gerald Kaufman had agreed with almost everything I said. I should have asked him why, if he agreed, he wasn't speaking out against his government's defence of the chief commissioner of the Met, who almost the entire country was demanding should be sacked. I'm fairly certain the reason I didn't challenge him was subconsciously I was thinking 'oh he's quite pleasant, and passed the pâté without asking'.

This is the process which dampens journalists and politicians. Formally they might stay as radical as when their career began, but the speeches lose their angry edge and evolve into playful banter. For Kenneth Clarke is probably charming. And Peter Mandelson, and even Ann Widdecombe. I bet there were journalists in Cambodia who said, 'But when you get to know him, Pol does tell the most delightful anecdotes.'

This was a big night for Sandwich, having been planned for a year. At the reception in the Guild Hall, someone made a speech that ended, 'Last but by no means least, may I thank Mrs Whittaker, who's surpassed herself once again with her delightful sausage rolls.'

An upright chap in a blazer and RAF tie approached me. 'I must say,' he said, 'I wasn't keen on that Forsyth fellow. I don't know how you restrained yourself from clocking him one.'

'You're making me feel I was soft on him,' I answered. To which he leaned into my ear, and replied, in a marvellously clipped militaristic accent, 'I rather think you were.'

In my own area of Crystal Palace, one side of the park was due to have a multi-screen cinema built on it, so a band of crusties moved into the area, living in the trees and on the mud below. And almost everyone in the area supported them. Shopkeepers took them food and most people signed their petitions. Political parties devote enormous resources into focus groups and opinion surveys. No party report would suggest that in order to win the middle ground, candidates at the next election should weave mud into their hair, wave a plastic cup outside Safeways and live under a sheet of tarpaulin. But the underlying reason for their level of support was, as so many people repeated, 'at least they're having a go'.

After over a year in the trees, a police operation involving over 1000 officers and 1000 security guards was launched to get them out. The woman from the shoe shop announced a demonstration, to which 300 people came, of which the paramilitary wing appeared to be the uppity middle class.

A policeman casually dropped a metal barrier near the demonstration, causing it to bounce towards us. This was a little arrogant but hardly Tiananmen Square. But a local businessman thrust his nose into the copper's face and boomed, 'How dare you? I pay your wages, young man.' And in twenty years of demonstrations, I don't think I'd ever seen a copper look so terrified.

The *liberal* middle class weren't quite so supportive. One day the *Guardian* comment editor rang me, to say he wanted to 'talk about the future'. If it had been anyone else, I'd have said, 'All right then, I reckon we'll all be living in giant pods on the moon.' But instead I subserviently agreed. Then he said, 'So shall we have a drink?' And at that point I thought, 'Ah, here's a sociable side to this man I wasn't aware of.' So I accepted, and said, 'You name a place because I don't know the pubs around the *Guardian*.'

And he said, 'I was thinking of the foyer of the Waldorf Hotel.'

So we met in the foyer of the Waldorf Hotel, and sat at a table with a bowl full of those crunchy cheesey balls that look as if they've been varnished, and waited for a Japanese man to take our orders, while someone played 'Feelings' on a harp. We had a stilted conversation in which we stumbled on to the subject of attitudes towards gays. I said I was impressed with the language of the current crop of eighteen-year olds, compared to my experience as a teenager in the pubs of Swanley, when 'you could call me anything, ANYTHING, but you don't call me a poof'. And he looked at me as if I was talking about the rituals of a planet in another galaxy. Eventually he said in a counsellor's pseudo-sympathetic voice, 'Oh, it must have been awful for you.'

Then he told me that when my contract expired, it wouldn't be renewed. The paper, he said, was 'realigning towards Blair'. This was 'not my decision', he assured me and added that 'certain people regard you as vulgar' though 'I shan't tell you who'.

Sacked in the foyer of the Waldorf Hotel! The manager of Express Dairies had just told me in his office behind the milk floats. But what snobbery. They revered writers whose genius is to place words in such an order that they are physically impossible to read. Reading some articles in the *Guardian* comment page is like trying to eat three dry cream crackers in a row. As you start, you think 'of course I'll get to the end, it's not much'. But by one-third of the way through, you're gagging and fighting for breath, shaking your head and reaching for water.

What seemed so ironically unjust was that most of what was written by the liberal types revered at the paper was about how we had to adhere to the line of New Labour and embrace the free market. But how well would they fare if the free market was let loose? Where would such people be without their privileged background, in a world in which no columnist was paid unless they could sell their writing. They'd be scrawling their unreadable sycophantic nonsense on sheets of cardboard and sitting next to it outside a railway station with a polystyrene cup.

So there was a protest letter, signed by various MPs, trade unionists and journalists. The stewards committee of the Liverpool dockers formally called a demonstration outside the *Guardian*'s office. I received several hundred letters from people who said they had sent copies to the *Guardian*, and the comment editor made a statement that the SWP had 'organized the demonstration and campaign of letter-writing'. How pleased the SWP would have been to know there were so many members dotted in remote corners of the country. Or perhaps there were a couple of full-time staff, writing letters pretending to be outraged pensioners, then flying by helicopter to post them from places like Cockermouth and Oswestry, to ensure an authentic postmark. And the speakers at the demonstration included the Liverpool dockers, an official from the National Union of Journalists, representatives from a Kurdish group and churchgoing Abdul Onibiyo.

One of the dockers' committee offered, 'we could go international on this,' which I thought was taking it a bit far. Though I quite like the idea of dockers in Copenhagen and Caracas refusing to unload apricots until this whimsical column was reinstated.

I spoke at rallies about low pay around this time, in which the chair would mention the *Guardian*, and the room packed with hundreds of people would jeer. Georgina Henry, the deputy editor, told me 'those people supporting you are all stupid'. As global injustice goes, the removal of a column from a newspaper comes well near the bottom of important causes. But that contempt

resulted from the same attitude that led the *Guardian*, and the rest
of the liberal establishment, to be the most vociferous cheerleaders
for the world's next atrocity; the Kosovo war.

Away we went again. But this time the war had a liberal veneer,
that it was conducted in defence of refugees. Blair wrung his hands
in anguish about their plight, but if he really cared about refugees,
I wondered, why didn't he appear to care about the hundreds of
thousands displaced from East Timor by the Indonesian army. I'm
no military expert, but there was one military option that might
have helped those people, which was to stop supplying the
weapons. As the war began, I spoke to a woman who ran the local
Kurdish centre. Three hundred thousand Kurds had been made
refugees by the Turkish army and 4,000 of their villages had been
destroyed. But no one wanted to know them. I was touched by the
way her reaction conveyed little anger, but rather utter bewilderment. 'Why they not show *us* on TV?' she kept saying, as if it was
a problem with the Kurdish PR department.

And the same papers and politicians deploring the plight of
refugees, were backing a new bill to keep refugees, many of whom
would be fleeing from Milosevic, from coming to Britain. A typical
story in the *Sun* revealed that refugees from Kosovo were being put
up in a bed and breakfast with 'a television and coffee-making
facilities'. So that explains it. They fake their own beatings, travel
across Europe under a crate in a lorry, sneak into Britain and say
to themselves 'we'll never see our friends or family again, but it was
worth it because this place has got a kettle and bloody marvellous
coffee-whitener'.

But the most obvious flaw in the argument that the bombing had
begun in response to the refugee crisis, was that the mass expulsion
of Albanians started after the Nato bombing had begun. Every
group opposed to Milosevic inside Serbia stated that the bombing
had strengthened him and weakened the opposition. A Serb said to
me at a meeting, 'I have always hated Milosevic. But when this
bombing started, I put my hatred in an envelope, and will take it
out again when it stops.'

One week into the war, there were hundreds of times as many
refugees as before. And then the debates began about whether the

campaign was 'achieving what it set out to do'. This, it seemed to me, was the wrong question. They should have been asking whether anything in history had ever been such a humiliating total disaster. Because it's fairly obvious whether or not you've achieved what you set out to do. If you go shopping and return with the shopping you've succeeded. If you met a mate and went to the pub, returning with no shopping, you failed. If you come home, not only with no shopping, but while you were out you burned Tescos to the ground, get a job at Nato.

And every day the civilian casualties mounted. Nato bombed market places, car factories, bridges, trains, convoys of the refugees they were supposed to be saving, a television centre and the Chinese embassy. And every day spokesman Jamie Shea would smirk that 'the campaign continues'.

This was the liberals' war. 'We have to do *something*,' they screamed at those of us opposed to it. They were like someone arriving at a burning house with no water and chucking petrol over it because 'at least it's *something*'. So the liberal bloodlust mounted. The problems of the world were to be sorted out by those with superior intellect and values, the sort of people you can discuss policy with without worrying they might become vulgar. All rational judgement was thrown out of the window. Jonathan Steele wrote on the front page of the *Guardian* that 'Pristina is now deserted except for tough-looking Serbs'. Really? No weedy frail Serbs were allowed in then. And if you were a borderline case, you had to go to make-up and get your head shaved and a tattoo etched on to your arm.

This time the main obstacle to the anti-war movement wasn't patriotism but confusion. If the war was wrong, weren't we abandoning the desperate refugees? The answer had to be that there *was* opposition to Milosevic, there *were* pockets of multi-ethnic community life in the Balkans. There were some Serbs who protected Albanians and some Albanians who protected Serbs, and that was where hope lay. But the bombing left all that in tatters. From the liberal point of view, ordinary people's actions are irrelevant. The answer is to follow the kind powerful man wringing his hands, especially if he chatted to you for a minute at a buffet lunch a couple of years back.

Amongst those opposed to the war, a new camaraderie was forged. Meetings were organized around the country and the circuit that resulted reminded me of the comedy scene. I'd meet Bruce Kent and ask him whether he'd done that place in Oxford. Conversations would open with phrases like, 'It's a shame you weren't at that one in Chesterfield, that was a very good audience. Tariq Ali stormed the place.' I did do that one in Chesterfield, where I had the honour of meeting Tony Benn for the first time. I went into the hall, found the room and it was locked. And there sat on the stairs was Benn, surrounded by a family of Greeks and a pile of papers. They were constituents of his, and he was listening to them intently, not with the blank glow of a politician itching to get away to someone important, but with deep concern. They all shook his hand, with a clasp that suggested they trusted him, and not just because he could solve their immediate problem. Tony Benn genuinely liked that Greek family. He would rather have spent time with them than at a House of Commons lunch. Which is why his party had poured nothing but contempt on him for the last ten years.

Just as appealing was speaking at the demonstrations, though invariably I was put on last. At Hyde Park, I hovered by a tent in the drizzle, as speaker after speaker made identical points, and various friends came up to tell me they were leaving. When the crowd had dwindled from 10,000 to around 300, I asked when I was on. The organizer looked at a sheet of paper, mouthed some calculations like a greengrocer totting up a bill, and said 'twenty-third'. 'No,' I screamed as if I'd stubbed my toe, suffering from the lethal combination of a political speaker's worthiness and a comedian's ego. 'I'll just be up here ranting like a lunatic to a bloke in the dark with his dog,' I wailed. And she hurriedly upgraded me to nineteenth.

Eventually Blair discarded much of the pretence and admitted the war was about 'the credibility of Nato'. After it was over, the usual process began. The bombing had killed more people and done less damage to the military than admitted. The Kosovo Liberation Army, having represented the victims, became the tyrants. Milosevic was stronger than ever. The films we'd been shown had been rigged. As time passed, amongst the liberal warmongers, some of them began to see, yet again, that they'd been duped. By the time ten years has passed, Britain will be full of such people lamenting the deceit and carnage. Then they'll add 'but this time, in Estonia, well we have to do *something*'.

And some people did gain from the experience. George Robertson became Lord Robertson, head of Nato. And Jamie Shea became a celebrity. We could expect him to present his own gardening show or cooking programme. Or perhaps *Changing Rooms* with Jamie Shea, where he comes round for the weekend while you're away and reduces the place to rubble.

And I gained something out of it. I got to know the president and priest of the local Greek church, who both came to a meeting the anti-war group organized. The president stood up, next to the priest dressed in immaculate long white robes, and made the most brilliant twenty-minute speech on the war, spitting and boiling with Greek passion. Those of us who had arranged the meeting, he said, should be blessed. As long as God is either muslim or Greek orthodox, I'm sorted.

But I was not, and never likely to be, 'in'.

Chapter 23

After Kosovo came the peak time for the notion that New Labour were unassailably popular. On the day the war ended an article in the *Observer* began, 'The outstanding political winner of the first humanitarian war is Tony Blair . . . the steeliness of his rhetoric put this instinctive bridge-builder so far out on a ledge that it alarmed some of those close to the Prime Minister . . . When Washington and the Europeans wobbled, he was resolute . . .' etc., etc., as if he learned journalism from the Russian Communist Party in 1936. I expected it to continue, 'The sun shines just half the day, but you o steely unwobbling one shine all night too.' On the night the article appeared, local election results were announced in which Labour got its lowest vote since 1919.

The statistic I'd liked to have seen from the pollsters was the length of time between the end of their question to the start of their answer. My guess is the most typical answer to the question 'who would you vote for' was not 'Tony Blair', but 'Phoo, er, tut, [two, three, four] Blair I suppose'. An accurate campaign slogan for New Labour would have been 'Well, what else is there?'. Labour activists began leaving the party in large numbers and the enthusiasm of election night evaporated. When Blair tried to impose his ally Alun Michael over Rhodri Morgan as leader of the Welsh assembly, the result was a mirror image of Tony Benn's campaign in 1981. This time the officials and union leaders almost all voted with the leadership, but every vote amongst the wider population was won overwhelmingly by the rebel. And in an uncanny twist, Peter Hain, who had been one of Benn's most committed supporters, was the campaign manager for Tony Blair/Alun Michael. Just as in 1981, he dismissed the votes that took place outside of small committees. When his man lost amongst members of UNISON, he said this was because 'Welsh UNISON is full of Trotskyists'. But Morgan won by 5,000 votes. Wouldn't someone have noticed before if there were 5,000 Trotskyists in Welsh UNISON? Anyone arriving at casualty in Swansea General Hospital would be treated to a lecture about petit-bourgeois vacillations. It would be impossible to walk across a park in Abergavenny without bumping into council gardeners giving out leaflets denouncing each other.

Just as significant, in its own way, was the dismissal of 'young people', by politicians and most of the media, as 'no longer interested in politics'. But having trampled on every outbreak of protest for several years, New Labour could hardly expect anyone who was young, angry and idealistic to look to them. It would be as likely as a seventeen-year-old deciding that she was so furious at the inhumanity of Western banks towards African nations, that she was going to join a wine-tasting society.

So a few weeks before the end of the millennium, tens of thousands protested in Seattle, temporarily halting the conference of the World Trade Organization. A few weeks later I had the pleasure of feeling woefully old at a Rage Against the Machine gig at Wembley. I felt as if everyone around me was thinking 'Who's that old bloke? He must be from the record company.' I looked down from my distant seat at twelve thousand people, roaring 'Free Mumia' and 'Fuck you, I won't do what you tell me'.

'Aah,' I thought to myself, 'our future is safe in their hands.'

A few days after the gig, I caught myself acting out a scene that was the synthesis of the eighteen-year-old and thirty-nine-year-old me, screaming to 'Fuck you, I won't do what you tell me' but while I was hoovering the carpet.

As the new century began, there was an enormous gap between the theories of the politicians and pundits at the top of society and the reality of life for most people. All the boasts about the thrills of mind-boggling new technology ignored the fact that most people were working longer hours than at any time for eighty years. The new consumer goods of the time had nothing like the time-saving impact of the vacuum cleaner, fridge and telephones that became household objects forty years earlier. For many people, the impact of mobile phones and lap-top computers was that now they had to work on the way to work and the way home from work as well. Even in the old cotton mills, workers weren't expected to drag their power looms out of the factory and carry on weaving all the way home. A new work culture developed, especially in areas such as hotels, printing and the media, in which set hours were abandoned and employees were expected to stay until whenever the job was done.

The trains from London became packed with people leaving work up until half past nine in the evening. Longer hours meant that for many people, eating out and grabbing take-aways became standard, while cooking became a luxury.

A general disquiet continued to grow, so any credible political figure who opposed the unrestrained rule of big business attracted support. Which is how New Labour stumbled from Rhodri Morgan to Ken Livingstone. Blair couldn't countenance Livingstone's ambition to be Labour's candidate for mayor of London, so they made it almost impossible for him to be selected.

Again Blair put forward his own man, this time Frank Dobson, and abuse was heaped on Livingstone. Neil Kinnock was resurrected to tell Labour members not to support him as Labour candidate, as he was bound to lose. In effect he was saying, 'Don't all vote for him, can't you see he's unelectable.' Besides which, if you wanted advice on the subject of winning elections, would the name 'Neil Kinnock' be the first to spring to mind? Kinnock was the political equivalent of the wheezing football supporter with an enormous beer gut, who shouts at the players 'get after the ball you lazy slobs'. Dobson announced that Livingstone's plans to bring back conductors on London buses would cost 'every household £1,600'. Though when the buses were converted to being one-man operated, I don't remember every household being *given* £1,600. Why pick such an unbelievable figure? If he'd said '£45' or '£32.50' a few people might have believed him. But £1,600 was the sort of figure a seven-year-old makes up in an argument. He might as well have said, 'Ken will cost everyone a million billion squillion thrillion drillion.'

So again, the support of MPs and trade union leaders was enough to make Dobson the official candidate, although every vote showed an overwhelming majority in support of Livingstone. Most spectacularly, in the Fire Brigades Union, Livingstone won 94 per cent of the votes, and Dobson 2 per cent. What, in effect, New Labour had done, was to go one better than Stalin. Because when Stalin rigged a vote, he made sure his man won 94 per cent, his opponent won 2 per cent, and his man won. But when Blair rigged a ballot, his man won 2 per cent, his opponent won 94 per cent, and his man *still* won.

The spreading discontent against New Labour created the possibility for the left of standing candidates against them. So a coalition of groups on the left, disaffected Labour members and unaligned activists formed the London Socialist Alliance, to contest the elections for the Greater London Assembly, which would take place at the same time as the vote for Mayor. I agreed to be LSA candidate for Croydon and Sutton. My first concern was whether this would appear as a joke. My greater worry was whether I could take it seriously myself. Can a comedian stand for election? The next time I did any stand-up, if someone shouted 'why don't you piss off mate', I might answer 'I'm very glad you asked me that question'.

In the meantime there was endless speculation about whether Livingstone would stand as an independent candidate. When he announced that he would, a buzz swept around London. The extent of New Labour's cluelessness as to what was happening was demonstrated one morning when I took part in a radio debate with Baroness Thornton. The interviewer asked her who she thought would become mayor. 'Frank,' she said, 'because from where he is in the polls, he can only go up. And from where Ken is in the polls, he can only go down. So by election day, the two should have crossed over.' The London Socialist Alliance, never having stood before, started on 0 per cent. So come election day we were sure to win unanimously.

In a pub my mate Martin agreed to be my election agent. We reckoned on three other definites but had no idea where the sixth vote would come from.

It occurred to me that in elections, the numbers you're playing with are completely different from the campaigns I was used to. If you get 100 people to a public meeting, that's excellent. But 100 votes is fucking useless.

But supporters gathered; people like Tommy who embodied the chaos of every vibrant political campaign. When I took out a map to work out a route for a campaign bus, he spluttered, 'It's no use showing that to me, I'm dyslexic when it comes to maps. The last time I read a map was when I was in the army and I ended up mortar bombing my own side.'

As Tommy took me around his estate to meet the people he was getting to campaign for the LSA, I realized that everyone he introduced me to had two unusual things about them. As we left the first one, he said, 'She's a good kid. She's a transsexual and she's out on bail for attempted murder.' As we left the next one he informed me, 'She's a lovely woman, she's on tranquilisers and she's got eighteen cats.' It was as if someone who only had one extraordinary aspect to them wasn't worth knowing. If you'd been to the moon but that was all, don't bother coming round. After meeting a supporter in the street, he said, 'His brother's just got seven years for blowing someone away. He lives in a bunker under his garden.'

Our next boost was in a debate with the other candidates at Croydon College. In response to a student asking about tuition fees and the level of the minimum wage, the Labour candidate replied, 'If you don't think you're paid enough, my advice to you is to value yourself higher, and get a job that pays more.'

So that's the problem with the low paid. If only they weren't so forgetful, and remembered to ask for more. The students organized a benefit for the campaign, with their mates and DJs. One student, cool, black and determined to impress asked me why he should bother voting for me. After a few minutes he said, 'Yeah man, you're for the people and not the rich, I'll vote for you.' Then his mate said, 'You can't vote, you're only seventeen,' and he replied, 'I can get round that, I've got connections man.'

One day I spent the afternoon at a stall we set up outside the mosque and the early evening at Croydon's first gay pub. Could two places be more opposite? You certainly wouldn't want to mix them up and start kneeling in the mosque, wailing 'Allah repeal section 28'. Yet they had more in common than they realized. Most of the muslims were appalled at New Labour's increasingly racist tone, including one who said 'I agree with you about New Labour, but for propagating a non-muslim ideology outside a mosque, you're going to the firehole my friend.' And everyone in the gay pub was equally appalled at New Labour breaking its promise to repeal section 28.

A teacher got his headmistress to extend the children's playtime one day, so they could invite me in to speak to the teachers. The Greek priest, remembering the campaign against the Balkans war, hugged me in his robes, pinned our leaflets to the door, and took me around the church just before a service, asking people to vote for the LSA. I did a speech to firefighters at the fire station, who shone with enthusiasm and spent an hour discussing how production could be organized in a socialist society. Just one firefighter stayed quiet, and I resigned myself to having one detractor. But as the meeting was ending he leaned meekly forward and said quietly 'I don't agree with you that New Labour are a disappointment. I knew they'd be shit from the start.'

The Ford convenor distributed LSA leaflets via the shop stewards, to every worker in the car plant. At the Kurdish centre I made a speech, which was translated sentence by sentence, to around forty Kurds, during which I received the best heckle of my career. It came in Kurdish, after which the translator told me, 'He says "Mark, you need to speak more about capitalism and imperialism".'

Perhaps the most surprising category of people voicing disgust at the Labour Party was the Labour Party. Almost all the local members told me how appalled they were and wished me luck. Except one who was hoping to become a local councillor and defended her party vigorously. Then, a cameraman, who was filming the campaign wandered off to change his battery, and as he left she said, 'Now he's gone I don't mind saying I agree with nearly everything you've said.'

But would any of these people vote for us? One of Tony Cliff's most insistent points was that bullshitters are eventually found out. From the Gravesend dole office onwards, I'd been aware that 'er yeah mate' wasn't the same as 'yes'. I started to fear the words 'Mark Steel (London Socialist Alliance) – 103'. Then one Sunday, halfway through the campaign, Tony Cliff died.

This was inconceivable. How could someone so joyous and

dedicated and funny and energetic die? And it was wrong. I'd heard him boast 'My family all live a long time. My grandfather lived to ninety-two when he choked to death on a prune. So I learn my lesson, when I get to ninety-two I will stop eating prunes.' And I believed him, but he'd lied. How many patients and staff at the hospital can have known the significance of what came to an end that day? There passed the link between my generation and the great historical events of the century. So many times I'd heard him talk about the difficulties of building socialist groups in the 1930s, when politics was dominated by the twin tyrannies of Hitler and Stalin. But never as a rambling old man, only ever as an incentive to aid the same task today. Somehow now he was dead his achievements seemed all the more extraordinary. After the war he defied the entire socialist movement to declare that Russia was now another capitalist country. At the same time he rejected the dominant Trotskyist view that capitalism was in terminal crisis, and insisted it was enjoying an unprecedented boom, fuelled by the production of arms in East and West. Both theories were backed up with complex documents, but they started at the bottom. He first doubted the idea that the post-war West was in slump, because he saw that for the first time every child had shoes. And it was the miserable accounts of Russian workers that alerted him to the idea that Russia was in no sense a worker's state.

His style of speaking, of weaving meandering jokes and anecdotes with poignant polemic, was a blend of the rural story-telling that reflected his upbringing, and the urban setting at which he aimed the ideas. One of his favourite routines involved reading a tatty leaflet, issued by the Labour Party in the 1930s, in response to accusations that their candidate John Strachey was a Jew. It said, 'We deny wholeheartedly that he is a Jew. We challenge anyone to find any evidence that he is a Jew.' Cliff would add that the only true socialist response would be to say 'not only is he Jewish, but we are *all* Jewish'. Three thousand people were at the funeral, marching silently through the avenues of Golders Green to the crematorium, holding little red flags behind a lone piper. Amongst the procession were trade unionists and socialists who had long since given up the rigour of daily confrontation, meetings, and living amidst bundles of leaflets and posters. Above the defiant silence of the march, astonished bystanders asked each other whose funeral this was, in an array of languages. I heard one exchange between two people who I think were Turkish, that went, 'It was Tony Cliff, a man for the workers.' 'Good,' said the second Turk, unshaven, about fifty, and in a little black hat, and he smiled and raised a fist.

The day after he died, I spent much of the time staring out of the window, contemplating how different my and many other lives would have been but for his presence. I would still have become a socialist, but maybe joined the Labour Party, becoming gradually disillusioned until I either gave up and dropped out, or gave up and pursued a career as a politician. Or maybe I'd have simply concluded there was no point in being in a tiny minority all my life and accepted all those offers to be on programs like the Jimmy Tarbuck Show. In other words, if it wasn't for that bastard I might be a millionaire with my own series on ITV.

On the day of the vote I felt absurdly important, wearing a rosette, voting for myself, and scooting up to London for a TV interview. Maybe everyone from the entertainment world should try it. Leaflets through every door in the borough, posters all over the town, megaphones calling your name and teams of people urging everyone to put you in charge of the area – that's got to be a bigger fix than being a guest on 'Call My Bluff'.

I stood in the corner of the Fairfield Halls and learned that 1,823 people had voted for us. In Lambeth and Southwark we won 6 per cent, and in Hackney and Islington 7 per cent. The initial reaction of many of our supporters was euphoric relief. Had we been invited on to the news to make an official statement it would have been, 'This commanding vote of an average 3 and a half per cent is the final nail in New Labour's coffin, which struggled to win only ten times as many votes as us.'

But to understand the importance of the result, you have to realize how insignificant socialists outside the Labour Party have been for so long. Twenty years earlier, we'd have been spat at by working-class people sick of socialism. Fifteen years earlier we'd have been spat at by people eagerly buying their council flat and shares. Five years earlier we'd have been gazed at in bewilderment, as an obstacle to getting rid of the Tories. For eighty years the far left in Britain has been dismissed as irrelevant. Now we could finally honestly say we were becoming a footnote.

In my area the Labour candidate came third. Ever since the debate at the college, she had been blaming me for everything wrong in her campaign and now she walked across to the camera-man filming the result and shoved the camera into his face as if she was a dodgy builder being interviewed by a consumer programme. So that was another cheerful result of twenty-five years' work. The angry young Trotskyist had learned to respect the etiquette of social institutions while the respectable politician went round thumping people. The most important vote that day, which clearly was an indication of widespread disillusionment with New Labour, was Ken Livingstone's election as Mayor of London. The following Sunday, I was on a radio show when the chair of the London Labour Party rang in to take part in a discussion on why Frank Dobson won only 13 per cent of the vote. He was Jimmy Fitzpatrick, the firefighter I'd admired so much in my early days as an activist, who had been employed for the last year doing everything Blair asked to stop Livingstone. I said, 'Jimmy, it's Mark Steel here. We knew each other better when we were *both* members of the Socialist Workers Party. So how does it feel to be back where you started, as part of a tiny minority?'

Chapter 24

One of the most common reasons given for the impossibility of socialism is that people are naturally selfish. But if everyone is selfish, why do people give blood? Presumably the cynic would say 'aha, typical, trying to get a free biscuit off the state'. Why do people knock on your door to let you know you've left your headlights on? Are they thinking 'well I don't want his battery to run down because I was going to nick that in half an hour'.

Activists are often told they're 'banging their head against a brick wall'. But unlike a brick wall, the situation and the people you come into contact with are constantly changing. So people who never imagined they would play a role in history find themselves face-to-face with those who rule the world. I wouldn't be surprised if one day I meet someone who's preparing to speak at a mass demonstration, who says to me, 'I know you from Swanley school, but I don't suppose you remember me. My name is Julie Jensen.'

In other respects it's harder than banging your head, because it takes enormous organization. Which is why even simple tasks like flyposting often get no further than two people saying simultaneously, 'I thought *you* were bringing the bucket.'

So I do fear the prospect of being seventy-five years old, sat in a room with seven other people and too many chairs saying 'if we can just get this mailing list sorted out, we can begin to have an influence in this area'. Demanding without success takes its toll. You shout 'stop the war' but the people with the power to stop the war take their instructions from higher authorities than the group with a stall in the shopping centre. How many times can you demand that it's vital something happens then see it not happen? How many public meetings can you speak at, in which half-way through the speech the poster behind you peels from its poorly applied blu-tac and collapses embarrassingly on to the floor? Nothing saps the will to fight for what you believe in like not having any influence. As someone once said, it's not power that corrupts but lack of power that corrupts. I was so certain we were going to change the world, and like anyone who felt that way in 1978, I confess to feeling slightly cheated.

That's why Blair and New Labour thrive on pessimism. Over the last twenty years, each time a battle against injustice has ground to defeat, whether on the scale of the miners' strike or the closure of a youth club, the concept of Blair has been at the death, feeding and gorging like bindweed. 'You see,' it whispers, with the hypnotic tone of the snake in the *Jungle Book*, 'you can't oppose inequality, just learn to live with it, then to praise it, and eventually invite it to lunch.'

The antidote to pessimism is the understanding that we do make a difference. Blair didn't scrap the poll tax – we did. New Labour didn't end apartheid – we did. What keeps campaigners going is not a naive faith that one sugary day we can make the world a better place, but the knowledge that defying authority *already* makes the world a better place. The welfare state may have come under attack for twenty years, but they haven't dismantled it. Because every time a ward, a classroom or a library was threatened, a handful of residents, staff and activists made a fuss. Multinational corporations lose no sleep over buying regions of land and evicting the local population. But how many times have they decided not to, or gritted their teeth and compensated the victims. Because they know that otherwise they'll have to deal with riots, boycotts, demonstrations, a stunt by crusties from Wiltshire and a documentary by John Pilger. Every strike, leaflet, petition, each act of defiance reminds them they can't have it all their own way because someone, somewhere will ignore the rules and eat their banana in the corridor.

And even if there are only two of you, it's better than being on your own. On your own, the urge to keep quiet can be overwhelming.

What gives someone the confidence to raise an awkward issue with the bloke at work or the next-door neighbour, is the feeling they're part of something bigger. As you read this, someone will be

arguing against racism, someone will be enthusing about the anti-
Vietnam War movement, and tired trade unionists, having got their
kids to sleep, will be studying the case of one of their members who
has been unfairly treated. Wherever there's a war, someone will be
thinking of ways to oppose it. And while the wealth of the richest
358 people in the world is equal to that of the poorest 40 per cent
of the planet, there will be people devising ways of exposing and
overturning that appalling state of affairs.

Who knows what impact each action has. You may speak up on
behalf of asylum-seekers in a room in which no one supports you,
but someone may be secretly admiring the stance you take and be
inspired by it for years. A.J. Cook will have had no idea, on the day
he made the speech seen by that old Welshman, that he'd created a
jewel in that man's memory that would glow for sixty years.

One afternoon in Edinburgh, sat on my own in a café, I was
reading an eyewitness account of the Warsaw ghetto. For page after
oppressive page the horror kept coming, as my coffee and cake
remained untouched. Until one man refuses to board a Nazi train.
He and his companions are immediately shot, but news of the
incident spreads, sparking a new defiant spirit. One group, of
which the author is one, acquires explosives smuggled from outside
the ghetto, and ambushes a Gestapo unit, blowing up the whole
convoy. 'YES,' I screamed spontaneously, and banged my fist on
the table in delight, sending cake and coffee rattling across the table
and on to the floor. The action was worth the courage and sacrifice,
because fifty years later, it made a dozen people in a café in
Edinburgh think 'the wee English boy's crazy'.

Many people at some point have felt a similar rush of inspired
adrenaline, maybe after a speech by a Liverpool docker, or a
Sandinista, or after reading about Tom Paine, Che Guevara or
Trotsky. Whereas no one will ever say 'the person who really
inspires me is Jack Straw'.

Most of those who submit to pessimism do so against their
instincts. Ask anyone when they were most inspired. It might have
been in the campaign against apartheid, as a member of CND, or
supporting the miners. No one will say 'my most exhilarating
moment was when I realized it was unrealistic to propose a higher
tax rate for the rich'.

The overwhelming majority are on the side of the weak when they stand up to bullies. That's why most of us admire the suffragettes, the French Resistance, the 15th century scientists who fought lone battles against mysticism, the ANC, opponents of dictators and the multitude of people who, at the time, were meeting in small groups, largely ignored and derided as nutcases.

The challenge and exhilaration comes from supporting such people at the time. Opposing injustice from a distance is easy. Anyone can get up in their workplace and say, 'I'd like to let everyone know that I'm completely opposed to the Spanish Inquisition.'

My advice is to value yourselves higher. Follow the instinct, don't be sensible. Massive events are made up of tiny acts. At the next act of injustice, take a gulp, open your mouth and be the one to run down the muddy bank, to start the booing, to stand in front of the tank, to refuse to get on the train – to kick out the irritating idiot at the party.

The happy ending is that one of the most popular films of all time is *Spartacus*. Whereas I wonder whether that film would have been as successful if the Romans had come into the field, asked 'Which one is Spartacus?', and received the answer, 'It's him over there mate. He's nothing to do with us. You see, we're *New* Spartacus.'